Learn, Teach...
Succeed...

With **REA's PRAXIS II® Middle School Mathematics (5169)**
test prep, you'll be in a class all your own.

WE'D LIKE TO HEAR FROM YOU!
Visit **www.rea.com** to send us your comments

REA: THE LEADER IN TEACHER CERTIFICATION PREP

3rd Edition

PRAXIS II® MIDDLE SCHOOL MATHEMATICS (5169)

Stephen Reiss, M.B.A.

Edited by
Sandra Rush

 Research & Education Association

Research & Education Association
61 Ethel Road West
Piscataway, New Jersey 08854
E-mail: info@rea.com

PRAXIS II Middle School Mathematics (5169) With Online Practice Tests, 3rd Edition

Published 2016
Copyright © 2015 by Research & Education Association, Inc.
Prior edition copyright © 2012 by Research & Education Association, Inc. All rights reserved. No part of this book may be reproduced in any form without permission of the publisher.

Printed in the United States of America

Library of Congress Control Number 2014911501

ISBN-13: 978-0-7386-1184-6
ISBN-10: 0-7386-1184-0

The competencies presented in this book were created and implemented by Educational Testing Service (ETS). For individual state requirements, including cut scores, consult your state education agency. For further information, visit the Praxis website at www.ets.org/praxis. Praxis®, Praxis II®, and The Praxis Series® are registered trademarks of ETS, which does not endorse this product. All other trademarks cited in this publication are the property of the their respective owners.

LIMIT OF LIABILITY/DISCLAIMER OF WARRANTY: Publication of this work is for the purpose of test preparation and related use and subjects as set forth herein. While every effort has been made to achieve a work of high quality, neither Research & Education Association, Inc., nor the authors and other contributors of this work guarantee the accuracy or completeness of or assume any liability in connection with the information and opinions contained herein. REA and the authors and other contributors shall in no event be liable for any personal injury, property or other damages of any nature whatsoever, whether special, indirect, consequential or compensatory, directly or indirectly resulting from the publication, use or reliance upon this work.

Cover image: © iStockphoto.com/Christopher Futcher

REA® is a registered trademark of
Research & Education Association, Inc.

Contents

CHAPTER 1
PASSING THE MIDDLE SCHOOL MATHEMATICS EXAM   1

CHAPTER 2 NUMBERS AND OPERATIONS   17

CONTENTS

CHAPTER 3 ALGEBRA   59

CONTENTS

CHAPTER 4 FUNCTIONS AND THEIR GRAPHS   107

CHAPTER 5 GEOMETRY AND MEASUREMENT   137

CHAPTER 6 PROBABILITY, STATISTICS, AND DISCRETE MATHEMATICS   **205**

PRACTICE TESTS

About Our Author

Stephen Reiss is the founder and owner of *The Math Magician*, a leading San Diego-based provider of supplementary mathematics instruction. His company specializes in seminar and private instruction, preparing students for a wide range of standardized tests including the GED® test. He earned his B.A. from Clark University and his M.B.A. from Arizona State University. Mr. Reiss has written many mathematics test preparation publications and is a proud member of Mensa, the largest and oldest high IQ society in the world.

About Our Editor

Sandra Rush earned a Bachelor of Arts degree in mathematics from Temple University in Philadelphia. While an undergraduate student, she served as a math tutor for members of the basketball team as well as for local public school students. In these early years of her own higher education, she realized that teaching mathematics had a special appeal. Ms. Rush's interest in education has extended beyond the classroom to the field of publishing, including writing and editing manuals on preparation for standardized tests at all levels.

About REA

Founded in 1959, Research & Education Association (REA) is dedicated to publishing the finest and most effective educational materials—including study guides and test preps—for students in middle school, high school, college, graduate school, and beyond.

Today, REA's wide-ranging catalog is a leading resource for students, teachers, and other professionals. Visit *www.rea.com* to see a complete listing of all our titles.

Acknowledgments

We would like to thank Pam Weston, Publisher, for setting the quality standards for production integrity and managing the publication to completion; John Paul Cording, Vice President, Technology, for coordinating the design and development of the REA Study Center; Larry B. Kling, Vice President, Editorial, for his supervision of revisions and overall direction; Diane Goldschmidt, Managing Editor, for coordinating development of this edition; Kathy Caratozzolo of Caragraphics for typesetting this edition; Ellen Gong for proofreading; and Claudia Petrilli, Graphic Designer, for designing our cover.

1

Passing the Praxis II Middle School Mathematics (5169) Exam

Let's assume for the moment that you are confident you really know your math (which will be the case when you finish this book). That's great, but you also need to know what's in this first chapter in order to pass the Praxis II Middle School Mathematics (5169) test. After all, if you don't know how to communicate your math competency because you're confused by the question format, unfamiliar with the online calculator, or you've made an innocent mistake that disqualifies you from taking the exam, how will you land a great teaching job?

Don't skip this chapter just because you want to get right to the math examples and test yourself with the exercises and practice tests presented in this book. Read this chapter through now, and then read it again after you finish studying the review chapters. The key to scoring well on the Praxis II Middle School Mathematics test is threefold:

1. Know the math (this goes without saying, but we said it anyhow).

2. Familiarize yourself with what you will face on the exam—no surprises to ambush you.

3. Be relaxed and at your best on exam day (e.g., wear comfortable clothes).

ABOUT THE PRAXIS II MIDDLE SCHOOL MATHEMATICS TEST

Educational Testing Service (ETS) administers the Praxis II tests. They are designed to evaluate the preparedness of an individual to teach subject-specific courses and are part of teaching certification and licensure in many U.S. states and territories.

The purpose of the Praxis II Middle School Math test (5169) is to assess the mathematical knowledge and competency for certification as a middle school math teacher. The people who take this exam come from a variety of backgrounds, but most are college seniors or recent graduates of a four-year college. Another contingent of people seeking certification include those who have had other occupations and are hoping to change careers, or teachers who are moving to a state that requires the Praxis for certification from a state that does not. The Praxis scores are transferable between states that both require the Praxis for certification.

The Middle School Mathematics test consists of 55 selected-response and numeric-entry questions. You have two hours to complete the test. Content categories include:

- Arithmetic and Algebra (approximately 34 questions)

    — Numbers and Operations

    — Algebra

    — Functions and Their Graphs

- Geometry and Data (approximately 21 questions)

    — Geometry and Measurement

    — Probability, Statistics, and Discrete Mathematics

For a more detailed list of subtopics covered on the exam, see the Praxis Middle School Math 5169 Study Companion, available for download from *www.ets.org/praxis*.

HOW THIS BOOK AND ONLINE PREP WILL HELP YOU

"Praxis tests are demanding enough to require serious review of likely content."

—Educational Testing Service

A demanding test . . . scary, yes? So, even if you think you know the math, this book will help you prepare for your test. Our review offers complete coverage of the material you will find on the Praxis Middle School Mathematics exam, along with plenty of practice exercises. After you've finished studying and practicing with our test prep, you'll be more than ready to tackle and pass this challenging test.

REA's comprehensive test prep gives you:

- An **online diagnostic test** to pinpoint your strengths and weaknesses. Your instant score report will show you where to focus your study.

- **Five chapters of review material** explaining all the math concepts tested on the exam.

- Plenty of **practice exercises** with step-by-step detailed explanations that show you why the incorrect answers are wrong. Working through the exercises and studying the detailed explanations is part of your learning—don't skip them!

— An **online posttest**. You've done your studying, now let's see what you've learned. Taking this posttest with instant scoring and topic-level feedback will let you know if you need more practice and review.

— **Four full-length practice tests** (two online and two in the book). Practice makes perfect, so practice as much as possible before taking the actual test.

Test Yourself at the Online REA Study Center

The REA Study Center *(www.rea.com/studycenter)* is where you'll find the online material that accompanies this book—the diagnostic test, the posttest, and two full-length practice tests.

The Praxis Middle School Math is a computer-based exam. Practicing online at the REA Study Center will simulate test-day conditions and help you become comfortable with the exam format.

The online content at the REA Study Center comes with these added benefits:

✓ **Automatic Scoring**—Find out how you did on your test, instantly.

✓ **Diagnostic Score Reports**—Get a specific score tied to each competency, so you can focus on the areas that challenge you the most.

✓ **Detailed Answer Explanations**—See why the correct response option is right, and learn why the other answer choices are incorrect.

✓ **Timed Testing**—Learn to manage your time as you practice, so you'll feel confident on test day.

As you read this book, you'll see icons telling you when to access the online material. Take your time as you work through the online practice—it's all been designed to help you thoroughly prepare for your Praxis exam. (You'll be taking the online Diagnostic Test when you finish this chapter, but keep reading.)

PREPARING FOR YOUR TEST

ETS states, "Research shows that test-takers tend to overestimate their preparedness." Don't get lulled into complacency. It is never too early to start studying for the test. Set a realistic time to review the material that will likely be on the test so you aren't cramming. Cramming equates to forgetting—try to remember rather than memorize the material covered in this book.

Work out a study routine and stick to it. Reviewing class notes and textbooks, along with this book, will provide you with a strong foundation for passing this exam.

STUDY SCHEDULE

Below is a six-week study schedule to help you plan and prepare for your test. If you don't have the recommended six weeks, combine each two-week period into one. Remember, however, that the more time you spend studying, the more prepared and relaxed you will be on test day.

PRAXIS Middle School Mathematics Study Schedule

Week	Activity
1	After reading Chapter 1, go to *www.rea.com/studycenter* and take the Diagnostic Test. Your detailed score report will identify the topics where you need the most review.
2	Study review Chapters 2 through 4. Highlight key terms and information and take notes as you read the review.
3	Study Chapter 5. Continue highlighting and taking notes as you read.
4	Study Chapter 6. When finished, take the online Posttest at the REA Study Center. Your score report will indicate topics you need to study again.
5	Take Practice Tests 1 and 2 at the online REA Study Center. Review your score reports and identify the topics you need to restudy.
6	If time allows, continue your preparation by taking Practice Tests 3 and 4 in this book.

WHAT TO EXPECT AT THE TESTING SITE

There are specific rules that need to be followed before and during the administration of the Praxis test. This section will make you aware of what to expect when you sit for the test. However, before you head out to the test site, make sure to leave the following things at home.

FOOD

DRINKS

YOUR OWN SCRATCH PAPER

WATCHES WITH A
CALCULATOR FUNCTION CELL

PHONES

CALCULATOR

ELECTRONICS

Be sure to consult the online registration center for official information updates. Some test sites provide storage lockers for personal items such as handbags, but unless you know for sure that these lockers are available, it is best to just leave these items behind. Approved scratch paper will be given to you and an on-screen calculator is provided.

Also note that all stop-clock functions and alarms on watches must be turned off. Your pockets must be empty—completely empty.

Simply put, come to the test center with only your picture ID, which has your name and signature on it, and your admission ticket. Be prepared for a thorough security check, mainly designed to ensure that you are taking the test for yourself.

Your photo ID will be checked, maybe more than once. You will have to sign your name, and you will be photographed. Your pockets will be checked. Your body may even be scanned. Be prepared for all of this, and realize you're not being singled out.

You can be dismissed from the test, even before it starts, for the following infractions:

- Taking the test for someone else (or having someone else take the test for you).

- Using a cell phone or watch calculator as well as notes or other aids. The only things allowed on the computer table are the supplied scratch paper, the supplied No. 2 pencils, and your picture ID.

- Bringing in any electronic, photographic, recording, or listening devices.

- Creating a disturbance.

- Tampering with the computer.

- Communicating with anyone during the test or during any breaks.

- Leaving the room without permission (raise your hand for permission for a break) or taking excessive breaks (only one break is normally allowed).

- Leaving the building at any time.

- Failing to follow directions.

Dismissal also means your test scores will be canceled and you will forfeit your test fees. If you are seen using any banned devices, they will be confiscated. For more information on what is allowed in the test center, visit *www.ets.org/praxis/test_day/bring*.

Since there are no scheduled breaks during the two-hour test, be prepared to stay seated for the whole time. If, however, you must take a break, be aware of two things: (1) the clock doesn't stop—the time you take for a break is counted—and (2) you may have to go through the screening process all over again before being allowed to reenter the testing room, taking up more of your precious time. Be sure to take your photo ID with you if you have to take a break.

The test site has video monitors and Test Center Administrators (TCAs) will be walking around, as well. This means if you have any technical questions, such as a problem with the computer, you will get immediate help by just raising your hand. The TCA cannot help you, however, with content queries on a particular test question.

YOUR COMPUTER TESTING STATION

Once you pass through the security screening, you will be seated at an assigned testing station. The first screen on the computer will show your personal data (including your photo), the name of the test you will be taking, your name, and your assigned ID number. If these are all correct, click **Continue** (upper right corner of each screen).

The next screens are all information screens, including a confidentiality statement that says you agree to not divulge any of the test questions after you leave the test site. You must agree to these terms by clicking **Continue**.

The rest of the screens will present general and testing-tool information, such as navigation instructions, question types, how to access math reference material, and (most important) how to mark questions that you want to come back to later during the test. This information is presented in the next sections of this chapter, but be sure to read each of these screens carefully before the test as a refresher, even if you think you know all about the test.

The clock countdown doesn't start until you have clicked **Continue** on each of the information screens, so take the time to read the information screens instead of wasting precious time to look something up during the test. The direction screens also include information on the test format, timing, and breaks.

Testing Tools

The testing tools information screen explains the buttons and tools on the screen, which are accessed by clicking on them. Click to select as well as to deselect. It is crucial that you become familiar with the navigation buttons that appear with each question. They are located on the upper right corner of the screen.

1. The **Review** button brings up a list of all the question numbers (the latest one is highlighted) and two columns for each. The first column is the "Marked" column, which has a check mark for each question that you marked for review (see below). The second column is a "Status" column, which tells whether the question was answered, not answered, or not yet seen. The **Review** feature

is immensely helpful and will show you which questions need to be revisited once you have navigated through all of the questions. If you go to `Review` at any time during the test, you will not lose your place on the test because a " `Return` " button (in the upper right corner) takes you back to where you were before you clicked `Review` .

2. Use the `Mark` button to mark a question for later review, especially if you are not sure of your answer. This button places a check mark on the question as well as on the `Review` list, but the check mark can be deleted by simply clicking `Mark` again.

3. The `Help` drop-down offers information on different topics. The choices for `Help` may vary, depending on where you are in the test. Note that the countdown clock does not stop while you are using the `Help` function. Click "Return" to go back to where you were before you clicked `Help` . If you have prepared well for the test (including knowing the information in this chapter), you probably won't have to refer to any of these `Help` options except the first one listed below. Typical entries under the `Help` function are the following:

   a. The *Math Reference* option displays a sheet of reference formulas and other math material that may be helpful in answering a question, such as notations and definitions. The content on the Math Reference sheet varies for each question, or it may not even be available for a particular question.

   b. *Testing Tools* explains the navigation tools (`Next` , `Back` , `Help` , `Mark` , and `Review`). It pays to be familiar with the navigation tools listed here before you take the test.

   c. *How to Answer* helps if any of the directions for a particular question are unclear.

   d. *How to Scroll* explains how to scroll the screen by using the up and down arrows. You should be familiar with scrolling before you take the test. You may have to scroll the screen for particularly long questions, but not to go to the next question (use the `Next` button for that).

   e. *General Directions* discusses the test format, timing, breaks, and other general information.

4. `Back` takes you back to the previous question.

5. Click the `Next` button to enter your response and move on to the next question. If you don't click `Next` , your response may not register. You may change responses to any question at any time by using the `Next` button, however. *Do not double-click* on `Next` or you may possibly click past (skip) the next question.

The Countdown Clock

Once you have navigated through the informational screens, you are ready to take the test. When you click the final `Continue` button, the timing will start. You will have two hours to finish the test. A countdown clock appears in the upper right-hand corner of the screen below the navigation buttons. If you find that distracting, you can hide it by pressing the "Hide Time" button to the left of the clock. To turn the clock back on, click the "Show Time" button. In the last five minutes of the test, the clock appears automatically and cannot be hidden. It will blink for a few seconds and then remain visible for the rest of the test until time runs out and the screen reads, "Your time for answering the questions in this section has ended."

Remember that the clock does not stop. If you have to take a break or if you access the `Help` button, the clock keeps running.

TYPES OF QUESTIONS AND STRATEGIES

The Praxis II Middle School Mathematics test has many question formats, although the majority will be multiple-choice. Below is a discussion of the types of questions you might encounter on the exam, examples of the questions and strategies for answering correctly.

1. Multiple Choice. Most questions will be multiple-choice questions in which you select the best answer from among four choices. The instruction at the bottom of the page for multiple-choice questions is, "Answer the question by clicking on the correct response." Be sure to read every answer choice, even if you think the first or second answer choice appears to be the correct answer. Do not automatically think that the answer you have chosen is the *best* answer until you have assured yourself that none of the others are better. Sometimes you may be asked to choose the *incorrect* response among correct responses. Although there are no "trick" questions on the test, you are expected to pay full attention. This isn't a time to skim over what is written.

For multiple-choice questions, you don't necessarily have to come up with the correct answer from scratch—you only have to be able to identify the correct answer from among the four choices. You should be able to eliminate one or more of the answer choices without any calculation if they are obviously wrong (for example, the problem asks for a whole number and one answer choice is a fraction or a decimal), or inappropriate (for example, the problem indicates that the answer will be in the set {1, 2, 3, 4, 5} and the answer choice is 6).

An example of a multiple-choice question would be:

Which of the following units would be most appropriate for measuring the length of a pencil?

(A) Miles

(B) Meters

(C) Feet

(D) Centimeters

The correct answer is (D).

Another variation of the multiple-choice question asks for *all* of the correct answer choices, so there may be more than one correct answer choice for the question, and *you must select all of them* to get credit. The instruction at the bottom of the page for these questions is, "Select multiple answers by clicking more than one checkbox."

An example of this type of multiple-choice question would be:

Which of the following units would be appropriate for measuring the length of a pencil (choose all that apply)?

(A) Miles

(B) Inches

(C) Feet

(D) Centimeters

The correct answers are (B) and (D).

2. Interactive Questions. Questions with interactive graphics may display a map, a table, or a grid. Your click may produce a checkmark or highlight an area. Directions would be, "Move over the image and click to choose an answer," or "Click on your choices." If you want to change your answer, click it and enter a new answer in the same way.

An example of an interactive question (with the answers filled in) would be:

Click to indicate which group the equations in the following table belong.

Equation	More than one solution	Only one solution	No solutions
$x^2 = 16$	✓		
$4x + 10 = 2x + 5$	✓		
$4x + 10 = 4x - 16$			✓
$3(x + 2) = 6$		✓	

3. Drag-and-Drop. Drag-and-drop questions ask you to move a phrase or expression to another part of the screen. Typically, you are given some choices to drag into boxes. Drag-and-drop items require computer dexterity in moving the cursor to drag and drop small images on the screen, such as words or parts of numerical expressions (e.g., numbers, operators, or variables) into boxes where they make sense.

Drag by pointing the cursor over the item to be moved, clicking on it and, while keeping the mouse button pressed, drag the item across the screen to where it belongs, and then release the mouse button to drop it. Replace any choice you have made by simply dragging a new item onto the old item. After you do this, the old item goes back into the area of choices and the new item you selected goes into the proper box in the question. Or you can change your answer by dragging and dropping to another location.

An example of a drag-and-drop question, based on the above interactive example, would be:

Drag each equation into the box that describes its solution(s).

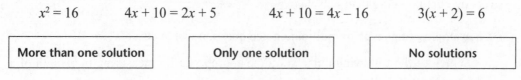

$$x^2 = 16 \qquad 4x + 10 = 2x + 5 \qquad 4x + 10 = 4x - 16 \qquad 3(x + 2) = 6$$

| More than one solution | Only one solution | No solutions |

4. Fill-in-the-Blank. Fill-in-the-blank questions leave a blank space or box into which you type your answer. It can be the value you got from doing a specific calculation, a one-word or one-phrase answer to a question, or an equation you would use to solve a problem. Fill-in-the-blank questions may have more than one blank to fill in. You can delete your answer by using the backspace key and then typing in a new answer, just as you would delete and type new text on any computer.

An example of a fill-in question would be:

The product of 27 and 66 to the nearest hundred is

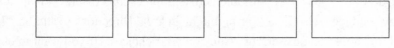

The answer is 1800.

TEST-TAKING STRATEGIES

Your score on the Praxis Middle School Mathematics test is based on the number of questions you get right. There is no penalty for wrong answers. Therefore, it cannot be overemphasized that you should *answer every question*. As an example, let's say the question asks something you haven't a clue about. If you leave the answer blank, you get 0 points for that question. If you blindly guess, you at least have a 25% chance of getting full credit. And if you guess wrong, you're no worse off than if you left the answer blank.

Now suppose you can eliminate just one choice, and then you have to guess. Your odds just increased to 33% that you will get full credit. With two eliminations, your odds go up to 50%. So answer every question on the test, even if you have to guess.

When you have finished the test, you will probably have time to select the Review button to see which questions were unanswered or marked for review. Often, your brain is working subconsciously while you continue the test, still mulling over the questions you marked, and when you return to them, the answers may come to you right away. You definitely do not want any unread questions at the end of the test just because you ran out of time because a question momentarily baffled you.

Use a four-part plan for reasoning skills to answer all questions.

1. Figure out what is known, necessary to solve the problem, what information is missing (usually your solution), and what is unnecessary (just because something is mentioned doesn't mean it has anything to do with your solution).

2. Devise a strategy to solve the problem. This may involve making a sketch or a grid (use your scrap paper) or looking for a pattern.

3. Solve the problem according to your strategy and choose or enter the correct answer.

4. Make sure the answer makes sense.

The test allows a little more than two minutes per question, on average. You will be able to answer several questions on the test right away. For these "easy" questions, you will be using a lot less than two minutes, which will allow more time at the end to go back to the questions that gave you trouble. But don't hurry through any question. The last step in the strategy above is very important—take the extra few seconds to make sure your answer makes sense.

For example, let's examine the following question:

How many people could an elevator hold if each person weighed 160 pounds and the capacity of the elevator was one ton?

(A) 12.5

(B) 12

(C) 13

(D) Cannot tell from the information given.

The correct answer is (B). One ton is 2,000 pounds, and $2000 \div 160 = 12.5$. If you chose (A), you would be wrong. Why? Who wants to be on an elevator with one-half of a person? In real-world problems, the answer must make sense in real-world terms—the elevator can hold 12 people, but not 13.

YOUR BEST FRIEND: SCRATCH PAPER

You will be supplied with scratch paper, which you can use in any way you want. But be aware that you receive no credit for what is written on the paper, and you must turn it in at the end of the test. It turns out that this scratch paper can be your best friend during the test.

Suppose there is one (or more than one) thing that you always seem to mis-remember (such as whether slope is rise over run or run over rise). If that comes up in the middle of the test after you have been focused on so many other topics, you may not be sure if you recall it correctly. That's where the scratch paper comes in handy. Once the test starts, write down anything you are afraid you might mis-remember during the test, so you will have a reference to go to later.

Here's another example of the usefulness of scratch paper: Set aside part of the scratch paper (draw a square around it so you can find it easily), then if you are able to eliminate one or two of the four answer choices on a multiple-choice question, but feel you need a little more time to think about the problem, write the question number and the choices that you didn't eliminate in that square. Thisway, when you are going back to answer the questions you marked (by using Mark) during the test, you won't have to reconsider the ones you already eliminated.

When you use the scratch paper for what it was intended for—sketching a geometry problem or doing some figuring—be sure to identify the problem number so you aren't wasting time looking for whatever it was you did before. This is a time to be neat without being nagged about it.

But don't spend time doing arithmetic on the scratch paper that isn't simple (that includes multiplying a two-digit number by a two-digit number and any kind of division) when you have the online calculator available. Not only will you waste precious time, you will also risk getting a problem wrong because, for example, you forgot to borrow in subtraction or didn't keep your columns straight in long division, even though you knew how to do the problem. It's surprising how many errors are due to such miscalculations.

THE ONLINE CALCULATOR

Your second best friend during the test is the online calculator because it will keep you from wasting time and, even more important, making "stupid" mistakes. If you don't know how to work the calculator, however, you may encounter other problems. Taking the time to learn about the online calculator is one of your most important preparation tasks.

To practice with the online calculator used on the Praxis Middle School Math test, go to *www.infinitysw.com/ets*, where you will be able to sign up for a 30-day free trial. The tutorial on that website is very helpful and will familiarize you with the functions of this calculator.

Consider using your 30-day free trial for the online calculator when you do the exercises and take the practice tests in this book. You may be familiar with a handheld calculator, but this one is different. Practice, practice, practice until you are comfortable with the online calculator.

The online calculator has three drop-down menus for the functions offered. Mostly, you will be in "math" mode (other choices are "trig," "number," and "Boolean"). The Praxis Middle School Math test doesn't necessarily include the others. For the second pull-down menu, choose "deg" rather than "rad." These choices stand for "degrees" and "radians," respectively. Radians are used in trigonometry and are not part of this test. The last pull-down gives a choice of "float" or "sci" modes. Most of the time, you will be using the "float" mode, which simply means the numbers will appear as they usually do: 30, 75.6, etc. However, you are expected to be familiar with scientific notation, so you may use "sci" for some problems.

CALCULATOR TIPS

When rounding answers, be careful to round to the units requested. If the problem says "round to the nearest hundredth" and the number is 1.1965, which rounds to 1.20, don't use 1.2 as the answer, even though 1.20 and 1.2 have the same value. "Nearest hundredth" means you can't drop the 0—it is a placeholder, and says there are no hundredths. Also, save any rounding until the end of the problem—do not round in intermediate steps. As an example, $3.28 \times 1.7 = 5.576$, which is 5.58 to the nearest hundredth, whereas $3.3 \times 1.7 = 5.61$.

Another common error when using the calculator is to assume that the answer on the calculator screen is the answer to the problem, when in fact, it may just be one of the steps to finding the answer. For example, if asked to find $(3.28 \times 1.7)^2$, you may do the multiplication first ($3.28 \times 1.7 = 5.576$) and forget that you are not done with the problem. Most likely 5.576 will be one of the answer choices, but it is not the correct answer. You still have to square it. You should read all questions and answer choices carefully, but especially so if you are using the calculator to get the answer.

It would be helpful (but not necessary) to know how to work with scientific notation as well as functions and graphs on the calculator, but even if you use it only for the basic arithmetic operations and calculations (e.g., exponents and roots), it will be a time-saver.

Remember, the calculator display is in calculator language. For example,

- Scientific notation appears on the screen as 6.12E5, meaning 6.12×10^5. The number after the E tells you the exponent of 10.

- Square root appears as sqrt(value), and then you simply fill in the value. For $\sqrt{4}$, you would use the $\sqrt{x}$ key and the screen would show sqrt(value), and then you enter 4 and the "ENT" button.

- For other roots, the key is $\sqrt[x]{y}$, but the screen looks like root(y;x), and you would enter the y value (the radicand) and then the x value (the root). So for the cube root of 8, you would choose the $\sqrt[x]{y}$ button, root(y;x) would appear on the screen with the y highlighted, and you would enter 8;3. The result would be the expected 2.

You have a choice of entering values on the calculator or using your computer keyboard. Note, however, that on your computer keyboard, the plus sign (+) and the multiplication sign (*) require using caps, which can be annoying. Also, note that the ENT (Enter) key on the calculator or computer keyboard is the equivalent of the equals sign (=). If you enter "6 + 3 =" and then ENT, you will get the error message "Missing or invalid operand." So don't use the equals sign, just ENT when you want the result.

SCORING THE TEST

The one advantage of a computer-based test is that you can get an idea of how well you did at the end of the test. This is only partially true. You will be given your raw score (the sum of correct answers), and you can get a general idea from that how much you can celebrate. Your official score (ranging from 100 to 200) may not be immediately available.

The official score, along with a pass/not pass designation, will come later because the raw score on each test is actually weighted according to its difficulty, which makes sense. The tests are not identical. Each edition of a test has its own table to convert from a raw score to the official score so there is a standard across all forms of the test. Your official score, if it is not available at the end of the test, will be available approximately two to three weeks after the test date.

You can access your official score via the web using your Praxis account number free of charge for one year following the test date. Scores are no longer mailed.

Passing scores vary by state. Visit the ETS website to see what your state requirement is. All states, however, require a minimum of 165 points for passing.

If you score in the top 15% of test-takers, you will be given a Recognition of Excellence (ROE), a prestigious award for outstanding individual performance on the Praxis test. Candidates who earn the ROE receive a formal recognition certificate and congratulatory letter from ETS. The honor is also indicated on score reports that are sent to you and your designated institutions.

CONTACTING ETS

If you need more information about the Praxis Middle School Mathematics (5169) test or if you're ready to register and schedule your test, visit the Educational Testing Service (ETS) website at *www.ets.org/praxis*.

Good luck on the Praxis II Middle School Mathematics (5169) test!

Diagnostic Test

Go to the online REA Study Center to take the diagnostic test to help focus your study.

(www.rea.com/studycenter)

Numbers and Operations

In this chapter, we will review the following topics:

- The real number system

- Exponents

- Fractions, decimals, and percentages

- Ratios and proportions

- Number theory

- Operations involving radicals

- Estimation

THE REAL NUMBER SYSTEM

Numbers in the real number system comprise the following:

Natural or counting numbers: 1, 2, 3, 4 ...

Whole numbers: 0, 1, 2, 3, 4 ...

Integers: ... −2, −1, 0, 1, 2 ...

Rational numbers: the quotients of two integers in the form of $\frac{a}{b}$. Rational numbers can be in the form of fractions such as:

$$\frac{1}{2}, \ \frac{9}{7}, \ 3\frac{5}{8}, \ \frac{6}{1}$$

or decimals that terminate:

0.6, 2.7, 0.0004

Any decimal that is infinite, but repeats a pattern, is also a rational number:

3.333... or 0.142561425614256...

Rational numbers that do not terminate but repeat a pattern are often expressed with a decimal bar above the repeating numbers:

$5.276276... = 5.\overline{276}$

Irrational numbers: numbers that cannot be written as the quotient of two integers. Examples are:

$5.2351758...$, π, $\sqrt{17}$

The symbol π has a value equal to 3.141592654...

$\sqrt{17}$ equals 4.123105626...

There is another set of numbers, the **complex** number system, which involves imaginary numbers, or $i = \sqrt{-1}$.

Note: There may be one question on the Praxis exam that deals with imaginary numbers, but the test taker will be reminded that i (the variable for an imaginary number) equals $\sqrt{-1}$.

Order of Operations

Consider the following example:

$6 + 2 \times 7$

Is the answer 56 or is it 20? Do we simply proceed from left to right or do we prioritize certain operations in arithmetic? The answer, 20, is the result of using the order of operations.

The order of operations is a system that sequences operations in mathematics. The order is:

Parentheses

Exponents

Multiplication

Division

Addition

Subtraction

The acronym *PEMDAS* is useful in remembering the precise order of operations (some teachers also use the expression "Please Excuse My Dear Aunt Sally" as an alternate method of remembering the order of operations). Regardless of which method you use to remember the order of operations, it is important to note that multiplication and division as well as addition and subtraction are considered equivalent operations. When encountering a line of math that is solely multiplication and division or addition and subtraction, proceed from left to right to make the correct calculation.

Practice Exercises

1. $12 \times 4 \div 6 = ?$

2. $9 \div 3 \times 4 = ?$

3. $12 + 8 - 10 = ?$

4. $9 - 4 + 6 = ?$

Solutions:

1.   **8**

This example contains both multiplication and division, so proceed from left to right:

$12 \times 4 \div 6 = 48 \div 6 = 8$

2.   **12**

This example contains both multiplication and division, so proceed from left to right:

$9 \div 3 \times 4 = 3 \times 4 = 12$

3.   **10**

This example contains both addition and subtraction, so proceed from left to right:

$12 + 8 - 10 = 20 - 10 = 10$

4.   **11**

This example contains both addition and subtraction, so proceed from left to right:

$9 - 4 + 6 = 5 + 6 = 11$

Let's try a more challenging example, this time using exponents and parentheses.

$$3(2 - 5)^3 - (-12) = ?$$

As PEMDAS tells us, simplify the parentheses first:

$$3(2 - 5)^3 - (-12) = 3(-3)^3 - (-12)$$

Work with exponents next:

$$3(-3)^3 - (-12) = 3(-27) - (-12)$$

Multiply:

$$3(-27) - (-12) = -81 - (-12)$$

Subtract:

$$-81 - (-12) = -81 + 12 = -69$$

Properties of the Real Number System

Addition and multiplication have important properties that are identified below.

Commutative Property: The order in which numbers are added or multiplied does not affect their sum or product.

Examples:

$$12 + 54 = 54 + 12 \qquad 15 \times 17 = 17 \times 15 \qquad (12 - x) + p = p + (12 - x)$$

Associative Property: The grouping of three or more numbers does not affect their sum or product.

Examples:

$$(12 + 15) + 9 = 12 + (15 + 9) \qquad\qquad 9 \times (5 \times 7) = (9 \times 5) \times 7$$

Distributive Property: A method for combining addition and multiplication.

Example:

$$9(8 - 12) = (9)(8) - (9)(12) = 72 - 108 = -36$$

Practice Exercises

Decide which property is illustrated below.

1. $3(8 + n) = 24 + 3n$

2. $\pi + 3n = 3n + \pi$

3. $(12 + 18) + 41 = 12 + (18 + 41)$

4. $(12)(n) = (n)(12)$

Solutions:

1.   Distributive property

2.   Commutative property of addition

3.   Associative property of addition

4.   Commutative property of multiplication

EXPONENTS

Exponents, also called **powers**, are the number of times a base number is multiplied by itself. For example, $3^3 = 3 \times 3 \times 3 = 27$.

EXAMPLE

$5^3 \times 2^2 \times 1^4 = ?$

SOLUTION

$5^3 \times 2^2 \times 1^4 = (5 \times 5 \times 5) \times (2 \times 2) \times (1 \times 1 \times 1 \times 1) = 125 \times 4 \times 1 = 500$

Notice that 1 raised to any power is always 1.

EXAMPLE

$(-4)^3 \times (-2)^2 = ?$

SOLUTION

$(-4)^3 \times (-2)^2 = -4 \times -4 \times -4 \times -2 \times -2 = (-64)(4) = -256$

Properties of Exponents

There are properties of exponents that facilitate their use.

When multiplying numbers with the same base, add the exponents.

$2^2 \times 2^4 = 2^{2+4} = 2^6 = 64$

This is because $2^2 \times 2^4 = (2 \times 2)(2 \times 2 \times 2 \times 2) = 4 \times 16 = 64$.

When raising an exponent to a power, multiply the exponents.

$(2^3)^2 = 2^{3 \times 2} = 2^6 = 64$

This is because $(2^3)^2 = (8)^2 = 64$.

When dividing numbers that have the same base, subtract the exponents.

$5^4 \div 5^2 = 5^{4-2} = 5^2 = 25$

This is because $5^4 \div 5^2 = 625 \div 25 = 25$.

Any base raised to the 0 power equals 1.

Negative Exponents

Numbers can be raised to negative exponents as well.

EXAMPLE

If $3^1 = 3$ and $3^0 = 1$, then $3^{-1} = ?$

SOLUTION

Since the exponent is negative, the answer must be less than 1. In order to convert a negative exponent into a positive one, we must first create a fraction with the base in the denominator. If there is no numerator already, place 1 in the numerator.

$$3^{-1} = \frac{1}{3^1} = \frac{1}{3}$$

Let's try a more challenging example using all of our knowledge of exponents.

EXAMPLE

Simplify the following expression

$$\frac{(2^3 \times 2^{-4})^5}{6^{-2}} = ?$$

SOLUTION

Using the order of operations, first simplify the quantity in the parentheses:

$$(2^3 \times 2^{-4})^5 = (2^{3+(-4)})^5 = (2^{-1})^5$$

Next, raise the quantity in the parentheses to the fifth power:

$$(2^{-1})^5 = 2^{-1 \times 5} = 2^{-5}$$

Finally, convert the negative exponents to positive ones and solve as you normally would:

$$\frac{2^{-5}}{6^{-2}} = \frac{\frac{1}{2^5}}{\frac{1}{6^2}} = \frac{\frac{1}{32}}{\frac{1}{36}} = \frac{1}{32} \times \frac{36}{1} = \frac{9}{8}$$

Practice Exercises

Simplify each expression.

1. $\left(-\frac{1}{8}\right)^{-2} =$

2. $\frac{(5^2)^3(5^3)}{5^8} =$

3. $\frac{(7^5)^2(7^3)}{7^{-11}} =$

4. $\frac{(-7m^{-2}n)^{-2}}{14mn^3} =$

Solutions:

1. 64

$$\left(-\frac{1}{8}\right)^{-2} = (-8)^2 = 64$$

2. 5

$$\frac{(5^2)^3(5^3)}{5^8} = \frac{5^{2\times3+3}}{5^8} = \frac{5^9}{5^8} = 5^{9-8} = 5^1 = 5$$

3. 7^{24}

$$\frac{(7^5)^2(7^3)}{7^{-11}} = \frac{(7^{10})(7^3)}{7^{-11}} = \frac{7^{13}}{7^{-11}} = 7^{13-(-11)} = 7^{24}$$

4. $\dfrac{m^3}{686n^5}$

$$\frac{(-7m^{-2}n)^{-2}}{14mn^3} = \frac{\left(-\frac{1}{7}\right)^2 m^{(-2)(-2)}n^{-2}}{14mn^3} = \frac{\frac{1}{49}m^4n^{-2}}{14mn^3} = \frac{m^3}{686n^5}$$

Scientific Notation

Scientific notation is a tool that makes managing large numbers more efficient. A number expressed in scientific notation is the product of two numbers:

1. A number greater than or equal to 1 and less than 10 ($1 \leq n < 10$).

2. 10 raised to some power.

The quantity 2.756×10^5 is in scientific notation because $1 \leq 2.756 < 10$ and 10 is raised to the power of 5. A number written in standard form, such as 432.7, can be converted to scientific notation by moving the decimal point to the right of the units digit. Count the number of places you moved the decimal: if you moved the decimal point to the left, add that many powers of 10. If you moved the decimal point to the right, subtract that many powers of 10.

$$432.7 = 4.327 \times 10^2$$

$$0.0435 = 4.35 \times 10^{-2}$$

EXAMPLE

A light year, the distance light travels in a year, is approximately 6,000,000,000,000 miles. The distance to the Andromeda Galaxy is 2,200,000 light years. How many miles distant is the Andromeda Galaxy from Earth? (Express your answer in scientific notation.)

SOLUTION

Convert miles in a light year to scientific notation:

$$6{,}000{,}000{,}000{,}000 = 6.0 \times 10^{12}$$

Next, convert the light years to the Andromeda Galaxy to scientific notation.

$$2{,}200{,}000 = 2.2 \times 10^{6}$$

Multiply 6.0×10^{12} and 2.2×10^{6} to find the number of miles to the Andromeda Galaxy.

$$(6.0 \times 10^{12})(2.2 \times 10^{6}) = 13.2 \times 10^{18}$$

The product is not in scientific notation because 13.2 is not between 1 and 10. Move the decimal point one place to the left and increase the power of 10 by 1.

$$13.2 \times 10^{18} = 1.32 \times 10^{19}$$

Notice how working with a cumbersome math problem is facilitated by using scientific notation.

Let's look at a scientific notation problem that integrates our knowledge of positive and negative exponents.

EXAMPLE

Evaluate $\dfrac{(8.19 \times 10^{9})(3.69 \times 10^{-4})}{(2.73 \times 10^{3})}$.

Express your solution in scientific notation.

SOLUTION

Multiply and divide the first numbers in each parentheses.

$$(8.19 \times 3.69) \div 2.73 = 11.07$$

Multiply and divide the 10s:

$$(10^{9} \times 10^{-4}) \div 10^{3} = 10^{(9 + (-4)) - 3} = 10^{2}$$

$$\frac{(8.19 \times 10^{9})(3.69 \times 10^{-4})}{(2.73 \times 10^{3})} = 11.07 \times 10^{2}$$

Convert the number to scientific notation by moving the decimal point one place to the left and adding 1 to the power of 10.

$$11.07 \times 10^{2} = 1.107 \times 10^{3}$$

FRACTIONS, DECIMALS, AND PERCENTAGES

Virtually all of the math questions on the Praxis II Middle School Math test probe your knowledge of fractions, decimals, and percentages. The test features an online scientific calculator, which will ensure that you can quickly and accurately answer questions.

Fractions

A **fraction** is the comparison of two integers in the form of $\dfrac{x}{y}$. The number above the fraction bar is called the **numerator** and the number below is the **denominator**. There are three types of fractions:

Proper fraction: A proper fraction is one in which the denominator is greater than the numerator.

$\dfrac{7}{11}$ and $\dfrac{74}{107}$ are examples of proper fractions.

Improper fraction: An improper fraction is one in which the numerator is greater than the denominator.

$\dfrac{11}{9}$ and $\dfrac{49}{6}$ are examples of improper fractions.

Mixed number (also called a mixed fraction): A mixed number has an integer component and a fraction component.

$7\dfrac{2}{3}$ and $-14\dfrac{5}{7}$ are examples of mixed numbers.

Adding and Subtracting Fractions

When adding and subtracting fractions with the same denominator, add the numerators while keeping the denominators the same. For example:

$$\dfrac{2}{7}+\dfrac{3}{7}=\dfrac{5}{7}$$

Sometimes, adding two proper fractions results in a sum that is an improper fraction.

$$\dfrac{5}{8}+\dfrac{4}{8}=\dfrac{9}{8}$$

The answer choices may be in the form of an improper fraction or a mixed number. You can convert $\frac{9}{8}$ to a mixed number by dividing 9 by 8.

$$
\begin{array}{r}
1\frac{1}{8} \\
8\overline{)9} \\
\underline{-8} \\
1
\end{array}
$$

When adding or subtracting fractions with different denominators, find a common denominator.

EXAMPLE

$$\frac{3}{8} - \frac{1}{6} = ?$$

SOLUTION

Find the smallest number that 8 and 6 will divide into evenly. This number is called the **least common multiple** or **LCM**. Begin by multiplying each denominator by 1, 2, 3 …

6: 6, 12, 18, **24**, 30, 36…

8: 8, 16, **24**, 32, 40 …

Since 24 is the LCM, it is also the **lowest common denominator (LCD)**. Multiply $\frac{3}{8}$ by $\frac{3}{3}$ and $\frac{1}{6}$ by $\frac{4}{4}$ to express both as fractions with the same denominator.

$$\frac{3}{8} \times \frac{3}{3} = \frac{9}{24}$$

$$\frac{1}{6} \times \frac{4}{4} = \frac{4}{24}$$

Now subtract the fractions as you normally would.

$$\frac{9}{24} - \frac{4}{24} = \frac{5}{24}$$

Now try adding $\frac{7}{11}$ and $\frac{2}{9}$ on your calculator.

$$\frac{7}{11} + \frac{2}{9} = \frac{85}{99}$$

The calculator automatically expresses every result in simplest terms; there is no need to simplify.

When adding mixed numbers, add the whole number portions and then the fractions. Sometimes the solution needs to be altered.

$$9\frac{1}{3} + 6\frac{7}{9} = 15\frac{10}{9}$$

Convert the improper fraction, $\frac{10}{9}$, into a mixed number and add it to 15.

$$10 \div 9 = 1\frac{1}{9}$$

$$15 + 1\frac{1}{9} = 16\frac{1}{9}$$

When subtracting mixed numbers, regrouping may be needed.

$$8\frac{1}{5}$$

$$-4\frac{2}{3}$$

First change each fraction part so they have the same denominator.

$$8\frac{1}{5} = 8\frac{3}{15}$$

$$4\frac{2}{3} = 4\frac{10}{15}$$

Since $\frac{3}{15}$ is less than $\frac{10}{15}$, we have to "borrow" 1 from the whole number 8. Remember, $1 = \frac{15}{15}$.

Then $8\frac{3}{15}$ changes to $7\frac{18}{15}$ and we can subtract.

$$7\frac{18}{15}$$

$$-4\frac{10}{15}$$

$$3\frac{8}{15}$$

Multiplying and Dividing Fractions

When multiplying fractions, simply multiply the numerators and denominators separately; there is no need for common denominators.

$$\frac{3}{7} \times \frac{4}{13} = \frac{12}{91}$$

EXAMPLE

$$\frac{18}{35} \times \frac{14}{27} = \frac{252}{945} \div \frac{63}{63} = \frac{4}{15}$$

SOLUTION

Notice how much easier it is to cross-divide the fractions first.

$$\frac{\overset{2}{\cancel{18}}}{\underset{5}{\cancel{35}}} \times \frac{\overset{2}{\cancel{14}}}{\underset{3}{\cancel{27}}} = \frac{4}{15}$$

By dividing 18 and 27 by 9 and 14 and 35 by 7, the product, $\frac{4}{15}$, is assured to be expressed in simplest form.

When multiplying mixed numbers, convert each to an improper fraction. Follow these steps to change a mixed number into an improper fraction:

1. Multiply the denominator of the fraction by the whole number.

2. Add that value to the numerator while maintaining the original denominator.

EXAMPLE

Change $7\frac{5}{8}$ to an improper fraction.

SOLUTION

$$7\frac{5}{8} = \frac{(8 \times 7) + 5}{8} = \frac{61}{8}$$

After converting a mixed number into an improper fraction, multiply and cross-divide as needed.

EXAMPLE

$$3\frac{1}{3} \times 1\frac{4}{5} =$$

SOLUTION

$$\frac{\overset{2}{\cancel{10}}}{\cancel{3}_{1}} \times \frac{\overset{3}{\cancel{9}}}{\cancel{5}_{1}} = 6$$

When dividing fractions, change the division sign to multiplication and exchange the values in the numerator and the denominator of the second fraction. This new fraction is called the *reciprocal* of the original.

$$\frac{3}{8} \div \frac{11}{16} = \frac{3}{8} \times \frac{16}{11} = \frac{6}{11}$$

Note: Many of the operations with fractions on the Middle School Mathematics test can be performed quickly and effortlessly with the online calculator. It is recommended that the prospective test-taker become familiar with ETS's instructional video for the online calculator.

Decimals

A decimal is a number to the right of a decimal point. In the number 148.768, .768 is the decimal.

Each value in a decimal is $\frac{1}{10}$ the value of the number to its left. Consider the following number:

235.0749

2 is in the hundreds place (200)

3 is in the tens place (30)

5 is in the ones (or units) place (5)

0 is in the tenths place $\left(\frac{0}{10}\right)$

·7 is in the hundredths place $\left(\frac{7}{100}\right)$

4 is in the thousandths place $\left(\frac{4}{1000}\right)$

9 is in the ten thousandths place $\left(\dfrac{9}{10{,}000}\right)$

In our daily lives, we say a normal body temperature is "ninety-eight point six degrees" (98.6°).

Mathematically we say "ninety-eight and six tenths degrees"; the decimal is connected to the whole number by the word "and."

Rounding Decimals

Rounding means expressing a number in terms of a specific place value. For example, we often round prices to the nearest dollar—we see $9.95 and say "10 dollars."

When rounding decimals, follow these steps:

1. Identify the digit to be rounded.

2. Look to that digit's immediate right. If that digit is 5 or greater, increase the digit to be rounded by 1. If the digit is less than 5, the digit to be rounded remains the same.

EXAMPLE

Round 19.278 to the nearest hundredth.

SOLUTION

1. 7 is the integer in the hundredths place.

2. The digit to its right, 8, is larger than 5, so round 7 up by 1.

Thus, 19.278 rounded to the nearest hundredth is 19.28.

Operations with Decimals

When **adding decimals**, align the decimal points and add as you normally would.

EXAMPLE

5.1 + 7.0003 + 8.35 = ?

SOLUTION

Some students find it useful to add zero place holders.

$$
\begin{array}{r}
5.1000 \\
7.0003 \\
+\ 8.3500 \\
\hline
20.4503
\end{array}
$$

The online calculator makes adding decimals effortless.

$7.071 + 9.5555 + 6.17 = ?$

Enter the numbers into the calculator, making sure to enter the decimal point as need.

$7.071 + 9.5555 + 6.17 = 22.7965$

When **subtracting decimals**, align the decimal points and subtract as you normally would. You may wish to use zero place holders as a visual aid.

$11.12 - 3.051 = ?$

$$
\begin{array}{r}
11.120 \\
- 3.051 \\
\hline
8.069
\end{array}
$$

The online calculator makes subtracting decimals effortless.

$13.1 - 8.0071 = ?$

Enter the numbers into the calculator, making sure to put the decimal point in the correct place.

$13.1 - 8.0071 = 5.0929$

When **multiplying decimals,** there is no need to align the decimal points. There are two steps to follow:

1. Ignore the decimal points and multiply the numbers as you normally would.

2. Count the number of decimal places in both numbers. Proceeding from the right, place a decimal point that number of places to the left.

EXAMPLE

$15.367 \times 14.602 = ?$

SOLUTION

1. Multiply the numbers as you normally would, ignoring the decimal points.

    $15,367 \times 14,602 = 224,388,934$

2. Since 15.367 and 14.602 contain a total of six decimal places, count six places from the right of 224,388,934.

    $15,367 \times 14,602 = 224.388934$

Use estimation to assess your answer by rounding each number to the nearest integer:

15.367 rounds to 15; 14.602 rounds to 15

$15 \times 15 = 225$, so our answer 224.388934 makes sense.

The online calculator makes multiplying decimals effortless.

$5.886 \times 3.41 = ?$

Enter the numbers as you normally would, making sure to enter the decimal point in the correct position.

$5.886 \times 3.41 = 20.07126$

When **dividing decimals**, such as $143.902 \div 4.22$, set it up as a division problem $4.22\overline{)143.902}$ and follow these steps.

1. Move the decimal point in the divisor, in this case 4.22, to the right as many places as needed to create an integer. (Here, that is two places.)

2. Move the decimal point in the dividend, in this case 143.902, an equal amount of places also to the right. Align the decimal point in the quotient with the new decimal point in the dividend.

$$4.22\overline{)143.902} = 422\overline{)14390.2} \quad \frac{34.1}{}$$

The online calculator makes dividing decimals effortless.

$148.55603 \div 36.89 = ?$

Enter the numbers as you normally would, making sure to enter the decimal point as needed.

$148.55603 \div 36.89 = 4.027$

Comparing Fractions and Decimals

A fraction can be converted to a decimal by dividing the numerator by the denominator.

EXAMPLE

Convert $\frac{5}{8}$ to a decimal.

SOLUTION

$$8\overline{)5.000} \quad 0.625$$

Thus, $\frac{5}{8}$ expressed as a decimal is 0.625.

You can easily compare fractions by converting each to a decimal.

EXAMPLE

Place $\frac{5}{8}$, $\frac{2}{5}$, and $\frac{13}{20}$ in ascending order.

SOLUTION

Convert the fractions into decimals:

$$\frac{5}{8} = 0.625$$

$$\frac{2}{5} = 0.40$$

$$\frac{13}{20} = 0.65$$

$$0.40 < 0.625 < 0.65$$

$$\frac{2}{5} < \frac{5}{8} < \frac{13}{20}$$

Percentages

Percent means "by the hundred." Percentages are a useful way of expressing values as some fraction of a hundred. For example, we can find 11% of $250.00 by multiplying 250 by $\frac{11}{100}$.

$$\frac{11}{100} \times 250 = 27.50$$

Thus, 11% of $250.00 is $27.50.

We will have more to say about percentages in our discussion of ratios and proportions. In this section, we will limit our discussion to applications of percentages using decimals.

We can change any percentage into a decimal by moving the decimal point two places to the left.

14.7% = 0.147

9.3% = 0.093

5% = 0.05

If a number has no decimal point, it can be added to the end because 14 = 14.0 = 14.000 and so on.

When we are asked what 37.1% of 89.2 is, we convert 37.1% into a decimal and multiply it by 89.2 (remember that "of" means multiplication).

$$37.1\% = 0.371$$

$$0.371 \times 89.2 = 33.0932$$

37.1% of 89.2 is 33.092.

Decimals can be converted into percentages. To convert a decimal into a percentage, move the decimal point two places to the right.

$$0.412 = 41.2\%$$

You can use the formula $\dfrac{\text{part}}{\text{whole}} \times 100$ to find a percentage.

EXAMPLE

During a recent history test, 13 of the 25 students received a grade of A or B. What percent of the students received an A or B?

SOLUTION

Define your terms:

Part = 13

Whole = 25

$$\text{Percent} = \dfrac{\text{part}}{\text{whole}} \times 100$$

$$\dfrac{13}{25} = 0.52$$

$$0.52 \times 100 = 52$$

52% of the students who took the history test received an A or a B.

Absolute Value

The absolute value of a number is the number of units a quantity is from 0. The absolute value uses the symbol "$| \quad |$". When you see $|x|$, it is read "the absolute value of x."

The absolute value is *always* expressed as a positive number. For example, $|3| = 3$ and $|-3| = 3$.

EXAMPLE

Evaluate the expression $|-7| + 3 = ?$

SOLUTION

$|-7| + 3 = 7 + 3 = 10$

When finding the absolute value of a variable, there will be two answers (unless the variable equals zero).

EXAMPLE

Solve for x.

$|x| - 7 = 12$

SOLUTION

Add 7 to isolate the variable.

$$|x| - 7 + 7 = 12 + 7$$

$$|x| = 19$$

Because $|x|$ equals 19, we say that $x = 19$ or $x = -19$ because $|19| = 19$ and $|-19| = 19$.

Practice Exercises

1. $|-12| - |12| =$

2. $|-17.6| + |12| =$

3. $|x| + |12| = 15$

    $x =$

Solutions:

1. 0

    $|-12| - |12| = 12 - 12 = 0$

2. 29.6

    $|-17.6| + |12| = 17.6 + 12 = 29.6$

3. 3 or –3

    $|x| + |12| = 15$

    $|x| + 12 = 15$

    $|x| = 3$

    $x = 3$ or $x = -3$

RATIOS AND PROPORTIONS

A **ratio** is the comparison of two numbers or quantities. When you travel at a rate of 50 miles per hour (mph), your speed is a ratio: it compares distance (miles) to time (hours).

Other examples of ratios include:

   Price per pound: compares money to weight

   Annual gym membership fees: compares money (your dues) to time (a year)

   Distance on maps: compares distance (in inches) to distance (in miles)

A ratio can be expressed three ways. The ratio of 5 cookies for $4.00 can be expressed as follows:

   5 to 4   5:4 $\dfrac{5}{4}$

Applications of Ratios

A ratio can be a useful tool when comparing prices.

EXAMPLE

One store offers 6 cans of vegetables for $5.00 and another store offers 5 cans of vegetables for the same price. Which is the better deal?

SOLUTION

If the cans of vegetables are of the same quality, then 6 cans of vegetables for $5.00 is preferred over 5 cans for the same price. We can see this comparison mathematically:

$$\frac{\$5.00}{6 \text{ cans}} = \$.833 \text{ per can}$$

$$\frac{\$5.00}{5 \text{ cans}} = \$1.00 \text{ per can}$$

Sometimes we cannot easily make a logical comparison between options because the units of measure are not equivalent.

EXAMPLE

Jim can buy a six-ounce cheesecake for $1.99 or a one-half pound cheesecake for $2.99. Which is the better deal?

SOLUTION

Notice that one cheesecake has its weight expressed in ounces while the other is expressed in pounds. Unless both units of weight are expressed in equivalent units, we cannot accurately gauge which is the preferred option. Although we can express both options in pounds or ounces, it is usually easier to convert to the smaller unit.

Option #1: The 6-ounce cheesecake: $\dfrac{\$1.99}{6 \text{ ounces}} = $ about $0.33 per ounce

Option #2: Convert pounds into ounces. Since 1 pound = 16 ounces, then $\dfrac{1}{2}$ pound equals 8 ounces $\left(\dfrac{1}{2} \times 16 = 8\right)$.

$$\frac{\$2.99}{8 \text{ ounces}} = \text{about } \$0.37 \text{ per ounce}$$

If the quality of both cheesecakes is equivalent, it is cheaper to buy the 6-ounce dessert.

Applications of Proportions

A **proportion** is a statement that two ratios are equal. For example, $\frac{1}{2} = \frac{8}{16}$ is a proportion because $\frac{1}{2}$ and $\frac{8}{16}$ are equal ratios. You can test if two ratios are equal by cross-multiplying the two fractions.

EXAMPLE

Prove that $\frac{1}{2} = \frac{8}{16}$ by cross-multiplying the two fractions.

SOLUTION

$$\frac{1}{2} = \frac{8}{16}$$

$$1 \times 16 = 2 \times 8$$

$$16 = 16$$

EXAMPLE

Show that $\frac{7}{19}$ and $\frac{12}{23}$ do *not* create a proportion.

SOLUTION

$$\frac{7}{19} = \frac{12}{23} \ ?$$

$$7 \times 23 = 12 \times 19 \ ?$$

$$161 \neq 228$$

Since their cross-products are not equal, $\frac{7}{19}$ and $\frac{12}{23}$ do not form a proportion.

We can use the fact that a proportion's cross-products are equal to solve many problems.

EXAMPLE

If 3 pizzas will feed 11 students, how many pizzas are needed to feed 14 students? (Round any decimal/fraction remainder up to the nearest whole pizza.)

SOLUTION

Solve this problem by comparing the ratios: $\dfrac{\text{pizzas}}{\text{students}}$ for each case.

We can let a variable, p, represent the number of pizzas needed to feed 14 students.

$$\frac{3}{11} = \frac{p}{14}$$

Cross-multiply fractions and solve for p.

$$\frac{3}{11} = \frac{p}{14}$$

$$11 \times p = 3 \times 14$$

$$11p = 42$$

$$\frac{11}{11}p = \frac{42}{11}$$

$$p = 3\frac{9}{11}$$

The question asks us to round any fraction of a pizza up to the nearest whole pizza, so we must purchase 4 pizzas to feed 14 students.

Scale Factor

Proportions are useful when finding distances using scale factors. A scale factor uses small units of measure, such as inches, to equal large units of measure, such as miles. Let's try a common example using a map.

EXAMPLE

The legend on a regional map of New England indicates that 1 inch = 47 miles. If the distance on the map between Danbury, Conn., and Boston, Mass., is 2.8 inches, what is the actual distance between the two cities?

SOLUTION

Use the ratio $\dfrac{\text{map distance}}{\text{actual distance}}$ for each case. Since the actual distance between Danbury and Boston is unknown, we will use a variable, d, to represent that distance.

$$\frac{1}{47} = \frac{2.8}{d}$$

Cross-multiply the fractions and solve for d.

$$1 \times d = 2.8 \times 47$$

$$d = 131.6$$

The distance between Danbury and Boston is 131.6 miles.

Percentages as Proportions

Earlier we discussed how percentage problems can be solved by using decimals. In this section we will show how percentages can also be calculated using proportions.

We can solve any type of percentage problem using the following proportion: $\dfrac{\text{part}}{\text{whole}} = \dfrac{n}{100}$, where n stands for the unknown percentage.

EXAMPLE

If 17 of 25 people in the math class are right-handed, what percentage are right-handed?

SOLUTION

Use $\dfrac{\text{part}}{\text{whole}} = \dfrac{n}{100}$ to solve the problem.

$$\frac{17}{25} = \frac{n}{100}$$

Solve for n:

$$\frac{17}{25} = \frac{n}{100}$$

$$17 \times 100 = 25 \times n$$

$$1{,}700 = 25n$$

$$\frac{1{,}700}{25} = \frac{25}{25}n$$

$$68 = n$$

In the math class, 68% of the students are right-handed.

Sometimes the percentage, n, is known, but the part is not.

EXAMPLE

An art class has 20 students. If 35% of the students in the class are male, how many males are in the class?

SOLUTION

In this class, the percentage is known, but the number of males is not. Use the variable m to represent the part of the whole class that is male.

$$\frac{\text{part}}{\text{whole}} = \frac{n}{100}$$

$$\frac{m}{20} = \frac{35}{100}$$

$$20 \times 35 = m \times 100$$

$$700 = 100m$$

$$\frac{700}{100} = \frac{100}{100}m$$

$$7 = m$$

There are 7 males in the art class made up of 20 students.

We also can use the proportion $\dfrac{\text{part}}{\text{whole}} = \dfrac{n}{100}$ to solve problems in which the percent and part are known, but the whole is not.

EXAMPLE

In a recent survey of computer users, 69 of the respondents use the Bytemaster brand. If the 69 users of those computers represent 37.5% of the respondents, how many computer users were surveyed?

SOLUTION

$$\frac{\text{part}}{\text{whole}} = \frac{n}{100}$$

$$\frac{69}{c} = \frac{37.5}{100}$$

$$c \times 37.5 = 69 \times 100$$

$$37.5c = 6,900$$

$$\frac{37.5}{37.5}c = \frac{6,900}{37.5}$$

$$c = 184$$

A total of 184 computer users were surveyed.

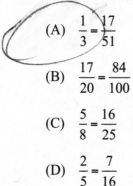

Practice Exercises

1. If a class has 9 men and 13 women, what is the ratio of men to the class?

   (A) 9:13

   (B) 13 to 9

   (C) $\frac{13}{22}$

   (D) $\frac{9}{22}$

2. If plums cost $3.20 per pound, what is the cost of a 3-ounce plum (1 pound = 16 ounces)?

   (A) $3.20

   (B) $2.40

   (C) $1.20

   (D) $0.60

3. Coaxial cable costs $2.70 per yard or $0.11 per inch. Which is the better deal? (1 yard = 3 feet = 36 inches.)

   (A) $0.11 per inch

   (B) $2.70 per yard

   (C) Both deals are the same.

   (D) It cannot be determined from the information provided.

4. Which of the following ratio pairs form a proportion?

   (A) $\frac{1}{3} = \frac{17}{51}$

   (B) $\frac{17}{20} = \frac{84}{100}$

   (C) $\frac{5}{8} = \frac{16}{25}$

   (D) $\frac{2}{5} = \frac{7}{16}$

5. The legend on a map shows that 1 inch = 80 miles. The distance on the map shows that Cleveland and Philadelphia are 5.05 inches apart. What is the actual distance?

   (A) 80 miles

   (B) 205 miles

   (C) 395 miles

   (D) 404 miles

6. Which proportion can be used to find 17% of 95?

   (A) $\dfrac{95}{p} = \dfrac{17}{100}$

   (B) $\dfrac{17}{95} = \dfrac{p}{100}$

   (C) $\dfrac{p}{95} = \dfrac{17}{100}$

   (D) $\dfrac{95}{100} = \dfrac{p}{17}$

7. The 35 members of a committee represent 28% of a group's members. How many members are in the group?

   (A) 125

   (B) 75

   (C) 49

   (D) 35

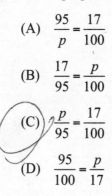

$$\frac{28}{100} = \frac{35}{p} \qquad 3500 = 28p$$

$$125$$

8. A machine produces 4,200 metal braces every hour. On the average, if 56 braces each hour are defective, what percent are defective? (Round your answer to the nearest tenth of a percent.)

   (A) 13.3%

   (B) 4.4%

   (C) 1.3%

   (D) 0.13%

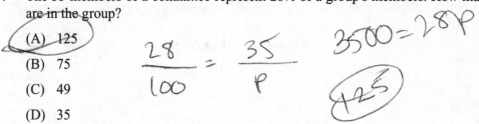

9. A store has discounted the price of its basketball shoes by 12.5%. If the original price of the shoes was $88.00, what is the sale price?

   (A) $11.00

   (B) $55.00

   (C) $75.50

   (D) $77.00

10. A vendor purchases sunglasses for $16 per pair and sells them for $30 in her store. What is her profit percentage (also known as a mark-up)?

(A) 87.5%

(B) 125%

(C) 144%

(D) 187.5%

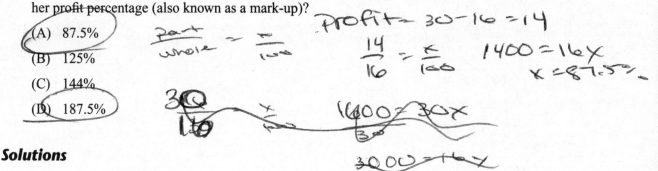

Solutions

1. **(D)**

   Since there are 9 men and 13 women in the class, the class roster consists of 22 students. The ratio of men to the class is $\dfrac{9}{22}$ (or 9 to 22 or 9:22).

2. **(D)**

   Convert pounds to ounces to find the cost of plums per ounce.

   $$\frac{\$3.20}{1 \text{ pound}} = \frac{\$3.20}{16 \text{ ounces}} = \$0.20 \text{ per ounce}$$

   Multiply $0.20 per ounce by 3 to get the cost of 3 ounces of plums.

   $$3 \times \$0.20 = \$0.60$$

3. **(B)**

   Convert the cost of cable per yard into cable per inch.

   $$\frac{\$2.70}{\text{yard}} = \frac{\$2.70}{36 \text{ inches}} = \$0.075 \text{ per inch}$$

   $0.075 per inch is more economical than $0.11 per inch.

4. **(A)**

   Two ratios form a proportion when their cross-products are equal.

   $$\frac{1}{3} = \frac{17}{51}$$

   $$1 \times 51 = 3 \times 17$$

   $$51 = 51$$

5. **(D)**

Use the ratios $\dfrac{\text{map distance}}{\text{actual distance}}$ to answer the question.

$$\frac{1}{80} = \frac{5.05}{d}$$

$$1 \times d = 80 \times 5.05$$

$$d = 404$$

6. **(C)**

Use the proportion $\dfrac{\text{part}}{\text{whole}} = \dfrac{n}{100}$ to find 17% of 95. The whole, 95, is known, but the part is not.

$$\frac{p}{95} = \frac{17}{100}$$

7. **(A)**

Use the formula $\dfrac{\text{part}}{\text{whole}} = \dfrac{n}{100}$ and input the known information.

$$\frac{35}{c} = \frac{28}{100}$$

$$35 \times 100 = 28 \times c$$

$$3,500 = 28c$$

$$\frac{3,500}{28} = \frac{28c}{28}$$

$$125 = c$$

8. **(C)**

Use the formula $\dfrac{\text{part}}{\text{whole}} = \dfrac{n}{100}$ and input the known information.

$$\frac{56}{4,200} = \frac{n}{100}$$

$$56 \times 100 = 4,200 \times n$$

$$5,600 = 4,200n$$

$$\frac{5,600}{4,200} = \frac{4,200n}{4,200}$$

$$1.333\ldots\% = n$$

1.333...% rounded to the nearest tenth of percent is 1.3%.

9. **(D)**

Use the formula $\dfrac{\text{part}}{\text{whole}} = \dfrac{n}{100}$ to calculate the discount, d.

$$\frac{d}{88} = \frac{12.5}{100}$$

$$100 \times d = 12.5 \times 88$$

$$100d = 1{,}100$$

$$\frac{100}{100}d = \frac{1{,}100}{100}$$

$$d = \$11.00$$

Subtract the discount, $11.00, from the original price of the shoes to find the sale price.

$$\$88.00 - \$11.00 = \$77.00$$

10. **(A)**

Use the formula $\dfrac{\text{part}}{\text{whole}} = \dfrac{n}{100}$ to find the store owner's profit percentage.

Profit = Selling price – purchase price

$$\$30.00 - \$16.00 = \$14.00$$

$$\frac{14}{16} = \frac{n}{100}$$

$$16 \times n = 14 \times 100$$

$$16n = 1{,}400$$

$$\frac{16}{16}n = \frac{1{,}400}{16}$$

$$n = 87.5\%$$

NUMBER THEORY

Divisibility

A number is divisible if it can be divided evenly (with no remainder) by another number. Without using a calculator or pencil and paper, do you think 40,002 is divisible by 3? This question can be answered quickly using divisibility rules.

A number is divisible by:

  2 if the number is even.

  3 if the sum of the digits is divisible by 3.

  4 if the last two digits are divisible by 4.

  5 if the number ends in 5 or 0.

  9 if the sum of the digits is divisible by 9.

  10 if the number ends in 0.

So 40,002 is divisible by 2 because it is even. It is also divisible by 3 because the sum of the digits is 6, which is divisible by 3.

EXAMPLE

Decide if 27,000 is divisible by 2, 3, 4, 5, 9, and 10.

SOLUTION

2: yes, because 27,000 is an even number.

3: yes, because $2 + 7 + 0 + 0 + 0 = 9$, which is divisible by 3.

4: yes, because 00 (or just 0) is divisible by 4. $0 \div 4 = 0$.

5: yes, because the number ends in 0.

9: yes, because $2 + 7 + 0 + 0 + 0 = 9$, which is divisible by 9.

10: yes, because the number ends in 0.

Prime Numbers

When using divisibility rules, remember that there are two different types of numbers. A number that is only divisible by itself and 1 is called a **prime number**. Numbers such as 7, 13, 29, and 67 are examples of prime numbers. Note that 1 is not a prime number and that 2 is the only even prime number. All other numbers, those that are divisible by numbers other than 1 and itself are called **composite numbers**. Numbers such as 14, 72, 121, and 480 are examples of composite numbers. All the numbers that divide evenly into a particular number are called its **factors**.

EXAMPLE

List all of the factors of 180.

SOLUTION

1, 2, 3, 4, 5, 6, 9, 10, 12, 15, 18, 20, 30, 36, 45, 60, 90, 180

Prime Factorization

Prime factorization tells which prime numbers multiply together to make a certain number. For example, the prime factorization of 6 is 2×3 because 2 and 3 are prime numbers. Sometimes, of course, the process is more complicated.

EXAMPLE

Find the prime factorization of 180.

SOLUTION

Begin dividing 180 by prime factors. It is convenient to use the same prime factor repeatedly until it no longer is a factor, and then continue, if possible, with other prime factors.

$$180 \div 2 = 90$$
$$90 \div 2 = 45$$
$$45 \div 3 = 15$$
$$15 \div 3 = 5$$
$$5 \div 5 = 1$$
$$180 = 2 \times 2 \times 3 \times 3 \times 5$$

It is customary to use exponents to streamline the prime factorization.

$$180 = 2^2 \times 3^2 \times 5$$

Greatest Common Factor (GCF)

The **greatest common factor (GCF)** is the largest common factor of two or more numbers. Look at the factors of 18 and 24.

18: 1, 2, 3, **6**, 9, 18

24: 1, 2, 3, 4, **6**, 8, 12, 24

Notice that 6 is the largest factor that is common to both 18 and 24. Thus, the greatest common factor of 18 and 24 is 6.

For larger numbers, arraying the factors becomes cumbersome. In this case, it was useful to find the prime factorization of the numbers.

EXAMPLE

Find the GCF of 144 and 216.

SOLUTION

Find the prime factorization of each number.

$$144 = 2^4 \times 3^2$$

$$216 = 2^3 \times 3^3$$

Look for common factors and use the **lesser** (or least when comparing three or more numbers) exponent. For 2, the lesser exponent is 3, and for 3, the lesser exponent is 2. Therefore, the GCF of 144 and 216 is $2^3 \times 3^2 = 72$.

Least Common Multiple (LCM)

The **least common multiple (LCM)** is the smallest multiple shared by two or more numbers. Look at the multiples of 8 and 12.

8: 8, 16, **24**, 32, 40…

12: 12, **24**, 36, 48…

Notice that 24 is the lowest number that appears in both lists. Therefore, the LCM of 8 and 12 is 24.

For larger numbers, arraying the multiples becomes cumbersome. In this case, it is useful to find the prime factorization of each number.

EXAMPLE

Find the LCM of 144, and 1,080.

SOLUTION

From our previous example, we know the prime factorization of 144 is $2^4 \times 3^2$. Further, we can determine that the prime factorization of 1,080 is $2^3 \times 3^3 \times 5$. Use the greatest power of all common factors. Thus, the LCM of 144 and 1,080 is $2^4 \times 3^3 \times 5 = 2,160$. Notice that when finding the LCM, every factor must be included even if it is not common to both numbers. In the example above, 5 was solely a prime factor of 1,080, yet it was included in the final calculation of the LCM.

Practice Exercises

1.   What is the prime factorization of 288?

2.   What is the GCF of 48 and 112?

3.   What is the least common multiple of 48 and 112?

Solutions

1. $2 \times 2 \times 2 \times 2 \times 2 \times 3 \times 3 = 2^5 \times 3^2$

2.   Find the prime factorization of 48 and 112.

   48: $2 \times 2 \times 2 \times 2 \times 3 = 2^4 \times 3$

   112: $2 \times 2 \times 2 \times 2 \times 7 = 2^4 \times 7$

   Raise each common prime factor to the lowest power in the array:

   $2^4 = 16$

3.   Find the prime factorization of 48 and 112.

   48: $2 \times 2 \times 2 \times 2 \times 3 = 2^4 \times 3$

   112: $2 \times 2 \times 2 \times 2 \times 7 = 2^4 \times 7$

   Raise each prime factor to its highest factor in the array:

   $2^4 \times 3 \times 7 = 336$

OPERATIONS INVOLVING RADICALS

The product of two equal quantities is called a **square**. Thus, 81 is a square because $9 \times 9 = 81$. Fractions can be squares, too. $\dfrac{36}{49}$ is a square because $\dfrac{6}{7} \times \dfrac{6}{7} = \dfrac{36}{49}$. The opposite of a square is a **square root**. Since 81 is the square of 9 (9^2), then 9 is the square root of 81. The symbol for finding the square root of a number is $\sqrt{}$ and is called a **radical**. Thus, $\sqrt{81} = 9$.

It is helpful to remember a few common squares, and square roots:

Common Squares		
$0^2 = 0$	$6^2 = 36$	$12^2 = 144$
$1^2 = 1$	$7^2 = 49$	$13^2 = 169$
$2^2 = 4$	$8^2 = 64$	$14^2 = 196$
$3^2 = 9$	$9^2 = 81$	$15^2 = 225$
$4^2 = 16$	$10^2 = 100$	
$5^2 = 25$	$11^2 = 121$	

Common Square Roots		
$\sqrt{0} = 0$	$\sqrt{36} = 6$	$\sqrt{144} = 12$
$\sqrt{1} = 1$	$\sqrt{49} = 7$	$\sqrt{169} = 13$
$\sqrt{4} = 2$	$\sqrt{64} = 8$	$\sqrt{196} = 14$
$\sqrt{9} = 3$	$\sqrt{81} = 9$	$\sqrt{225} = 15$
$\sqrt{16} = 4$	$\sqrt{100} = 10$	
$\sqrt{25} = 5$	$\sqrt{121} = 11$	

Approximating and Simplifying Square Roots

Not all numbers under the radical are rational numbers. The value of a square root can be approximated from the values of common square roots listed above.

EXAMPLE

Approximate the value of $\sqrt{29}$.

SOLUTION

The value has to be between 5 and 6, since $\sqrt{29}$ is between their square roots, $\sqrt{25}$ and $\sqrt{36}$.

Some square roots, even though they are irrational, can still be simplified, since the square root of a product equals the product of the square roots of its factors.

EXAMPLE

Simplify $\sqrt{18}$.

SOLUTION

$\sqrt{18} = \sqrt{9} \times \sqrt{2} = 3\sqrt{2}$

Simplifying some square roots can be more challenging.

EXAMPLE

Simplify $\sqrt{147}$.

SOLUTION

A factor of 147 is 3 because the digits total 12, which is divisible by 3.

$$\sqrt{147} = \sqrt{49} \times \sqrt{3} = 7\sqrt{3}$$

Adding and Subtracting Square Roots

Square roots can be added or subtracted if the number under the radical is the same.

EXAMPLE

Simplify $6\sqrt{7} - 5\sqrt{7} + \sqrt{7}$.

SOLUTION

$$6\sqrt{7} - 5\sqrt{7} + \sqrt{7} = 2\sqrt{7}$$

It is important to note that $\sqrt{7}$ is the same as $1\sqrt{7}$, even though the 1 rarely appears.

Multiplying and Dividing Square Roots

When multiplying square roots, simply multiply the numbers under the radicals and simplify as needed.

EXAMPLE

$\sqrt{8} \times \sqrt{18} = ?$

SOLUTION

$\sqrt{8} \times \sqrt{18} = \sqrt{144} = 12$

EXAMPLE

$\sqrt{8} \times \sqrt{6} = ?$

SOLUTION

$$\sqrt{8} \times \sqrt{6} = \sqrt{48} = \sqrt{16} \times \sqrt{3} = 4\sqrt{3}$$

When dividing square roots, divide the numbers under the radicals.

EXAMPLE

$\sqrt{192} \div \sqrt{3} = ?$

SOLUTION

$\sqrt{192} \div \sqrt{3} = \sqrt{64} = 8$

Let's add some variables into our exercises.

EXAMPLE

Simplify $\sqrt{12x^3 y^8}$.

SOLUTION

Separate the squares: $\sqrt{12x^3 y^8} =$

$$\sqrt{4}\sqrt{3}\sqrt{x^2}\sqrt{x}\sqrt{y^8} =$$

$$2xy^4\sqrt{3x}$$

Rationalizing the Denominator

When simplifying a radical such as $\dfrac{8}{\sqrt{3}}$, we are faced with an irrational denominator. This situation is remedied by rationalizing the denominator. By multiplying the numerator and denominator by $\sqrt{3}$, we eliminate the irrational number in the denominator.

$$\frac{8}{\sqrt{3}}\frac{\sqrt{3}}{\sqrt{3}} = \frac{8\sqrt{3}}{3}$$

Sometimes rationalizing the denominator takes additional steps.

EXAMPLE

Simplify $\dfrac{7}{6-\sqrt{3}}$

SOLUTION

Note that the denominator is a mixture of a rational and an irrational number. In order to create a rational denominator (hence the name "rationalizing" the denominator), we multiply the numerator and the denominator by $6+\sqrt{3}$. When the expression has the same numbers in the same order but a different sign, the new expression is called the **conjugate** of the original.

$$\left(\frac{7}{6-\sqrt{3}}\right)\left(\frac{6+\sqrt{3}}{6+\sqrt{3}}\right) = \frac{7(6+\sqrt{3})}{36-3} = \frac{42+7\sqrt{3}}{33}$$

You can multiply by the conjugate even when both the numerator and the denominator are irrational.

EXAMPLE

Simplify $\dfrac{\sqrt{6}+\sqrt{2}}{\sqrt{10}+\sqrt{5}}$.

SOLUTION

Multiply the numerator and denominator by the conjugate, $\sqrt{10}-\sqrt{5}$.

$$\left(\frac{\sqrt{6}+\sqrt{2}}{\sqrt{10}+\sqrt{5}}\right)\left(\frac{\sqrt{10}-\sqrt{5}}{\sqrt{10}-\sqrt{5}}\right) =$$

$$\frac{\sqrt{60}-\sqrt{30}+\sqrt{20}-\sqrt{10}}{10-5} =$$

$$\frac{2\sqrt{15}-\sqrt{30}+2\sqrt{5}-\sqrt{10}}{5}$$

You will see that the numerator remains an irrational number; it is acceptable and customary to only rationalize the denominator.

Practice Exercises

1. $4\sqrt{20} - 5\sqrt{5} =$

    (A) $3\sqrt{5}$

    (B) $-\sqrt{15}$

    (C) $-\sqrt{5}$

    (D) 25

2. $(3\sqrt{10})(4\sqrt{18}) =$

    (A) $9\sqrt{6}$

    (B) $24\sqrt{7}$

    (C) $72\sqrt{5}$

    (D) $7\sqrt{5}$

3. $\dfrac{\sqrt{360}}{\sqrt{20}} =$

    (A) 18

    (B) $3\sqrt{2}$

    (C) $6\sqrt{2}$

    (D) $6\sqrt{3}$

4. $\dfrac{8}{\sqrt{6}} =$

    (A) 24

    (B) $\dfrac{2\sqrt{3}}{3}$

    (C) $\dfrac{4\sqrt{3}}{3}$

    (D) $\dfrac{4\sqrt{6}}{3}$

5. $\dfrac{3-\sqrt{5}}{2-\sqrt{3}} =$

   (A) $9\sqrt{29}$

   (B) $6+3\sqrt{3}-2\sqrt{5}-\sqrt{15}$

   (C) $\dfrac{3+\sqrt{6}}{7}$

   (D) $\dfrac{3-\sqrt{6}}{7}$

Solutions

1.   **(A)**

   $4\sqrt{20}-5\sqrt{5}=8\sqrt{5}-5\sqrt{5}=3\sqrt{5}$

2.   **(C)**

   $(3\sqrt{10})(4\sqrt{18})=12\sqrt{180}=72\sqrt{5}$

3.   **(B)**

   $\dfrac{\sqrt{360}}{\sqrt{20}}=\sqrt{18}=3\sqrt{2}$

4.   **(D)**

   $\dfrac{8}{\sqrt{6}}=\dfrac{8\sqrt{6}}{\sqrt{6}\sqrt{6}}=\dfrac{8\sqrt{6}}{6}=\dfrac{4\sqrt{6}}{3}$

5.   **(B)**

   $\dfrac{3-\sqrt{5}}{2-\sqrt{3}}=\left(\dfrac{3-\sqrt{5}}{2-\sqrt{3}}\right)\left(\dfrac{2+\sqrt{3}}{2+\sqrt{3}}\right)=6+3\sqrt{3}-2\sqrt{5}-\sqrt{15}$

ESTIMATION

Estimation is a useful tool to assess the reasonableness of results. For example, when multiplying 19.8 and 102.7, would the answer 5,254.7 be a reasonable result?

Using Rounding for Estimation

Estimating 19.8 and 102.7 as 20 and 100, respectively, we would expect the answer to be close to 2,000 (the actual answer is 2,033.46). Thus, 5,254.7 is *not* a reasonable answer.

Estimating works well with fractions as well.

EXAMPLE

$$3\frac{2}{3} \times 7\frac{9}{11} = ?$$

If we came up with $20\frac{3}{7}$, would that be a good estimate?

SOLUTION

$3\frac{2}{3}$ rounds to 4

$7\frac{9}{11}$ rounds to 8

Since $4 \times 8 = 32$, we would expect our answer to be in that vicinity, so $20\frac{3}{7}$ would not be a good estimate.

CHAPTER

Algebra  3

In this chapter, we will discuss the following topics:

- Algebraic terms and expressions

- Equations

- Graphing linear equations

- Equations with two variables

- Systems of equations

- Quadratics

- Patterns

Think about a balancing scale with a 2-pound weight on each side. The scale will balance because the same weight is on each side. What will happen when a half-pound weight is added to one of the sides? Since the weight on one side is now 2.5 pounds, the scale will no longer be balanced. The scale will resume its balance, however, if another half-pound weight is placed on the other side.

The image of a balancing scale provides a useful visual tool in our discussion of algebra. To keep an equation balanced, we must always perform the same operation on both sides. Before we begin our discussion of equations, we must first review the building blocks of algebra: terms and expressions.

ALGEBRAIC TERMS AND EXPRESSIONS

A **term** is the product of a real number and one or more variables raised to powers. A variable is an unknown quantity, usually symbolized by a letter, such as x or n. The following are examples of terms:

$$2x^3 \qquad -7n^2 \qquad \frac{2}{3}x^3y \qquad r^{-2}$$

An exponent that is not expressly noted is understood to be 1. The term $7x$ is understood to be $7x^1$. If a number (called a coefficient) does not precede a variable, it is also understood to be 1. Thus the variable x can be understood as $1x^1$.

Any collection of terms is called an **expression**. The following are examples of expressions:

$$-7x + 5y \qquad 2.8x^3y - 3.2x \qquad 9xy - 5mn$$

Expressions are undefined when the denominator is zero because division by zero is not permitted.

EXAMPLE

For what value of x is the expression $\dfrac{3}{x-5}$ undefined?

SOLUTION

Since an expression is undefined when the denominator is equal to zero, set $x - 5$ equal to zero to find the value of x that renders the expression undefined.

$$x - 5 = 0$$
$$x = 5$$

When $x = 5$, the expression $\dfrac{3}{x-5}$ is undefined.

Order of Operations

In Chapter 2, we discussed the order of operations. A brief review follows.

The order of operations is a system that sequences operations in mathematics. The order is:

Parentheses

Exponents

Multiplication

Division

Addition

Subtraction

Let's simplify some expressions that contain variables by using the order of operations.

EXAMPLE

Find $-3x^3y^2 - \dfrac{2yz^3}{x}$ if $x = -1$, $y = 2$, and $z = -2$

SOLUTION

1. Substitute the value for each variable:

$$-3(-1)^3(2)^2 - \frac{2(2)(-2)^3}{-1}$$

2. Since all the values inside the parentheses are simplified, proceed to the exponents.

$$-3(-1)^3(2)^2 - \frac{2(2)(-2)^3}{-1} = -3(-1)(4) - \frac{2(2)(-8)}{-1}$$

3. Multiply and divide, proceeding from left to right.

$$-3(-1)(4) - \frac{2(2)(-8)}{-1} = 12 - \left(\frac{-32}{-1}\right) = 12 - 32$$

4. Add and subtract from left to right.

$$12 - 32 = -20$$

Practice Exercises

1. Which of the following describes $7ab^2$?

   (A) Term

   (B) Expression

   (C) Equation

   (D) Undefined

2. Which of the following describes $-0.27x^3 + 3.8xy^5$?

   (A) Term

   (B) Expression

   (C) Equation

   (D) Undefined

3. Simplify $\dfrac{-3xy^2 - z}{-3xz}$ if $x = 2$, $y = -2$, and $z = 4$.

   (A) 7

   (B) 6

   (C) $\dfrac{7}{6}$

   (D) -6

Solutions

1. **(A)**
   A term is the product of a real number and one or more variables raised to powers.

2. **(B)**
   A collection of terms is called an expression.

3.   **(C)**

Input the values for each variable, then use the order of operations to simplify.

$$\frac{-3(2)(-2)^2 - 4}{-3(2)(4)}$$

All of the values in the parentheses are expressed in simplest form, so proceed to working with the exponents.

$$\frac{-3(2)(-2)^2 - 4}{-3(2)(4)} =$$

$$\frac{-3(2)(4) - 4}{-3(2)(4)}$$

Next, multiply the quantities in the numerator and the denominator.

$$\frac{-3(2)(4) - 4}{-3(2)(4)} =$$

$$\frac{-24 - 4}{-24}$$

Use subtraction to simplify the numerator.

$$\frac{-24 - 4}{-24} = \frac{-28}{-24}$$

Finally, simplify the numerator and denominator by dividing each by –4.

$$\frac{-28 \div -4}{-24 \div -4} = \frac{7}{6}$$

Expressions with Like Terms

Expressions can be simplified if they contain like terms. **Like terms** are those that possess the same variable raised to the same power. Consider the following expression:

$3x + 5y + 6x$

The like terms in this expression are $3x$ and $6x$. They can be combined as follows:

$3x + 5y + 6x = 9x + 5y$

When combining like terms, add or subtract the coefficients but leave the variables and exponents the same. In this example, $5y$ is not a like term because it contains a y, not an x, and cannot be combined with $9x$.

Let's try a more challenging example:

$$7xy + 2x^2y - xy + 3xy^2$$

Notice that each term contains both x and y, yet not every term is a like term. In order for terms to be like terms, the variables *and* the exponents must be identical. Therefore, in the expression

$$7xy + 2x^2y - xy + 3xy^2$$

only $7xy$ and xy can be combined to create

$$7xy + 2x^2y - xy + 3xy^2 = 6xy + 2x^2y + 3xy^2$$

(Remember: $xy = 1xy$)

EQUATIONS

An **equation** is a mathematical statement that indicates two quantities are equal. The following are examples of equations:

$x + 9 = 12$

$3x + 2 = 5x - 7$

$r \times t = d$

EXAMPLE

$x + 5 = 8$

$x = ?$

SOLUTION

It is obvious that x must equal 3 because $3 + 5 = 8$. However, in some equations, the solutions may not be so obvious.

EXAMPLE

$x + 19 = -371$

$x = ?$

SOLUTION

Most people cannot perform such sophisticated calculations mentally. However, if you use algebra's two simple rules, you can solve any equation. In rule 1, isolating a variable means putting it alone on one side of the equal sign. Addition and subtraction are opposite operations, as are multiplication and division.

Rule 1: To isolate a variable, perform the opposite operation.

Rule 2: Whatever changes are made to one side of the equation must be done to the other side as well.

Let's go back to the example shown above.

$$x + 19 = -371$$

Since 19 is added to x, subtract 19 from both sides to isolate x:

$$x + 19 - 19 = -371 - 19$$

Simplify both sides:

$$x = -371 - 19 = -390$$

Let's solve some equations using the basic operations (addition, subtraction, multiplication, and division).

EXAMPLE

Solve for x.

$x - 17 = 43$

SOLUTION

Solve for x by adding 17 to both sides.

$$x - 17 + 17 = 43 + 17$$

Simplify: $x = 60$

EXAMPLE

Solve for x.

$7x = 98$

SOLUTION

Divide both sides by 7 to isolate the variable:

$$\frac{7x}{7} = \frac{98}{7}$$

Simplify: $x = 14$

EXAMPLE

Solve for x.

$$\frac{x}{15} = -12$$

SOLUTION

Multiply both sides by 15 to isolate the variable:

$$15\left(\frac{x}{15}\right) = (-12)15$$

Simplify: $x = -180$

Multistep Equations

Solving equations often requires more than one step.

EXAMPLE

Solve for n.

$$2n - 12 = -38$$

SOLUTION

Although both subtraction and multiplication are in this problem, we still use the two rules of algebra to solve for n. To isolate n, add 12 to both sides of the equation:

$$2n - 12 + 12 = -38 + 12$$

Simplify:

$$2n = -26$$

Divide both sides by 2:

$$\frac{2n}{2} = \frac{-26}{2}$$

Simplify: $n = -13$

You can check your solution by replacing it for the variable in the original equation.

$$2(-13) - 12 = -38$$

$$-26 - 12 = -38$$

$$-38 = -38$$

Equations with Decimals

An equation can contain decimals.

EXAMPLE

Solve for n.

$$-8.4 = 0.28n$$

SOLUTION

Divide both sides by 0.28 to isolate n.

$$\frac{-8.4}{0.28} = \frac{0.28n}{0.28}$$

When dividing decimals, move the decimal point in the divisor as many places to the right as needed to make it an integer. Remember to move the decimal point the same number of places to the right in the number being divided.

$$0.28\overline{)-8.4} \text{ becomes } 28\overline{)-840}$$

Simplify: $n = -30$

Equations with Fractions

Some equations may contain fractions.

EXAMPLE

Solve for r.

$$\frac{2}{3}r = 10$$

SOLUTION

Solve for r by multiplying both sides of the equation by $\frac{3}{2}$, the reciprocal of $\frac{2}{3}$. (This is the equivalent of dividing both sides by $\frac{2}{3}$.)

$$\frac{3}{2}\left(\frac{2}{3}r\right) = \frac{3}{2}(10)$$

Simplify: $r = 15$

Multivariable Equations

Equations can be solved for a particular variable, even if they have more than one variable.

EXAMPLE

Rate × Time = Distance

$$r \times t = d$$

Solve for t.

SOLUTION

Divide both sides by r.

$$\frac{r \times t}{r} = \frac{d}{r}$$

Simplify: $t = \dfrac{d}{r}$

Practice Exercises

1. Solve for x.

    $$x - (-15) = -12$$

    (A) −3
    (B) −27
    (C) 3
    (D) 27

2. Solve for x.

    $$-2x = -47$$

    (A) 49
    (B) 23.5
    (C) 47
    (D) −23.5

3. Solve for *x*.

$$\frac{2}{3}x + 5 = 9$$

(A) 21

(B) $\frac{8}{3}$

(C) 6

(D) −21

4. Solve for *r*.

$$-2.7r = 0.729$$

(A) 27

(B) 2.7

(C) −0.27

(D) 0.027

5. Solve $C = 2\pi r$ for *r*.

(A) $\frac{2\pi}{r}$

(B) $\frac{2C}{\pi}$

(C) $\frac{C}{2\pi}$

(D) πC

Solutions

1. (B)

$$x - (-15) = -12$$
$$x + 15 = -12$$
$$x + 15 - 15 = -12 - 15$$
$$x = -27$$

2. (B)

$$-2x = -47$$

$$\frac{-2x}{-2} = \frac{-47}{-2}$$

$$x = 23.5$$

3. (C)

$$\frac{2}{3}x + 5 = 9$$

$$\frac{2}{3}x + 5 - 5 = 9 - 5$$

$$\frac{2}{3}x = 4$$

$$\frac{3}{2}\left(\frac{2}{3}x\right) = \frac{3}{2}(4)$$

$$x = 6$$

4. (C)

$$-2.7r = 0.729$$

$$\frac{-2.7r}{-2.7} = \frac{0.729}{-2.7}$$

$$r = -0.27$$

5. (C)

$$C = 2\pi r$$

$$\frac{C}{2\pi} = \frac{2\pi r}{2\pi}$$

$$\frac{C}{2\pi} = r$$

Equations with Exponents and Square Roots

Some equations contain exponents and/or square roots.

$$3x^2 = 75$$

$$\sqrt{2x} = 8$$

As we learned earlier, whenever we wish to isolate a variable we perform the opposite operation to both sides of the equation. In this case, squares and square roots are opposite operations.

EXAMPLE

Solve for n.

$$\sqrt{2n} = 6$$

SOLUTION

Isolate the variable by squaring both sides of the equation.

$$\sqrt{2n} = 6$$
$$(\sqrt{2n})^2 = 6^2$$
$$2n = 36$$
$$\frac{2n}{2} = \frac{36}{2}$$
$$n = 18$$

Check your answer by replacing n with 18 in the original equation.

$$\sqrt{(2)(18)} = 6$$
$$\sqrt{36} = 6$$
$$6 = 6 \checkmark$$

Let's try another example.

EXAMPLE

Solve for x.

$$x^2 = 961$$

SOLUTION

Isolate the variable by performing the opposite operation (here, that is taking the square root) on both sides of the equation.

$$x^2 = 961$$
$$\sqrt{x^2} = \sqrt{961}$$
$$x = 31$$

Check your answer by replacing x with 31 in the original equation.

$$31^2 = 961$$
$$961 = 961 \checkmark$$

Practice Exercises

1. Solve for n.

    $$3n^2 - 11 = 136$$

2. Solve for x.

    $$\sqrt{2x+1} - 3 = 6$$

Solutions

1. **Step 1:** Begin isolating the variable by adding 11 to both sides of the equation.

    $$3n^2 - 11 + 11 = 136 + 11$$
    $$3n^2 = 147$$

    Step 2: Continue to isolate the variable by dividing both sides of the equation by 3.

    $$\frac{3n^2}{3} = \frac{147}{3}$$
    $$n^2 = 49$$

    Step 3: Isolate the variable by taking the square root of each side of the equation.

    $$\sqrt{n^2} = \sqrt{49}$$
    $$n = 7$$

    You can check your answer by substituting 7 for n in the original equation.

    $$3(7)^2 - 11 = 136$$
    $$3(49) - 11 = 136$$
    $$147 - 11 = 136$$
    $$136 = 136 \checkmark$$

2. **Step 1:** In order to isolate the variable, first isolate the radical. Add 3 to both sides of the equation.

    $$\sqrt{2x+1} - 3 + 3 = 6 + 3$$
    $$\sqrt{2x+1} = 9$$

    Step 2: Isolate the expression $2x + 1$ by squaring both sides of the equation.

    $$(\sqrt{2x+1})^2 = 9^2$$
    $$2x + 1 = 81$$

Step 3: Finish the calculations as you would for any equation.

$$2x+1=81$$
$$2x+1-1=81-1$$
$$2x=80$$
$$\frac{2x}{2}=\frac{80}{2}$$
$$x=40$$

Check your answer by replacing x in the original equation with 40.

$$\sqrt{2(40)+1}-3=6$$
$$\sqrt{81}-3=6$$
$$9-3=6$$
$$6=6 \checkmark$$

Direct and Inverse Variation

We can use our knowledge of solving equations to solve problems concerning direct and inverse variation. Imagine that you are running at 6 miles per hour. How far would you run if you ran for 3 hours? 4 hours? As the number of hours increases, so does the distance traveled. This situation is an example of **direct variation**. Use the model $y = kx$ where k is some constant.

EXAMPLE

The value of y varies directly with x. If $x = 12$ and $y = 30$, find the value of y when $x = 18$.

SOLUTION

$$y = kx$$
$$30 = (k)(12)$$
$$2.5 = k$$
$$y = (2.5)(18) = 45$$

Let's go back to the running example used above. If the race is 12 miles, how fast will you run in 3 hours? In 6 hours? In this case, the constant is the distance run, so the faster you run, the less time you need. As one variable increases, the other decreases. This is an example of **indirect variation**. Use the model $xy = k$.

EXAMPLE

The value of y varies indirectly with x. If $x = 12$ and $y = 30$, find the value of y when $x = 18$.

SOLUTION

$$xy = k$$
$$(12)(30) = k$$
$$360 = k$$
$$18y = 360$$
$$y = 20$$

When x increased from 12 to 18, y decreased from 30 to 20.

Using Equations to Model Real-World Contexts

Equations are very useful in solving everyday problems. Before we begin to use equations to model real-life situations, let's first review how words translate into algebraic expressions.

Word or Expression	Operation
more than	addition
greater than	addition
increased by	addition
decreased by	subtraction
less than	subtraction
times	multiplication
double, triple, etc.	multiplication
split	division

There are specific names for the answers to problems using mathematical operations.

Operation	Result
addition	sum
subtraction	difference
multiplication	product
division	quotient

Let's use this knowledge to solve a word problem.

EXAMPLE

Marcia and John ran a total of 48 miles in one week. If Marcia ran 14 miles more than John, how many miles did each of them run?

SOLUTION

Whenever using equations to model real-life situations in a word problem, use a five-step process.

Step 1: Define the variable.

Step 2: Create an equation that models the situation in the word problem.

Step 3: Solve the equation.

Step 4: Answer the question posed in the word problem.

Step 5: Assess the validity of your answer.

We will use the five-step process to answer the word problem about Marcia and John.

Step 1: Define the variable.

We can define either John's or Marcia's running distance as a variable. Let's choose n to represent John's running distance.

Let n = John's running distance.

Since Marcia ran 14 miles farther than John, we can say:

$n + 14$ = Marcia's running distance

Step 2: Create an equation that models the situation.

John's distance + Marcia's distance = 48 miles

$$n \quad + \quad (n + 14) \quad = 48$$

Step 3: Solve the equation.

$$n + (n + 14) = 48$$

$$2n + 14 = 48$$

$$2n + 14 - 14 = 48 - 14$$

$$2n = 34$$

$$\frac{2n}{2} = \frac{34}{2}$$

$$n = 17$$

Step 4: Answer the question posed in the problem.

Although we have successfully solved for the variable, the question asks how many miles *both* Marcia and John ran.

John: $n = 17$ miles, so John ran 17 miles.

Marcia: $n + 14 = 17 + 14 = 31$ miles. Marcia ran 31 miles.

Step 5: Assess the validity of your answer.

The problem states that Marcia ran 14 miles farther than John and that the sum of their distances is 48.

Did Marcia's distance exceed John's by 14 miles?

$$31 - 17 = 14$$

$$14 = 14 \checkmark$$

Do Marcia's and John's distances add up to 48 miles?

$$31 + 17 = 48$$

$$48 = 48 \checkmark$$

Let's try another word problem, this time using ratios.

EXAMPLE

A local philanthropist donated $192,000 to three charities: the Girl Scouts, the Boy Scouts, and the Girls Club. The ratio of the contributions to the Girl Scouts, the Boy Scouts, and the Girls Club was 5:2:1, respectively. What amount was donated to the Boy Scouts?

SOLUTION

Step 1: Define the variable.

Although any of the charities can be symbolized by the variable, it would be wise to let the smallest donation be the variable. Thus,

Let x = the donation to the Girls Club

Let $2x$ = the donation to the Boy Scouts

Let $5x$ = the donation to the Girl Scouts

Step 2: Create an equation that models the situation.

Girl Scouts + Boy Scouts + Girls Club = $192,000

$$5x \quad + \quad 2x \quad + \quad x \quad = \$192,000$$

Step 3: Solve the equation.

$$5x + 2x + x = 192,000$$
$$8x = 192,000$$
$$\frac{8x}{8} = \frac{192,000}{8}$$
$$x = 24,000$$

Step 4: Answer the question posed in the problem.

Since the Boy Scout contribution is represented by the term $2x$, multiply $24,000 by 2 to find the contribution made to the Boy Scouts.

$$(2)(\$24,000) = \$48,000$$

Step 5: Decide if the answer makes sense.

Substitute 24,000 for x in the original equation.

$$5(24,000) + 2(24,000) + 1(24,000) = 192,000$$
$$120,000 + 48,000 + 24,000 = 192,000$$
$$192,000 = 192,000 \checkmark$$

Since our calculations are correct, we conclude that the contribution to the Boy Scouts was $48,000.

GRAPHING LINEAR EQUATIONS

Thus far, all of the equations in this chapter have been linear equations. From the word *line*ar, we see the root of the word is **line**. Any equation raised to the first power can be graphed as a line.

Linear Equations

Any equation with a variable or variables raised to the first power is called a **linear equation**. Linear equations can be graphed on a number line.

EXAMPLE

Graph the solution to the equation $4x + 12 = x + 15$.

SOLUTION

Solve the equation.

$$4x + 12 = x + 15$$

$$3x = 3$$

$$x = 1$$

Place a dark circle at 1 on the number line.

Linear Inequalities

Linear inequalities mean one quantity is larger than another. The following symbols are used in linear inequalities:

Symbol	Meaning
<	less than
>	greater than
≤	less than or equal to
≥	greater than or equal to

EXAMPLE

Which of the following statements are true?

1.　$9 > -2$

2.　$-2 < -3$

3.　$2 \leq 2$

SOLUTIONS

1.　True. $9 > -2$ because 9 lies to the right of -2 on a number line

2.　False. -2 is not less than -3 because -2 lies to the right of -3 on a number line.

3.　True. $2 \leq 2$. Although 2 is not less than 2, it is equal to 2. Only one condition, less than **or** equal to, needs to be true to make the statement true.

We can use principles of algebra to solve many inequalities. Solve the inequality as you would normally solve an algebraic equation, retaining the inequality sign. However, when multiplying or dividing an equality by a negative number, reverse the direction of the inequality sign. In the examples below, we will review the basics of solving an algebraic inequality.

EXAMPLE

Solve and graph $4x - 16 > 20$.

SOLUTION

$$4x - 16 > 20$$
$$4x - 16 + 16 > 20 + 16$$
$$4x > 36$$
$$\frac{4}{4}x > \frac{36}{4}$$
$$x > 9$$

The solution can be graphed on a number line. We darken in the values greater than 9 on the number line. There is an open circle at 9 because 9 is not included in the solution.

Another way to express solution sets on a number line is by using brackets and parentheses. The brackets denote that the number next to it is included in the solution; a parenthesis means the number is not included. For example, in the graph above, we can refer to the solution as $(9, \infty)$ which indicates all numbers greater than 9 heading toward positive infinity. The infinity sign, both positive and negative, is always adjacent to parentheses.

If the equation was $4x - 16 \geq 20$, the solution would be $x \geq 9$. The new solution is graphed below.

The circle is darkened at 9, denoting that 9 is part of the solution set. Using brackets and parentheses, we get $[9, \infty)$.

EXAMPLE

Solve and graph $-2x + 8 < 12$.

SOLUTION

$$-2x + 8 < 12$$
$$-2x + 8 - 8 < 12 - 8$$
$$-2x < 4$$
$$\frac{-2}{-2}x > \frac{4}{-2}$$
$$x > -2$$

When we divided the inequality by -2, the direction of the inequality sign reversed. We can check our solution with an included value. If $x > -2$, we can substitute 1 for x because $1 > -2$.

$$-2(1) + 8 < 12$$
$$-2 + 8 < 12$$
$$6 < 12$$

Our solution set, $x > -2$, is verified by replacing x with 1. The graph of the inequality is shown below.

Graphs of Absolute Value Equations

Absolute value problems can also be graphed on a number line. The expression inside the absolute value signs can be positive or negative, so solve the equation both ways.

EXAMPLE

Graph the solution to $|6x - 3| = 18$ on a number line.

SOLUTION

$$6x - 3 = 18 \quad \text{or} \quad 6x - 3 = -18$$

$$6x = 21 \qquad\qquad 6x = -15$$

$$x = 3.5 \qquad\qquad x = -2.5$$

The graph is shown below.

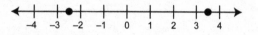

Absolute value inequalities can be graphed on a number line as well.

EXAMPLE

Graph the solution to the inequality:

$$|6x - 3| > 18$$

SOLUTION

Remember, the value within the absolute value symbol can be negative.

$$6x - 3 > 18 \quad \text{or} \quad -(6x - 3) > 18$$

$$6x > 21 \qquad\qquad -6x + 3 > 18$$

$$x > 3.5 \qquad\qquad -6x > 15$$

$$x < -2.5$$

The solution is graphed below. There are multiple solutions to the inequality, though 3.5 and −2.5 are not included in the solution (hence the open circles at those values). Using brackets and parentheses we get $(-\infty, -2.5)$ or $(3.5, \infty)$.

Practice Exercises

1. Solve for x: $-4x - 4 > 14$.

2. Graph $\frac{1}{3}y > 1$ on a number line.

3. Graph $7n - 6 \geq 15$ on a number line.

Solutions

1. $-4x - 4 > 14$

   $-4x - 4 + 4 > 14 + 4$

   $-4x > 18$

   $\dfrac{-4x}{-4} < \dfrac{18}{-4}$

   $x < -4.5$

2. $\dfrac{1}{3}y > 1$

   $3\left(\dfrac{1}{3}y\right) > (1)3$

   $y > 3$

3. $7n - 6 \geq 15$

   $7n - 6 + 6 \geq 15 + 6$

   $7n \geq 21$

   $\dfrac{7n}{7} \geq \dfrac{21}{7}$

   $n \geq 3$

EQUATIONS WITH TWO VARIABLES

The Coordinate Plane

The coordinate plane consists of an x- and y-axis. Each axis consists of negative and positive values. The point at which the two axes intersect is called the **origin**.

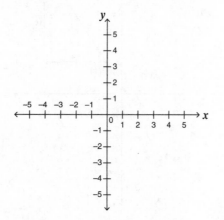

Each point on the coordinate plane consists of an x and y value; each value is called a **coordinate**.

A point on the coordinate plane is represented by a **coordinate pair** in the form of (x, y). A coordinate plane is shown below with certain points described by their coordinate pairs.

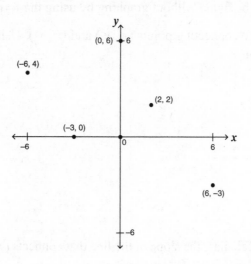

Slopes of Lines

A line can be drawn between any two points on the coordinate plane. Look at the line drawn between the points (1, 2) and (5, 8).

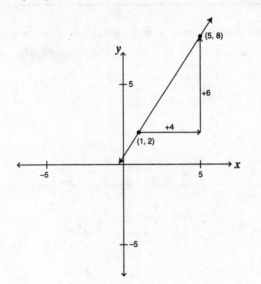

To move from (1, 2) to (5, 8) we move up 6 units and to the right 4 units. The slope of this line, defined as $\dfrac{\text{rise}}{\text{run}}$, is $\dfrac{6}{4}$, which simplifies to $\dfrac{3}{2}$.

The slope of a line can be found without graphing by using the formula $m = \dfrac{y_2 - y_1}{x_2 - x_1}$ where m represents the slope of a line connecting points (x_1, y_1) and (x_2, y_2). Using the slope formula from the previous example we get:

$(x_1, y_1) = (1, 2)$

$(x_2, y_2) = (5, 8)$

$m = \dfrac{y_2 - y_1}{x_2 - x_1} = \dfrac{8 - 2}{5 - 1} = \dfrac{6}{4} = \dfrac{3}{2}$

EXAMPLE

Without graphing, calculate the slope of the line that connects (7, –5) and (–4, –6).

SOLUTION

Use the slope formula $m = \dfrac{y_2 - y_1}{x_2 - x_1}$ and input the coordinates.

$(x_1, y_1) = (7, -5)$

$(x_2, y_2) = (-4, -6)$

$$\frac{-6-(-5)}{-4-7} = \frac{-1}{-11} = \frac{1}{11}$$

Note what happens when we consider (x_1, y_1) and (x_2, y_2) to be $(-4, -6)$ and $(7, -5)$, respectively.

$$\frac{-5-(-6)}{-7-(-4)} = \frac{1}{11}$$

Regardless of which point is designated (x_1, y_1) and (x_2, y_2), the result will be the same.

The Slope-Intercept Form of a Line

Any equation of a line is called a linear equation. The equation of a line in the form of $y = mx + b$ is called the **slope-intercept form of a line**. In this general equation, m represents the slope of the line and b stands for the line's y-intercept. The y-intercept of a line is the point at which the line intersects the y-axis.

EXAMPLE

In the equation $y = -\frac{2}{3}x - 3$, what are the line's slope and y-intercept?

SOLUTION

The slope, m, is $-\frac{2}{3}$ and the y-intercept, b, is -3.

The slope-intercept form of a line is a useful tool for quickly graphing a line. Let's graph the equation $y = -\frac{2}{3}x - 3$ by first plotting five points individually.

Let $x = -6$, so $y = -\frac{2}{3}(-6) - 3 = 1$

Let $x = -3$, so $y = -\frac{2}{3}(-3) - 3 = -1$

Let $x = 0$, so $y = -\frac{2}{3}(0) - 3 = -3$

Let $x = 3$, so $y = -\frac{2}{3}(3) - 3 = -5$

Let $x = 6$, so $y = -\frac{2}{3}(6) - 3 = -7$

We can summarize our findings with the following chart.

x	y
–6	1
–3	–1
0	–3
3	–5
6	–7

Plot the points (–6, 1), (–3, –1), (0, –3), (3, –5), and (6, –7).

Draw the line that connects the points.

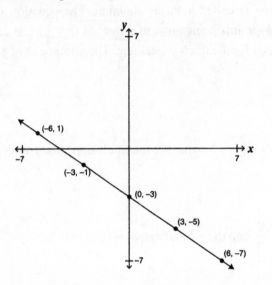

Now we'll graph the same line by using the slope-intercept form of the line.

In the equation $y = -\dfrac{2}{3}x - 3$, the slope is $-\dfrac{2}{3}$ and –3 is the y-intercept. Follow these two steps to graph the line.

1. Place a dot at the y-intercept, –3 on the y-axis.

2. The slope is defined as $\dfrac{\text{rise}}{\text{run}}$. From the point (0, –3), move down 2 units and to the right 3 units. Repeat this process one more time, each time making a dot. Connect all the dots, making a straight line that covers a large portion of the graph.

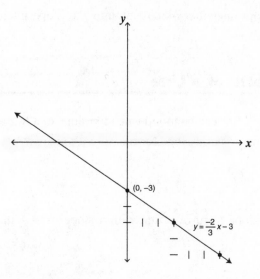

Graphing a line using the slope-intercept form is easier and quicker than substituting x-values and plotting points. Notice in the chart that when $x = 0$, $y = -3$, which is the y-intercept. A line's y-intercept is found by letting the x-coordinate equal 0.

Deriving the Equation of a Line

We can derive the equation of a line in slope-intercept form by using only two points on the line.

EXAMPLE

What is the equation of a line in slope-intercept form that connects the points $(6, -8)$ and $(5, -12)$?

SOLUTION

Follow these steps to derive the equation of the line.

1. Find the slope using the formula $m = \dfrac{y_2 - y_1}{x_2 - x_1}$.

$$\frac{-12 - (-8)}{5 - 6} = \frac{-4}{-1} = 4$$

2. Replace m with 4 in the slope-intercept form of a line.

$$y = mx + b \qquad y = 4x + b$$

3. To find b, substitute for x and y one of the coordinate pairs. In this example, we will use $(6, -8)$.

$$y = 4x + b$$
$$-8 = 4(6) + b$$
$$-8 = 24 + b$$
$$-32 = b$$

4. Put the slope and the y-intercept into the slope-intercept form to get $y = 4x - 32$.

The Point-Slope Form of a Line

The point-slope form of a line can be found when the slope of a line and a point on that line are known. The formula for a line in point-slope form is $y - y_1 = m(x - x_1)$.

EXAMPLE

What is the point-slope form of a line with a slope of $-\dfrac{5}{8}$ that passes through $(2, -8)$?

SOLUTION

Use the formula $y - y_1 = m(x - x_1)$ and input the known data.

$$y - (-8) = -\frac{5}{8}(x - 2)$$

$$y + 8 = -\frac{5}{8}(x - 2)$$

Practice Exercises

1. The line connecting the points $(2, -5)$ and $(-8, 3)$ has which slope?

   (A) $-\dfrac{11}{7}$

   (B) $-\dfrac{5}{4}$

   (C) $-\dfrac{4}{5}$

   (D) $\dfrac{4}{5}$

2. A line with the coordinates $(x, 7)$ and $(-4, -2)$ has slope $\dfrac{2}{3}$. What is the value of x?

   (A) 9.5

   (B) 6

   (C) −6

   (D) −9.5

3. What is the equation of a line in slope-intercept form that contains the points $(7, -4)$ and $(-5, 0)$?

(A) $y = \dfrac{5}{3}x - \dfrac{1}{3}$

(B) $y = -\dfrac{1}{3}x + \dfrac{5}{3}$

(C) $y = -\dfrac{1}{3}x - \dfrac{5}{3}$

(D) $3x - 12$

4. What is the equation in point-slope form of a line with slope 6 passing through $(6, 7)$?

(A) $y = 6x - 6$

(B) $y - 6 = 6(x - 7)$

(C) $y - 7 = 6(x - 6)$

(D) $2x + 6y = 7$

Solutions

1. **(C)**
Use the formula $m = \dfrac{y_2 - y_1}{x_2 - x_1}$ to find the slope.
$$\frac{3 - (-5)}{-8 - 2} = -\frac{8}{10} = -\frac{4}{5}$$

2. **(A)**
Place the known values into the slope formula and solve for x.
$$\frac{-2 - 7}{-4 - x} = \frac{2}{3}$$
$$\frac{-9}{-4 - x} = \frac{2}{3}$$

Cross-multiply and solve for x.
$$-9(3) = 2(-4 - x)$$
$$-27 = -8 - 2x$$
$$-19 = -2x$$
$$\frac{-19}{-2} = \frac{-2}{-2}x$$
$$9.5 = x$$

3.   **(C)**

Find the slope of the line connecting $(7, -4)$ and $(-5, 0)$.

$$\frac{0-(-4)}{-5-7} = -\frac{4}{12} = -\frac{1}{3}$$

Using $y = mx + b$, replace x and y with one of the coordinate pairs, $(-5, 0)$.

$$0 = -\frac{1}{3}(-5) + b$$

$$0 = \frac{5}{3} + b$$

$$-\frac{5}{3} = b$$

The equation of the line in slope-intercept form that connects $(7, -4)$ and $(-5, 0)$ is $y = -\frac{1}{3}x - \frac{5}{3}$.

4.   **(C)**

The point-slope form of a line is $y - y_1 = m(x - x_1)$, where x_1 and y_1 are the coordinates of the point. Thus, we get $y - 7 = 6(x - 6)$.

SYSTEMS OF EQUATIONS

Graphing Systems of Linear Equations

A system of equations is a set of two or more equations with two or more variables. A system of equations can be solved by graphing. Let's graph the equations $y = x + 1$ and $y = -2x + 4$.

1.   Graph $y = x + 1$ by starting at $(0, 1)$ and rising 1 and running 1. Connect the dots to graph a line.

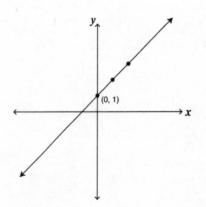

2. On the same coordinate plane, graph the equation $y = -2x + 4$ by starting at $(0, 4)$ and shifting down 2 and moving to the right 1. Connect the dots to graph a line.

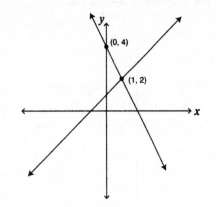

Notice that the lines intersect at $(1, 2)$. You can check your solution by substituting the x and y coordinate in each equation.

$y = x + 1$

$2 = 1 + 1$

$2 = 2$ ✓

$y = -2x + 4$

$2 = (-2)(1) + 4$

$2 = 2$ ✓

Graphing Systems of Linear Inequalities

The rules of graphing inequalities on a number line also apply to graphing linear inequalities in the coordinate plane. Earlier in this chapter we learned about the slope-intercept form of a line. This format can be used to graph linear inequalities as well.

EXAMPLE

Graph the following inequality:

$$y \geq -\frac{2}{3}x + 4$$

SOLUTION

First, graph the line for the equality $y = -\dfrac{2}{3}x + 4$.

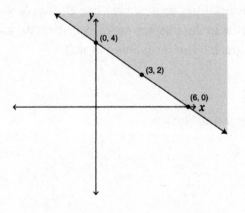

Choose a point on either side of the line and input the coordinates for x and y. If the test point satisfies the inequality, shade its side of the line. If it does not satisfy the inequality, shade the other side of the line. Unless $(0, 0)$ is on the line, it is usually the easiest point to test.

$$y \geq -\frac{2}{3}x + 4$$

$$0 \geq -\frac{2}{3}0 + 4$$

$$0 \geq 4$$

0 is not greater than or equal to 4, so $(0, 0)$ does not satisfy the inequality. Thus, the area above the line is shaded.

EXAMPLE

Graph $y < \dfrac{1}{4}x - 2$.

SOLUTION

Notice that the inequality sign is < not ≤. This means the line $y = \dfrac{1}{4}x - 2$ is not part of the graph. We show this by drawing a dashed line rather than a solid line.

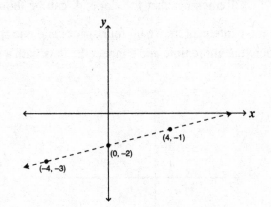

Use a test point to determine where to shade. Since (0, 0) is not on the line, it will serve as the test point again.

$$y < \frac{1}{4}x - 2$$

$$0 < \frac{1}{4}(0) - 2$$

$$0 < -2$$

Since 0 is not less than −2, shade below the line.

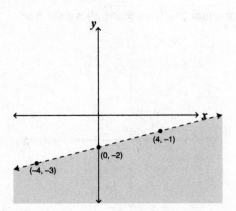

More than one inequality can be graphed on the same coordinate plane.

EXAMPLE

Graph $y \geq 4x - 7$ and $y < -\dfrac{2}{3}x + 3$ on the same coordinate plane.

SOLUTION

Graph $y = 4x - 7$ first. Remember that the slope, 4, can be thought of as $\dfrac{4}{1}$, so starting at $(0, -7)$, the y-intercept, move up four spaces and one space to the right. Repeat this procedure one more time and connect the dots with a solid line.

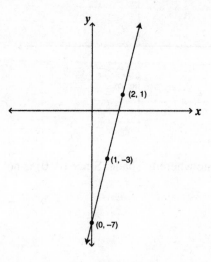

Use the point $(0, 0)$ to decide which side of the line to shade.

$$0 \geq 4(0) - 7$$

$$0 \geq -7$$

0 is greater than or equal to -7, so shade above the line.

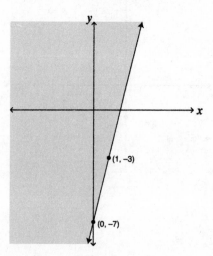

Now graph $y < -\dfrac{2}{3}x + 3$. Remember, the line in this graph is dashed, not solid.

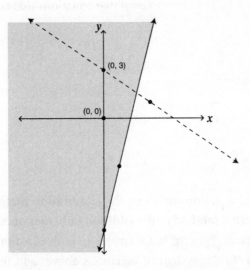

Use (0, 0) to assess which side of the line should be shaded.

$$0 < -\frac{2}{3}(0) + 3$$

$$0 < 3$$

0 < 3 is a true statement, so shade below the line.

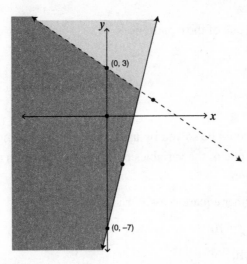

The solution to both problems is the area in which the shading from each inequality intersects.

Solving Systems of Equations Algebraically

Sometimes you will be asked to solve a set of two equations that contain two variables.

EXAMPLE

Solve the system of equations

$$x + y = 10$$

$$x - y = 6$$

SOLUTION

Solve this system of equations by using the **elimination method** (also known as the **linear combination method** or the **addition-subtraction method**). The elimination method eliminates one of the variables in both equations, permitting a solution for the other. In the system of equations above, add the two equations to eliminate y.

$$x + y = 10$$
$$\underline{+\, x - y = 6}$$
$$2x = 16$$
$$x = 8$$

Substitute 8 for x in one of the equations.

$$x + y = 10$$

$$8 + y = 10$$

$$y = 2$$

The same problem could be solved by using the substitution method, in which we find an equation for one of the variables by using one equation and then substitute it in the other equation.

Step 1: Solve either equation for x or y.

$$x + y = 10$$

$$x = 10 - y$$

Step 2: Substitute the value of x, or $10 - y$, into the second equation.

$$x - y = 6$$

$$(10 - y) - y = 6$$

$$10 - 2y = 6$$

$$-2y = -4$$

$$y = 2$$

$$x = 10 - 2 = 8$$

We get the same answers by using either the elimination or substitution methods.

Sometimes we have to multiply one or both of the equations by a number to eliminate a variable.

$$4x + 2y = 8$$

$$x + 3y = 7$$

Since adding the equations does not eliminate a variable, let's multiply the bottom equation by -4 to eliminate x.

$$-4(x + 3y = 7) = -4x - 12y = -28$$

Now add the original top equation to the modified bottom equation.

$$4x + 2y = 8$$
$$+ \ -4x - 12y = -28$$
$$\overline{ -10y = -20}$$
$$y = 2$$

Substitute $y = 2$ into either original equation.

$$4x + 2y = 8$$
$$4x + 2(2) = 8$$
$$4x + 4 = 8$$
$$4x = 4$$
$$x = 1$$

The solution to the system of equations is $x = 1$ and $y = 2$.

Practice Exercises

1. Graph the inequalities $y \geq 4x - 2$ and $y = -\dfrac{1}{2}x + 3$ on the same coordinate plane.

2. Solve the system of equations using the substitution method.

    $$y = 2x - 1$$
    $$2x + 3y = 21$$

    (A) $x = 3$ $y = 5$

    (B) $x = 5$ $y = 3$

    (C) $x = 7$ $y = 2$

    (D) $x = 2$ $y = 7$

Solutions

1. Graph the line $y = 4x - 2$, making sure it is a solid line. Use $(0, 0)$ to test which area to shade.

    $$0 \geq 4(0) - 2$$
    $$0 \geq -2$$

    0 is greater than or equal to –2, so shade above the line.

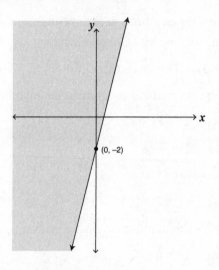

Next graph $y = -\frac{1}{2}x + 3$, making sure to draw a dotted line. Use $(0, 0)$ to test which area to shade.

$$0 < -\frac{1}{2}(0) + 3$$
$$0 < 3$$

0 is less than 3, so shade below the line.

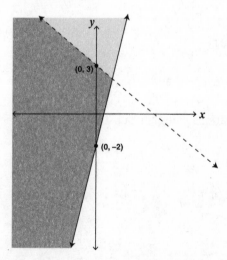

The solution to both inequalities is the shaded area that is the intersection of the two inequalities.

2.   **(A)**

Substitute $2x - 1$ for y in the other equation.

$$2x + 3(2x - 1) = 21$$
$$2x + 6x - 3 = 21$$
$$8x - 3 = 21$$
$$8x - 3 + 3 = 21 + 3$$
$$8x = 24$$
$$\frac{8x}{8} = \frac{24}{8}$$
$$x = 3$$

Substitute 3 for x in either equation.

$$y = 2(3) - 1$$
$$y = 5$$

QUADRATICS

Quadratic Expressions and Equations

A **quadratic expression** has a degree of two. Examples of quadratic expressions are:

$2x^2 + 6x - 7$

$-5x^2 + 3x$

$\frac{1}{2}x^2 - 2x - 11$

Questions on the Praxis exam might ask you to multiply quantities that create quadratic expressions.

EXAMPLE

Find the product of $(3x)(2x - 7)$.

SOLUTION

Use the distributive property to multiply the terms:

$(3x)(2x) - (3x)(7)$

Remember to add the exponents when multiplying like terms.

$(3x)(2x) - (3x)(7) = 6x^2 - 21x$

Some examples use the FOIL method to find the product of certain terms. FOIL is an acronym that means:

F: **F**irst terms get multiplied

O: **O**uter terms get multiplied

I: **I**nner terms get multiplied

L: **L**ast terms get multiplied

EXAMPLE

Find the product of $(2x + 3)(x - 5)$.

SOLUTION

Use FOIL to find the product.

First: $(2x)(x) = 2x^2$

Outer: $(2x)(-5) = -10x$

Inner: $(3)(x) = 3x$

Last: $(3)(-5) = -15$

List the terms in descending order of exponent and simplify.

$$2x^2 - 10x + 3x - 15 = 2x^2 - 7x - 15$$

Factoring Quadratic Expressions

Quadratic expressions can be factored by extracting the greatest common factor (GCF).

EXAMPLE

Factor $3x^2 + 9x$.

SOLUTION

The GCF of $3x^2 + 9x$ is $3x$. Divide each term by $3x$.

$$3x^2 + 9x = 3x(x + 3)$$

You can verify that the expression is correctly factored by multiplying $3x$ by the terms in the parentheses.

$$3x(x + 3) = (3x)(x) + (3x)(3) = 3x^2 + 9x$$

Some quadratic expressions use a more sophisticated form of factoring.

EXAMPLE

Factor $x^2 + 9x + 20$.

SOLUTION

By inspection, we see the expression does not have a GCF other than 1. When the leading coefficient is 1, we ask: What two numbers have a product of 20 and a sum of 9?

$$2 \times 10 = 20 \qquad 2 + 10 = 12$$
$$1 \times 20 = 20 \qquad 1 + 20 = 21$$
$$4 \times 5 = 20 \qquad 4 + 5 = 9$$

4 and 5 have a sum of 9 and a product of 20, so place each in parentheses as follows:

$$(x + 4)(x + 5)$$

Use FOIL to check your work.

First: $(x)(x) = x^2$

Outer: $(x)(5) = 5x$

Inner: $(4)(x) = 4x$

Last: $(4)(5) = 20$

Arrange the terms and simplify.

$$x^2 + 5x + 4x + 20 = x^2 + 9x + 20$$

Let's try a few more.

Practice Exercises

Factor the following quadratic expressions.

1. $x^2 + 7x + 12$

2. $x^2 + 2x - 8$

3. $x^2 - x - 56$

Solutions

1. $x^2 + 7x + 12 = (x + 4)(x + 3)$

2. $x^2 + 2x - 8 = (x + 4)(x - 2)$

3. $x^2 - x - 56 = (x + 7)(x - 8)$

Remember, the coefficient of x in $x^2 - x - 56$ is -1.

Quadratic Equations

Solving quadratic equations is easy once you have mastered factoring quadratic expressions.

EXAMPLE

Solve $2x^2 - 22x = 0$.

SOLUTION

Factor the left side of the equation.

$$2x^2 - 22x = 0$$

$$(2x)(x - 11) = 0$$

Since $(2x)(x - 11) = 0$, one of the quantities in parentheses must equal 0. Set each quantity equal to 0 and solve.

$$2x = 0 \text{ or } x - 11 = 0$$

$$x = 0 \text{ or } x = 11$$

You can check each value to verify its accuracy.

$$x = 11: \ 2(11)^2 - 22(11) = 0$$

$$242 - 242 = 0 \ \checkmark$$

$$x = 0: \ 2(0)^2 - 22(0) = 0$$

$$0 - 0 = 0 \ \checkmark$$

EXAMPLE

Solve $x^2 - 6x - 72 = 0$.

SOLUTION

Factor the left side of the equation:

$$x^2 - 6x - 72 = 0$$
$$(x - 12)(x + 6) = 0$$
$$x - 12 = 0 \text{ or } x + 6 = 0$$
$$x = 12 \text{ or } x = -6$$

Radical equations are challenging when the side without the radical is also an expression.

EXAMPLE

Solve for x: $\sqrt{5x+4} = x - 4$.

SOLUTION

Solve by squaring both sides:

$$(\sqrt{5x+4})^2 = (x-4)^2$$
$$5x + 4 = x^2 - 8x + 16$$

Subtract $5x + 4$ from both sides and solve for x.

$$5x + 4 = x^2 - 8x + 16$$
$$0 = x^2 - 13x + 12$$
$$0 = (x - 12)(x - 1)$$
$$x = 12 \text{ or } x = 1$$

In radical equations, it is important to check all solutions. Sometimes incorrect solutions, called **extraneous solutions**, will arise.

$$\sqrt{5x+4} = x - 4$$
$$\sqrt{5(1)+4} = 1 - 4$$
$$3 \neq -3$$
$$\sqrt{5(12)+4} = 12 - 4$$
$$\sqrt{64} = 8$$
$$8 = 8$$

We find that $x = 12$; $x = 1$ is an extraneous solution.

The Quadratic Formula

The general form for a quadratic formula is $ax^2 + bx + c = 0$, where a and b are coefficients of x^2 and x. The third term, c, is called a **constant**. Earlier we learned how to solve a quadratic equation by factoring. Look at the example we used in the last section.

$$x^2 - 6x - 72 = 0$$

$$(x - 12)(x + 6) = 0$$

$$x - 12 = 0 \text{ or } x + 6 = 0$$

$$x = 12 \text{ or } x = -6$$

Another way to solve quadratic equations is by using the quadratic equation.

$$x = \frac{-b \pm \sqrt{b^2 - 4ac}}{2a}$$

From the equation, $x^2 - 6x - 72 = 0$, we get $a = 1$, $b = -6$, and $c = -72$. Place each value in the quadratic equation and solve:

$$x = \frac{-b \pm \sqrt{b^2 - 4ac}}{2a}$$

$$x = \frac{-(-6) \pm \sqrt{(-6)^2 - 4(1)(-72)}}{2(1)}$$

$$x = \frac{6 \pm \sqrt{(36) - (-288)}}{2}$$

$$x = \frac{6 \pm \sqrt{324}}{2}$$

$$x = \frac{6 \pm 18}{2}$$

$$x = 12 \text{ or } x = -6$$

The quadratic formula is useful if you find factoring difficult. The quadratic equation always works. Consider the following equation.

$$x^2 + 4x - 6 = 0$$

There are no values that have a product of –6 and a sum of 4. Use the quadratic equation to solve.

$$a = 1 \qquad b = 4 \qquad c = -6$$

$$x = \frac{-4 \pm \sqrt{(4)^2 - 4(1)(-6)}}{2(1)}$$

$$x = \frac{-4 \pm \sqrt{40}}{2}$$

$$x = \frac{-4 \pm 2\sqrt{10}}{2}$$

$$x = -2 \pm \sqrt{10}$$

The two solutions are irrational and could not have been derived by using factoring.

PATTERNS

There will be at least one question on the Praxis exam that will test your ability to discern arithmetic and geometric sequences, as well as a combination of both. Patterns can apply to shapes as well as numbers.

EXAMPLE

What is the sixth term in the series 8, 3, –2, –7 …

SOLUTION

Test to see if the progression from term to term is arithmetic (the same number is added repeatedly) or geometric (the same number is multiplied repeatedly). In this series, –5 is added to each term to progress to the next. Thus:

Fifth term: –7 + –5 = –12

Sixth term: –12 + –5 = –17

Let's try another series:

EXAMPLE

Find the next term in the series.

7, 10.5, 15.75, 23.625…

SOLUTION

The series adds 3.5 to 7, but 5.25 to 10.5. Since the same value is not being added repeatedly, the series is not arithmetic. Check to see if the series is geometric. If it is not immediately obvious what number is multiplied, try dividing the second term by the first, the third term by the second, and so on.

$$10.5 \div 7 = 1.5$$
$$15.75 \div 10.5 = 1.5$$
$$23.625 \div 15.75 = 1.5.$$

The series is geometric, so multiply each term by 1.5 to arrive at the successive term. The next term is $23.625 \times 1.5 = 35.437$.

Sometimes a series uses an algorithm (we'll discuss algorithms again in Chapter 6), a pattern that involves using multiple operations.

EXAMPLE

4, 9.8, 17.92, 29.288…

SOLUTION

Each term after the first is found by adding 3 and then multiplying by 1.4.

Find the next two terms.

Fifth term: $29.288 + 3 = 32.288$ $32.288 \times 1.4 = 45.20322$

Sixth term: $45.2032 + 3 = 48.2032$ $48.2032 \times 1.4 = 67.48448$

Sometimes the sequence involves shapes or figures instead of numbers.

EXAMPLE

What is the next figure in the sequence below?

SOLUTION

The next figure should be since the pattern is to turn each figure a quarter turn clockwise.

Functions and Their Graphs

CHAPTER 4

In this chapter we will review the following topics:

- Relations

- Functions

- Linear functions

- Quadratic functions

- Other functions

- Modeling functions based on data

RELATIONS

A **relation** is any set of ordered pairs. The following is a relation:

(2, 0) (–3, 5) (7, 4) (–2, –5)

This same relation can expressed graphically.

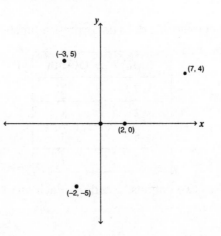

We can also express the relation in an input-output table.

Input	Output
2	0
–2	–5
7	4
–3	5

The set of all inputs is called the **domain**. The set of all outputs is called the **range**. The domain for the relation above is –3, –2, 2, and 7. The range for the relation is –5, 0, 4, and 5.

FUNCTIONS

A **function** establishes a relationship between inputs and outputs. It is important to note that in a function, each input has exactly one output.

EXAMPLE

Does the following input-output table express a function?

Input	Output
6	–3
12	–6
18	–9
24	–12
30	–15

SOLUTION

This input-output table expresses a function because each input has exactly one output.

The following input-output table does *not* express a function.

Input	Output
7	2
3	8
5	–3
7	–7

Notice that input 7 has two outputs, 2 and –7. Each input in a function can have only one output.

EXAMPLE

Does the following input-output table express a function?

Input	Output
7	3
8	3
9	3
23	3

SOLUTION

Although the outputs are identical, each input has only one output. Therefore, this input-output table expresses a function.

Let's see what a function looks like when it is graphed. Let's graph the points (–3, 3), (–2, 2), (–1, 1), (0, 0), (1, 1), (2, 2), (3, 3).

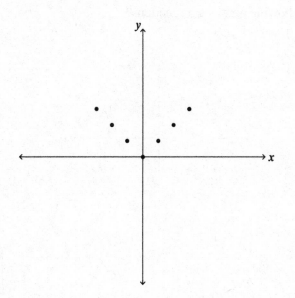

We can use a **vertical line test** to verify the graph is a function. If a vertical line passes through no more than one point on the graph, then the graph represents a function.

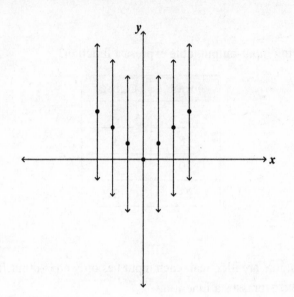

EXAMPLE

Which of the following graphs are functions?

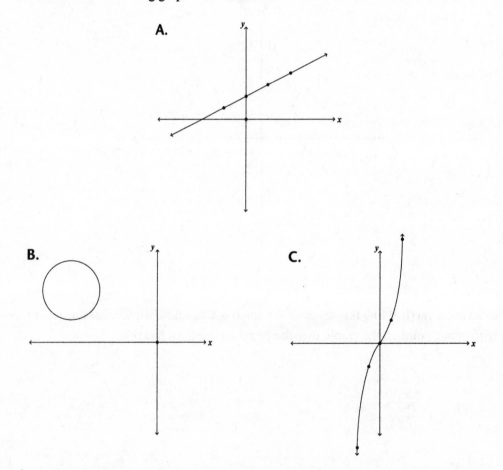

A.

B.

C.

SOLUTION

Draw vertical lines through each graph.

A.

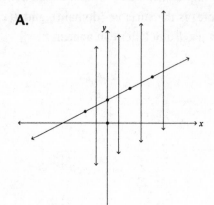

Graph A is a function.

B.

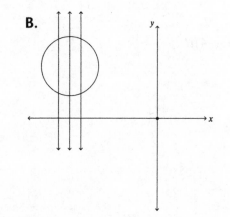

Graph B is not a function.

C.

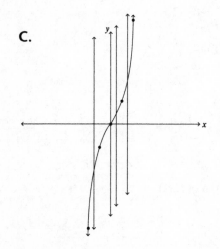

Graph C is a function.

Functional Notation

A function is usually named by a letter. For example $f(x) = 2x - 2$ can be read as "the function of x equals $2x - 2$." The letter in parentheses (x here) is the variable (domain), and $f(x)$, the function, is the range. Although $f(x)$ is most frequently used, any letter can appear.

EXAMPLE

If $g(x) = x^2$, what is $g(-2)$?

SOLUTION

Replace x with -2 in the function.

$$g(-2) = (-2)^2 = 4$$

Sometimes two functions appear in what is known as a **composite function**.

EXAMPLE

If $f(x) = x^2$ and $g(x) = -3x + 2$, what is $f(g(-4))$?

SOLUTION

Substitute $x = -4$ into $g(x)$:

$$g(-4) = -3(-4) + 2 = 14$$

So $g(-4) = 14$

Thus, $f(g(-4))$ means $f(14)$.

$$f(14) = (14)^2 = 196$$

Thus, $f(g(-4)) = 196$

Sometimes the questions can be more challenging.

EXAMPLE

If $g(x) = x^2 - 7$ and $f(x) = x - 6$, what is $g(f(x))$?

SOLUTION

Since $f(x) = x - 6$, substitute $x - 6$ for $f(x)$ in $g(f(x))$.

$$g(x - 6) = (x - 6)^2 - 7$$

Then expand by using the FOIL method and simplify.

$$g(x - 6) = (x^2 - 12x + 36) - 7$$
$$= x^2 - 12x + 29$$

Thus, $g(f(x)) = x^2 - 12x + 29$

Domains of Functions

Earlier we discussed the domain of relations. We will now discuss the **domain of functions**. It is important to note in advance if a function has restrictions.

EXAMPLE

What is the domain of $h(x) = 3x - 5$?

SOLUTION

The value of x can be any number, so the domain is all real numbers (sometimes shown by $\mathbb{R}$), and there are no restrictions.

In the next example, we do find some restrictions, however.

EXAMPLE

What is the domain of $f(x) = \dfrac{1}{x^2 - 9x + 20}$?

SOLUTION

A fraction, expression, or function is undefined when its denominator equals 0. Set the denominator equal to 0 to assess the restrictions:

$$x^2 - 9x + 20 = 0$$
$$(x - 4)(x - 5) = 0$$
$$x = 4, \quad x = 5$$

Thus, function $f(x) = \dfrac{1}{x^2 - 9x + 20}$ is undefined when $x = 4$ and $x = 5$. Using set notation, the domain can be expressed as $(-\infty, 4)$ $(4, 5)$ $(5, \infty)$. This can be interpreted as all real numbers from negative infinity to 4 (but not including 4), all real numbers between 4 and 5 (but not including 4 or 5), and all real numbers greater than 5 (but not including 5).

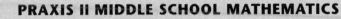
Practice Exercises

1. Is the relation below a function?

    (7, 4) (8, 2) (9, 5) (3, 2)

    (A) No, because the 2 is repeated.

    (B) Yes, because the 2 is repeated.

    (C) No, because each input has exactly one output.

    (D) Yes, because each input has exactly one output.

2. Is the following input-output table a function?

Input	Output
−1	0
0	1
1	3
5	3
1	2

    (A) Yes, the input-output table is a function

    (B) No, the input-output table is not a function.

3. What are the domain and range of the function (7, 5) (8, 4) (9, 3) (10, 2)?

4. Which test can be used to determine if a graph represents a function?

    (A) Vertical line test

    (B) Horizontal line test

    (C) Diagonal line test

    (D) Straight line test

5. Which of the following graphs does *not* express a function?

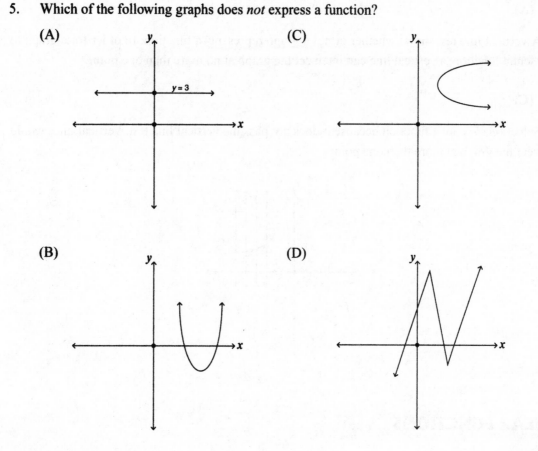

(A)

$y = 3$

(C)

(B)

(D)

Solutions

1. **(D)**

   The relation is a function because each input has exactly one output. A relation can still be a function if different inputs have the same output.

2. **(B)**

   The input-output table does not represent a function because the input 1 has two outputs, 3 and 2.

3. The domain is the set of all inputs: 7, 8, 9, 10. The range is the set of all outputs: 5, 4, 3, 2.

4.   **(A)**

A vertical line test shows whether or not a graph represents a function. In order for a graph to represent a function, a vertical line can intersect the graph at no more than one point.

5.   **(C)**

Selection C is not a function because it does not pass the vertical line test. Vertical lines would intersect the graph at more than one point.

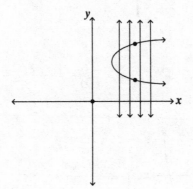

LINEAR FUNCTIONS

The Praxis exam will feature several questions about linear functions. Previously, we learned about the slope-intercept form of a line. In this section, we also use the concept of a straight line, only this time it will be used as a linear function that can predict future data.

A linear function, when graphed, forms a straight line. The following are examples of linear functions:

$$f(x) = -2x + 3$$

$$f(x) = 4$$

In the latter case, the linear function is a horizontal line. Although the y-value repeatedly occurs in the graph, the x-values (the inputs) do not repeat.

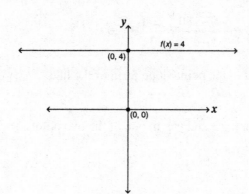

The equation $x = 7$ is a vertical line and is not a function. In the graph below, the x-value (7) always repeats and has much more than one y-value.

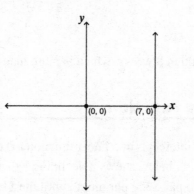

Applications of Linear Functions

Real-life situations can be modeled with linear equations.

EXAMPLE

The third grade class at a local school is raising funds for a school field trip. The class plans to raise funds for eight weeks with the intent of earning $750, the amount needed for the trip. After two weeks, the class had raised $180, and after five weeks, it had raised $540. If the class continues raising money at the same rate, will it have enough money after eight weeks?

SOLUTION

The expression "continues raising money at the *same rate*" means that a linear function is needed to answer the question. The slope of the line represents the rate of change. Let x represent time (in weeks) and y represent the money raised. Thus, we have the points (2, 180) and (5, 540). Find the equation of a line that connects these two points.

$$m = \frac{y_2 - y_1}{x_2 - x_1} = \frac{540 - 180}{5 - 2} = \frac{360}{3} = 120$$

Replace m with 120 in the point-slope form of the line.

$$y = 120x + b$$

Solve for b by replacing x and y with one of the two points, say, (2, 180):

$$180 = 120(2) + b$$

$$180 = 240 + b$$

$$-60 = b$$

The equation of the line connecting (2, 180) and (5, 540) is $y = 120x - 60$. Replace x with 8 to see if the class will raise at least $750 for the field trip in 8 weeks.

$$y = 120(8) - 60$$

$$y = \$900.$$

The class will raise $900 in 8 weeks, which is more than the $750 needed.

Intercepts of a Linear Function

The horizontal and vertical intercepts of a linear function are useful tools for quickly evaluating important information. The graph below shows a declining balance due of a certain debt between two friends. The agreement is to pay $320 per month until the $1,600 balance is paid off.

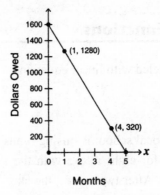

Upon inspection, we can see two important points:

Vertical intercept (0, 1600): The y-intercept indicates what the debt balance is at time 0, before the first payment is made.

Horizontal intercept (5, 0): The x-intercept indicates the number of months needed to pay off the debt.

QUADRATIC FUNCTIONS

A **quadratic function** is a function that uses the model $f(x) = ax^2 + bx + c$, where $a \neq 0$. For example, the outputs of the function $f(x) = 2x^2 - 6x + 8$ for the inputs -3, 0.5, and 7 are:

$$f(-3) = (2)(-3)^2 - (6)(-3) + 8 = 44$$

$$f(0.5) = (2)(0.5)^2 - (6)(0.5) + 8 = 5.5$$

$$f(7) = (2)(7)^2 - (6)(7) + 8 = 64$$

This quadratic function can be expressed by using the following input/output table.

x	$f(x)$
-3	44
0.5	5.5
7	64

Graphing Quadratic Functions

In Chapter 3 we learned to solve quadratic equations in the form of $ax^2 + bx + c = 0$.

EXAMPLE

Solve the quadratic equation $x^2 + 2x - 24 = 0$.

SOLUTION

$x^2 + 2x - 24 = 0$

$(x + 6)(x - 4) = 0$

$x + 6 = 0$ or $x - 4 = 0$

$x = -6$ or $x = 4$

Quadratic equations in the form of $y = ax^2 + bx + c$ can be graphed in the coordinate plane. The graph of a quadratic equation is called a **parabola** and can take several forms. On the Praxis exam, you will be responsible to know the following forms of a parabola:

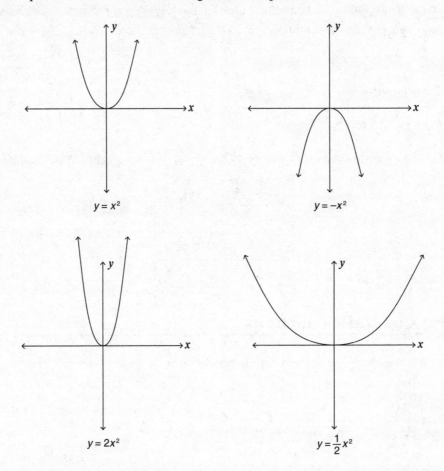

$y = x^2$

$y = -x^2$

$y = 2x^2$

$y = \frac{1}{2}x^2$

When the coefficient of x^2 is negative, the parabola opens downward; when the coefficient of x^2 is positive, the parabola opens upward. Further, larger coefficients of x^2 narrow the opening of the parabola, while smaller ones widen it.

A parabola always has a **vertex** and an **axis of symmetry**. The vertex is the minimum value of y when the parabola is in the form of $y = x^2$ and the maximum value when the form of the graph is $y = -x^2$. The axis of symmetry, usually shown as a dashed line, separates the halves of the parabola. Many parabolas contain x- and y-intercepts.

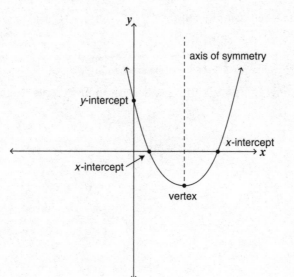

Follow these steps when graphing a parabola.

EXAMPLE

Graph $y = x^2 - 8x + 12$.

SOLUTION

Step 1: Find the axis of symmetry by using the formula $x = -\dfrac{b}{2a}$.

$$y = x^2 - 8x + 12$$
$$a = 1, b = -8, c = 12$$
$$x = -\frac{(-8)}{2(1)} = 4$$

Step 2: Find the vertex by replacing x with the value of the axis of symmetry.

$$y = (4)^2 - 8(4) + 12 = -4$$

The coordinates of the vertex are $(4, -4)$.

Step 3: Find the x-intercepts by letting $y = 0$ in the original equation.

$$0 = x^2 - 8x + 12$$
$$0 = (x - 6)(x - 2)$$
$$x - 6 = 0, x - 2 = 0$$
$$x = 6, x = 2$$

The x-intercepts are $(6,0)$ and $(2,0)$.

Step 4: Find the y-intercept by letting $x = 0$.

$$y = (0)^2 - 8(0) + 12 = 12$$

The y-intercept is $(0, 12)$.

Graph the axis of symmetry, vertex, and x- and y-intercepts to get an idea of the graph's shape.

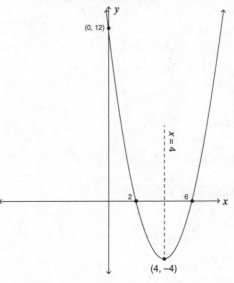

You can add some more values of x and evaluate y to get a better idea of the parabola's shape.

$$y = x^2 - 8x + 12$$

x	y
1	5
3	−3
7	5

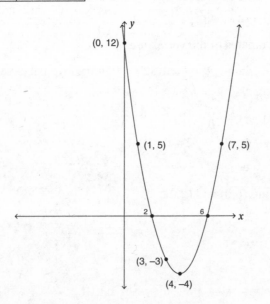

Domain and Range of Quadratic Functions

The domain of a parabola is the set of all possible x-values when it is in the form of $f(x) = x^2$. Similarly, the range of a parabola is the set of all possible y-values when it is in the form of $f(x) = x^2$. Let's use our previous example and graph to find the domain and range of a quadratic function.

Although the graph of $y = x^2 - 8x + 12$ cannot be shown in its entirety, it should be clear that the domain is all real numbers; any value of x is permitted in this function. Using set notation, the domain is defined as $(-\infty, \infty)$.

In contrast to the domain, there are restrictions on the range. Note that the least value of y occurs at the vertex, so the range is defined as $y \geq -4$. Using set notation, the range is defined as $[-4, \infty)$.

Practice Exercises

1. Diane makes extra money by word processing pages for a fee. She charges $3.00 per page. The following table represents her earnings for one recent week.

x = Pages	y = $ earned
0	0
5	15
2	6
3	9

The following is a graph of the function.

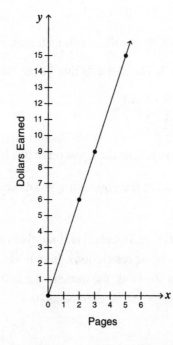

a.   Do the table and the graph express a linear function?

b.   What is the slope of the function?

c.   What equation models this function?

d.   How much would Diane earn if she word processed a document that was 17 pages long?

e.   What are the domain and range of the function?

2.   An auto repair shop charges $48.00 to inspect a car and $75.00 per hour subsequently for every hour of labor to repair the car. What linear model represents the fee schedule (disregard the cost of parts)?

(A) $f(x) = 48x + 75y$

(B) $f(x) = 75x + 48$

(C) $f(x) = 48x + 75$

(D) $f(x) = 75x - 48$

3.   If $f(x) = x^2 + 6x + 9$, what are the x- and y-intercepts of the function?

(A) $x = 9, y = -3$

(B) $x = -3, y = 9$

(C) $x = 3, y = 9$

(D) $x = 1, y = 16$

Solutions

1.

a. Both the table and the graph express a linear function. The points lie along a straight, non-vertical line.

b. Look at the points (2, 6) and (3, 9). As the x-value increases by 1 (run), the y-value increases by 3 (rise). Therefore, $\dfrac{\text{rise}}{\text{run}}$ is $\dfrac{3}{1}$ or 3. The slope of this linear function is 3. We could also use the slope formula to find $m = \dfrac{y_2 - y_1}{x_2 - x_1} = \dfrac{9 - 6}{3 - 2} = \dfrac{3}{1} = 3$.

c. The slope is 3 and the y-intercept is 0, so the equation of this linear function is $f(x) = 3x + 0 = 3x$.

d. Substituting 17 for the x-value in the equation $y = 3x$, we calculate that Diane would earn $51 for the job.

e. Although the linear function $f(x) = 3x$ has all real numbers as both the domain and range, the practical applications of the function bring restrictions. In real life, there can be no time before time 0 and no dollar amount is lower than $0. Thus, the domain is $x \geq 0$ and the range is $y \geq 0$. Using set notation, both the domain and the range can be defined as $[0, \infty)$.

2. **(B)**

The fixed cost, $48.00, is the *y*-intercept; it does not vary. The cost of labor, $75.00 per hour, varies according to the number of hours worked. Thus, the rate $75 is the slope. The linear model that represents this fee schedule is $f(x) = 75x + 48$.

3. **(B)**

The function $f(x) = x^2 + 6x + 9$ can also be written as $y = x^2 + 6x + 9$. Find the *x*-intercept by letting $y = 0$ and solve for *x*:

$$x^2 + 6x + 9 = 0$$
$$(x + 3)(x + 3) = 0$$
$$x + 3 = 0 \text{ or } x + 3 = 0$$
$$x = -3$$

The *x*-intercept of the function is –3. Find the *y*-intercept by letting $x = 0$ and solving for *y*:

$$y = (0)^2 + 6(0) + 9 = 9$$

The *y*-intercept of the function is $y = 9$.

OTHER FUNCTIONS

Many relationships that aren't linear or quadratic can also be functions. Here we will look at two: absolute value functions and exponential functions. Both of these pass the vertical line test.

Absolute Value Functions

The basic absolute value function is $f(x) = |x|$, and its graph always looks like the graph below.

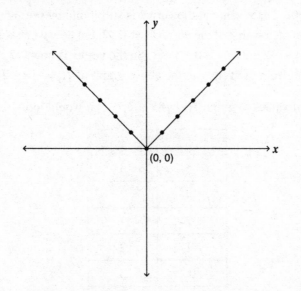

This is a function since for every value of x, there is only one value of $f(x)$. Notice that the vertex, or lowest point, is at the origin and that there are two lines, which are symmetric around the y-axis, where $x = 0$. Also, the slopes of the lines are $+1$ and -1.

Not all absolute value equations are this simple. They may shift up or down, left or right, or have a slope that is different than $m = 1$ or $m = -1$.

Let's change the value inside the absolute value signs. For example, let $f(x) = |x + 2|$. What does that do to the basic graph? The value inside the absolute value signs isn't just x anymore, so we must set the value within the signs equal to 0 to find the x-value of the vertex. When $x + 2 = 0$, $x = -2$, and if $x = -2$, then $f(x) = |x + 2| = |0| = 0$, so the vertex for $f(x) = |x + 2|$ is $(-2, 0)$. We haven't changed anything else in the basic absolute value equation—it will still have slopes of $+1$ and -1, it will still be symmetric, but not around the y-axis since the vertex is $(-2, 0)$. Now it will be symmetric around the line $x = -2$. In other words, the whole basic graph is shifted to the left 2 units, as shown.

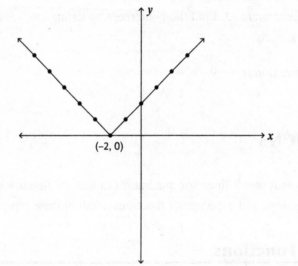

$(-2, 0)$

Now, what if we add a value to the basic equation? For example, let's look at the absolute value equation $f(x) = |x + 2| + 1$. The x-value of the vertex is still found by setting what is in the absolute value signs equal to 0. So the x-value of the vertex is still -2, but now when we substitute $x = -2$ into the equation, we get $f(x) = |-2 + 2| + 1 = 0 + 1 = 1$. So the vertex is now $(-2, 1)$. In other words, the vertex is shifted up 1 unit from the vertex in the above graph of $f(x) = |x + 2|$.

If we make a table of values to graph $f(x) = |x + 2| + 1$, it would look like:

x	y
−5	3
−4	2
−2	1
−1	2
0	3

Let's plot these points to see what this graph would look like. It is similar to the last one, but now the vertex is shifted from the basic absolute value equation not only 2 units to the left, but also up 1 unit.

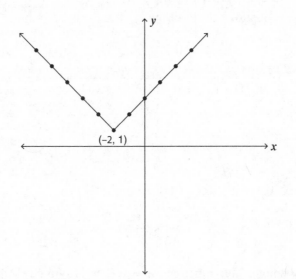

So, adding a positive constant to the absolute value moves the graph up. If the constant were negative, the graph would move down.

EXAMPLE

In what quadrant would the vertex of the graph of $f(x) = |x - 3| - 2$ be?

SOLUTION

The graph has a vertex to the right of the y-axis (because –3 is negative) and below the x-axis (because –2 is negative), so it would be (3, –2), in the fourth quadrant.

Finally, let's consider an absolute value function such as $f(x) = -3|x + 2| + 1$. What does the –3 do to the graph? It actually tells the slope of the right-hand side of the graph, $m = -3 = \dfrac{-3}{1}$, which means for every 3 units down, it goes 1 unit to the right. Since the graph is symmetrical around the vertical line that passes through the vertex, we can also easily figure out the left-hand side of the graph. Notice that the graph of $f(x) = -3|x + 2| + 1$ has a vertex of (–2, 1), but it is "flipped," or in a ^ shape. That is because the sign of –3 is negative. If the equation had a positive factor in front of the absolute value quantity, the graph would be in a V shape.

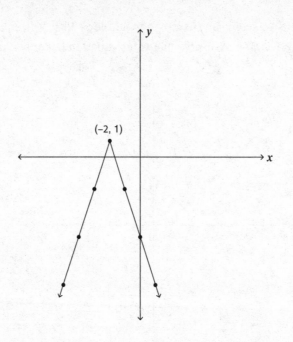

To summarize, an absolute value function has a vertex, is symmetric around the vertical line through the vertex, and its location and shape are determined by the values of a, b, and c in the function

$$f(x) = a|x + b| + c$$

where:

a tells the slope of the right-hand portion of the graph (the left-hand portion is a mirror image with slope $-a$). If a is positive, the graph looks like V; if a is negative, the graph looks like ^.

b tells whether the graph shifts left or right of the origin. If b is negative, the graph shifts to the right; if b is positive, the graph shifts to the left. (This seems the opposite of the number line, where + is to the right and – is to the left, but it is because this shift is determined by setting $x + b = 0$.)

c tells whether the vertex is raised or lowered from the x-axis. If c is positive, it is raised c units; if c is negative, it is lowered c units.

Exponential Functions

An exponential function is a special function that is used to depict very rapid changes that aren't linear. Powers of 2 are a good example, $f(x) = 2^x$. The first several values are (1, 2), (2, 4), (3, 8), (4, 16), (5, 32). But it goes sky high in a very short order. The point for $x = 10$ is (10, 1024), and for $x = 20$, it is (20, 1048576). That is very rapid growth.

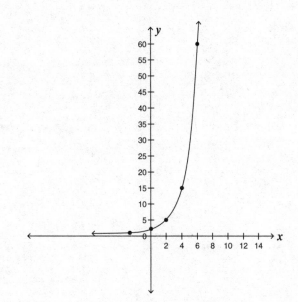

An exponential function $f(x) = b^x$ differs from the formula for a power function $f(x) = x^b$, for example, because now x is the exponent. The base, b, is a number that cannot be negative, nor can it be 0 or 1. If it were negative, its value would alternate between a positive and negative number, and if it were 0 or 1, its value would be a constant 0 or 1, respectively, with no exponential change.

The graph of an exponential function has some interesting features:

1. It will never cross the x-axis, although it can get quite close to it.

2. x (the domain) can be any real number, positive or negative.

3. $f(x)$ (the range) can be all real numbers greater than 0.

4. The graph always passes through the point $(0, 1)$ because $b^0 = 1$.

5. The graph passes the vertical line test.

6. The ends of the graph get close to a value but never reach it. This value is called an **asymptote**.

7. If b is greater than 1, the graph shows an exponential increase; if b is between 0 and 1 (a fraction), the graph shows an exponential decrease.

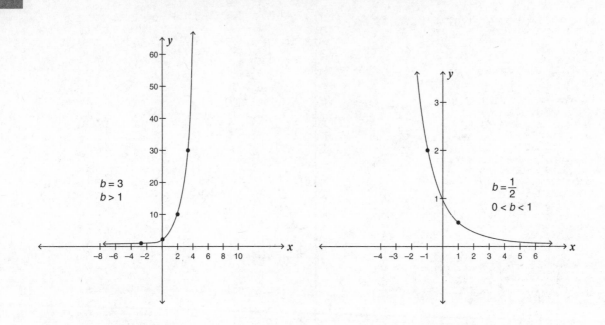

$b = 3$
$b > 1$

$b = \dfrac{1}{2}$
$0 < b < 1$

An example of an exponential increase is shown by bacteria, which multiply rapidly unless killed or kept under control by medicine. An example of an exponential decrease is the subject of a well-known math puzzle: If you take a step half the distance to a wall every few seconds, at what time would you reach the wall? The answer is never. You would get quite close, but never reach it.

Practice Exercises

1. What is the equation for the following graph?

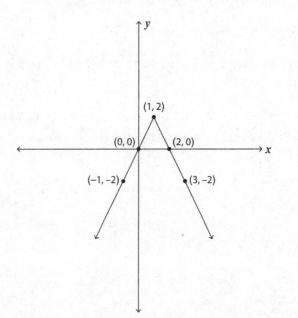

(A) $f(x) = |x - 2| + 1$

(B) $f(x) = 2|x - 1| + 1$

(C) $f(x) = -2|x - 1| + 2$

(D) $f(x) = -2|x + 1| - 2$

2. If the slope of the right-hand side of an absolute value function is +3, what is the slope of the left-hand side?

(A) +3

(B) −3

(C) $+\dfrac{1}{3}$

(D) $-\dfrac{1}{3}$

3. Absolute value equations are symmetric on either side of

(A) the vertical line that contains the vertex

(B) the horizontal line that contains the vertex

(C) the x-axis

(D) the y-axis

4. In the following graph of an exponential function, identify the two possible asymptotes.

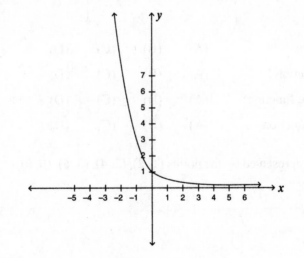

(A) $x = 0, y = 0$

(B) $x = -2, y = 0$

(C) $x = 0, y = 1$

(D) $x = 0, y = -2$

5. Four fruit flies are used in a biology experiment. Fruit flies can reproduce shortly after birth. The researcher expects more than 16,000 fruit flies from these two pairs in less than a month. This is an example of

   (A) absolute value

   (B) exponential decay

   (C) exponential growth

   (D) a linear function

6. Which of the following graphs is an example of exponential decay?

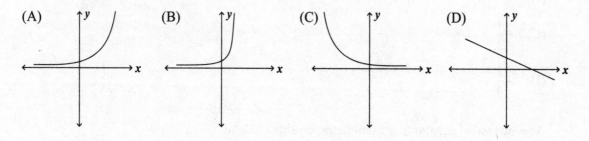

7. Match the following graphs to their function names according to the following choices:

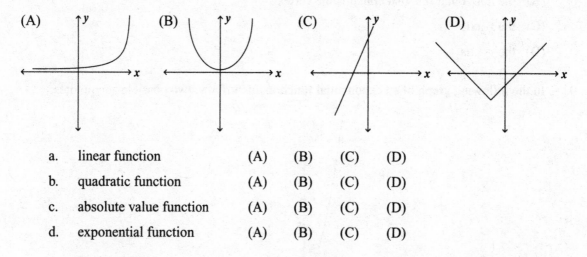

   a. linear function   (A)   (B)   (C)   (D)

   b. quadratic function   (A)   (B)   (C)   (D)

   c. absolute value function   (A)   (B)   (C)   (D)

   d. exponential function   (A)   (B)   (C)   (D)

8. Find the equation represented by the points $(1, 2)$, $(2, 4)$, $(3, 6)$, $(0, 0)$, $(-1, 2)$, $(-2, 4)$, $(-3, 6)$.

   (A) $f(x) = 2x$

   (B) $f(x) = -2|x|$

   (C) $f(x) = 2|x|$

   (D) $f(x) = \dfrac{1}{2}|x|$

Solutions

1. **(C)**

    For the vertex to be (1, 2), the term inside the absolute value signs must be $x - 1$. Also, since the graph opens downward, the sign before the absolute value sign must be negative. Choice (C), $f(x) = -2|x - 1| + 2$ is the only answer with these attributes. Other clues are that since the vertex is (1, 2), the y-axis must be 2 units above the x-axis, and the slope of the right-hand side is –2, so the factor in front of the absolute value sign must be –2.

2. **(B)**

    The slopes of the two sides of an absolute value graph have different signs (but have the same numerical value).

3. **(A)**

    Symmetry of an absolute value function is around a line x = constant, where the constant is the x-value of the vertex.

4. **(B)**

    The x-asymptote must be negative, and the y-asymptote is the x-axis ($y = 0$).

5. **(C)**

    Rapid growth that isn't linear is exponential growth.

6. **(C)**

    Exponential decay is curved with a negative-type slope.

7a. **(C)**

7b. **(B)**

7c. **(D)**

7d. **(A)**

8. **(C)**

    The graph is an absolute value function with the vertex at (0, 0) and the slope at 2.

MODELING FUNCTIONS BASED ON DATA

Data descriptions can be displayed in a table that can be transformed into an equation or graph.

EXAMPLE

Given the following pairs of numbers (x, y), construct a table and determine whether they express a function. Sketch the graph of these points. If the points represent a function, find the equation for that function: $(-2, -3)$, $(0, 1)$, $(1, 3)$, $(2, 5)$.

SOLUTION

The table is

x	y
−2	−3
0	1
1	3
2	5

These points represent a function because for each x there is only one y value.

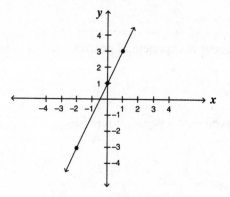

These points form a straight line, so find the slope by choosing any two points,

$$m = \frac{y_1 - y_2}{x_1 - x_2} = \frac{5 - 3}{2 - 1} = \frac{2}{1} = 2$$

Then use any of the points in the slope equation $m = \dfrac{y - y_3}{x - x_3}$ to find the equation of the line. Using the point $(0, 1)$:

$$2 = \frac{y - 1}{x - 0}$$

$$2x = y - 1$$

$$y = 2x + 1$$

Practice Exercises

1. Determine which table represents the following scenario: Julio banks $10 plus half of his take-home pay from his second job. Let x = his take-home pay, and $f(x)$ = the amount he banks.

(A)

x	$f(x)$
50	30
60	35
70	40
80	45

(B)

x	$f(x)$
50	60
60	70
70	80
80	90

(C)

x	$f(x)$
50	25
60	30
70	35
80	40

(D)

x	$f(x)$
50	35
60	40
70	45
80	50

2. Which equation represents the amounts that Julio banks, according to the scenario in Exercise 1?

(A) $f(x) = \dfrac{x}{2} + 10$

(B) $f(x) = \dfrac{x+10}{2}$

(C) $f(x) = x + \dfrac{10}{2}$

(D) $f(x) = \dfrac{x}{2} - 10$

3. Sketch a graph that shows the scenario from Exercise 1.

Solutions

1. **(D)**

    If Julio makes $50, he would bank $10 more than $25 (half of the $50), or $35.

2. **(A)**

    The function is 10 plus $\dfrac{1}{2}$ of x, which can be written as $f(x) = \dfrac{x}{2} + 10$.

3.   Plot points that correspond to part D of Exercise 1.

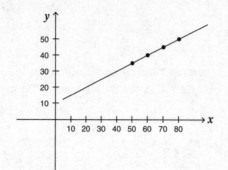

Geometry and Measurement

In this chapter we will review the following topics:

- Points, lines, and planes

- Angles

- Polygons

- Triangles

- Quadrilaterals

- Congruence and similarity

- Perimeter and area of polygons

- Circles

- Three-dimensional figures

- Volume

- Transformations, nets, and constructions

- Units of measure

POINTS, LINES, AND PLANES

The building blocks of geometry are points, lines, and planes.

Points

A **point** is represented by a dot. A point has no dimension.

•A is called point A

Lines

A **line** can be drawn through any two points. A line has one dimension and extends infinitely in opposite directions.

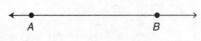

The line above can be labeled as $\overleftrightarrow{AB}$ (called line AB) or $\overleftrightarrow{BA}$.

The line above can also be labeled by a lowercase letter such as l.

If three or more points lie on the same line, they are called **collinear points**. Points that do not lie on the same line are called **non-collinear points**.

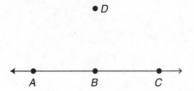

Points A, B, and C are collinear; points A, B, and D are non-collinear.

A part of a line that begins at one point (called an **endpoint**) and extends infinitely in the opposite direction is called a **ray**. A ray is shown below.

Since the endpoint is A, the ray is labeled $\overrightarrow{AB}$. It is important to note that the ray cannot be labeled $\overrightarrow{BA}$; the endpoint must always come first.

A part of a line that has a beginning and an end (that is, two endpoints) is called a **line segment**.

This line segment can be labeled $\overline{AB}$ or $\overline{BA}$.

The Distance Formula

The **distance formula** is used to determine the length of a line segment. The formula is:

$$\text{Distance} = \sqrt{(x_1 - x_2)^2 + (y_1 - y_2)^2}$$ where the endpoints are (x_1, y_1) and (x_2, y_2).

EXAMPLE

Find the length of $\overline{AB}$ if the coordinates of A are $(2, -4)$ and B are $(2, -12)$.

SOLUTION

Input the coordinates into the distance formula.

x_1: 2

x_2: 2

y_1: -4

y_2: -12

$$\text{Distance} = \sqrt{(2-2)^2 + (-4-(-12))^2} = \sqrt{64} = 8$$

Either point can be designated as (x_1, y_1); the results will be the same.

The Midpoint Formula

All line segments have a midpoint, which is the exact middle of the segment. The formula to calculate the midpoint of a segment with endpoints (x_1, y_1) and (x_2, y_2) is:

$$\left(\frac{x_1 + x_2}{2}, \frac{y_1 + y_2}{2} \right)$$

EXAMPLE

Find the midpoint of the segment with endpoints $(8, -3)$ and $(7, -1)$.

SOLUTION

Use the midpoint formula.

$$\left(\frac{8+7}{2}, \frac{-3+(-1)}{2} \right)$$

$$\left(\frac{15}{2}, -2 \right)$$

Planes

A **plane** extends indefinitely in two dimensions. A minimum of three non-collinear points determine a plane. Points that lie in the same plane are called **coplanar points**. Planes can be drawn using three coplanar points. Planes are named by an uppercase letter.

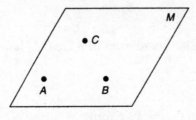

Planes *A, B,* and *C* are coplanar on plane *M*.

The intersection of two lines is a point, and the intersection of two planes is a line.

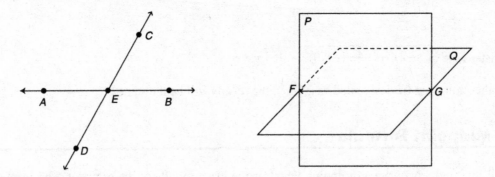

Lines $\overleftrightarrow{AB}$ and $\overleftrightarrow{CD}$ intersect at point *E*. Planes *P* and *Q* intersect at line $\overleftrightarrow{FG}$.

ANGLES

An **angle** is a pair of rays with a common endpoint. The endpoint is called the **vertex** of the angle.

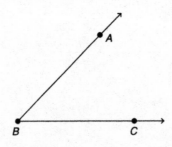

This angle can be named in several ways:

∠*ABC*, ∠*CBA*, or ∠*B*

Note that an angle can be named solely by its vertex. However, to avoid confusion, sometimes three letters must be used.

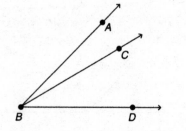

In the diagram above, referring to ∠B is confusing. Does ∠B in the diagram mean ∠ABC, ∠CBD, or ∠ABD?

Angles that share a side and a vertex, such as ∠ABC and ∠CBD are called **adjacent angles**.

Types of Angles

Angles are measured in units called **degrees,** which are indicated by the symbol °. Angles are classified by their size:

Acute: measures less than 90°

Right: measures exactly 90°

Obtuse: measures more than 90° and less than 180°

Straight: measures exactly 180°

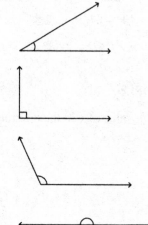

Special Angle Pairs

Two angles with measures that add up to 90° are called **complementary angles**. They do not have to be adjacent angles.

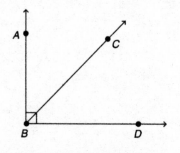

∠ABC and ∠CBD are complementary angles.

Two angles with measures that add up to 180° are called **supplementary angles**. Again, they do not have to be adjacent angles.

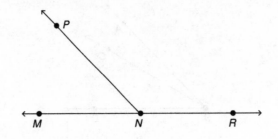

∠*MNP* and ∠*PNR* are supplementary angles.

EXAMPLE

∠*ABC* and ∠*CBD* are complementary angles. If *m* ∠*ABC* (read as "the measure of angle *ABC*") is 67.2°, what is *m*∠*CBD*?

SOLUTION

Complementary angles have a sum of 90°. Subtract 67.2° from 90° to find *m*∠*CBD*.

$$90° - 67.2° = 22.8°$$

$$m∠CBD = 22.8°$$

EXAMPLE

Find the value of *x* in the diagram below.

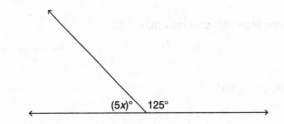

SOLUTION

The two angles are supplementary because they create a straight angle. Find their sum and set it equal to 180°.

$$5x + 125° = 180°$$

$$5x = 55°$$

$$x = 11°$$

Perpendicular and Parallel Lines

Perpendicular lines are two lines that cross at 90° angles, forming four 90° angles. The symbol for "is perpendicular to" is ⊥.

Parallel lines are lines in the same plane that never intersect. The addition of more arrowheads on the lines denotes that the lines are parallel. Parallelism can also be shown by indicating $l \parallel m$, where the symbol ∥ means "is parallel to."

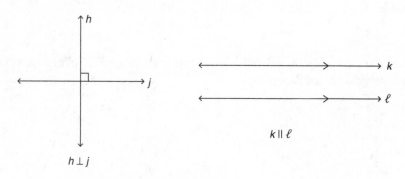

Angles Formed by Parallel Lines and a Transversal

When parallel lines are intersected by another line (called a **transversal**), several angle relationships are created.

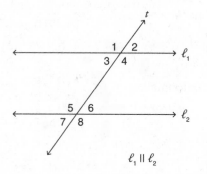

Corresponding angles are ∠1 and ∠5, ∠3 and ∠7, ∠2 and ∠6, ∠4 and ∠8. They are called **corresponding angles** because they are in the same position at each parallel line. Corresponding angles are equal.

$m\angle 1 = m\angle 5$

$m\angle 3 = m\angle 7$

$m\angle 2 = m\angle 6$

$m\angle 4 = m\angle 8$

Alternate interior angles are $\angle 3$ and $\angle 6$, $\angle 4$ and $\angle 5$. They are on alternate sides of t and are interior to ℓ_1 and ℓ_2. Alternate interior angles are equal.

$$m\angle 3 = m\angle 6$$

$$m\angle 4 = m\angle 5$$

Alternate exterior angles are $\angle 2$ and $\angle 7$, $\angle 1$ and $\angle 8$. They are on alternate sides of t and are exterior to ℓ_1 and ℓ_2. Alternate exterior angles have equal measures.

$$m\angle 2 = m\angle 7$$

$$m\angle 1 = m\angle 8$$

Vertical angles are $\angle 1$ and $\angle 4$, $\angle 3$ and $\angle 2$, $\angle 5$ and $\angle 8$, $\angle 7$ and $\angle 6$. They are vertically across from each other. Vertical angles are equal.

$$m\angle 1 = m\angle 4$$

$$m\angle 3 = m\angle 2$$

$$m\angle 5 = m\angle 8$$

$$m\angle 7 = m\angle 6$$

All other angle pairs in the figure that are not listed above (for example, $\angle 1$ and $\angle 2$ or $\angle 6$ and $\angle 8$) are supplementary because they form a straight line or total 180°.

Practice Exercises

1. Three non-collinear points determine a

    (A) line

    (B) ray

    (C) line segment

    (D) plane

2. The endpoints of $\overline{AB}$ are A (–6, 2) and B (4, –8). What is the length of $\overline{AB}$?

    (A) 200

    (B) $2\sqrt{10}$

    (C) $10\sqrt{2}$

    (D) $\sqrt{20}$

3. A segment has endpoints (5, –4) and (3, –8). What are the coordinates of the segment's mid-point?

    (A) (4, –6)

    (B) (–4, 6)

    (C) (4, 6)

    (D) (–4, –6)

4. Two supplementary angles have measures of $(7x)°$ and $(5x)°$. What is the measure of the smaller angle?

    (A) 180°

    (B) 105°

    (C) 75°

    (D) 15°

5.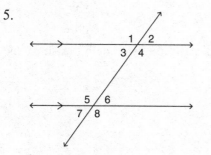

    $m\angle 1 = (6x)°$ and $m\angle 5 = (4x + 40)°$. What is the value of x?

    (A) 20

    (B) 30

    (C) 40

    (D) 60

Solutions

1. **(D)**

    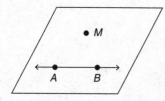

    Points *A*, *B*, and *M* are non-collinear points because they do not lie on the same line. A minimum of three non-collinear points is needed to determine a plane. Since non-collinear points determine a plane, they are also called coplanar points.

2. **(C)**

Use the distance formula to calculate the length of $\overline{AB}$.

$$\text{Distance} = \sqrt{(x_1 - x_2)^2 + (y_1 - y_2)^2}$$

$$\text{Distance} = \sqrt{(-6-4)^2 + (2-(-8))^2} = \sqrt{100 + 100} = \sqrt{200} = 10\sqrt{2}$$

3. **(A)**

Use the midpoint formula to calculate the midpoint.

$$\left(\frac{x_1 + x_2}{2}, \frac{y_1 + y_2}{2} \right)$$

$$\left(\frac{5+3}{2}, \frac{-4+(-8)}{2} \right)$$

$$(4, -6)$$

4. **(C)**

Supplementary angles are angle pairs with a sum of 180°. Add the two angle measures and solve for x.

$$5x + 7x = 180°$$

$$12x = 180°$$

$$x = 15°$$

The question requires the measure of the smaller angle, which is $5x$, so multiply 5 and 15°.

$$5 \times 15° = 75°$$

5. **(A)**

$\angle 1$ and $\angle 5$ are corresponding angles. When lines are parallel, corresponding angles have equal measures. Set $6x$ equal to $4x + 40$ to find the value of x.

$$6x = 4x + 40$$

$$2x = 40$$

$$x = 20$$

POLYGONS

A **polygon** is a plane figure in which three or more sides meet to form angles, or vertices (plural of vertex). Thus, they are **closed** figures. There are two general types of polygons:

A **convex polygon**, such as *ABCD*, is a closed polygon in which no line containing a side has a point within the polygon's interior.

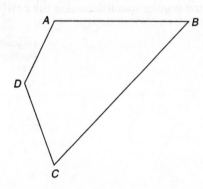

A **concave polygon**, such as *STUVW*, is a closed polygon that is not convex. Notice how line *WV* has points in the interior of *SWVUT*.

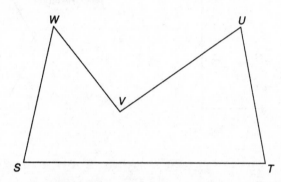

Polygons are named for the number of sides:

Number of Sides	Name
3	Triangle
4	Quadrilateral
5	Pentagon
6	Hexagon
7	Heptagon
8	Octagon
9	Nonagon
10	Decagon
12	Dodecagon
n	*n*-gon

An *n*-gon means a polygon with *n* sides, so a polygon with 15 sides is called a 15-gon, and a polygon with 30 sides is called a 30-gon.

An important subset of convex polygons is the set of **regular polygons**. Regular polygons are **equiangular** (all angles are equal) and **equilateral** (all sides are equal). Equal sides are shown with the same tick mark. Notice that the regular quadrilateral is the easily recognizable square.

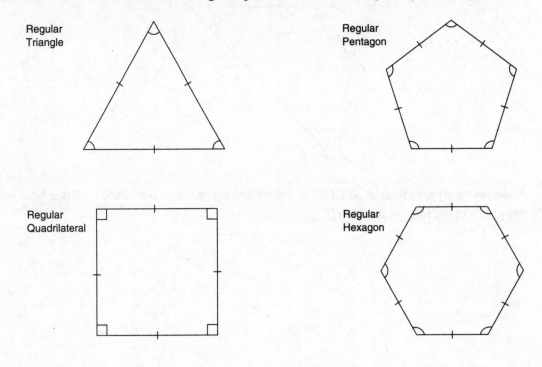

Regular Triangle

Regular Pentagon

Regular Quadrilateral

Regular Hexagon

TRIANGLES

A **triangle** is a closed figure with three sides and three angles. Each side of a triangle meets the others to form a vertex.

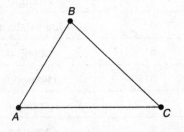

Sides: $\overline{AB}$, $\overline{BC}$, $\overline{AC}$

Angles: $\angle A$, $\angle B$, $\angle C$

The sum of the measures of the angles in a triangle is 180°.

$m\angle A + m\angle B + m\angle C = 180°$

A triangle can be classified by the length of its sides.

Equilateral: All sides have equal measures. Notice that all sides have the same tick mark.

Isosceles: Two sides have equal measures. Notice that only two sides have the same tick mark.

Scalene: No sides have equal measures. Notice that all sides have different tick marks.

A triangle can also be classified by its angle measures.

Acute: All angles measure less than 90°.

Right: Contains one right (90°) angle (shown by a small box).

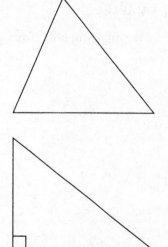

Obtuse: Contains one angle greater than 90° but less than 180°.

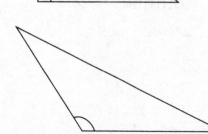

Angle – Side Relationship

In a triangle, the largest angle is opposite the longest side. Similarly, the middle and smallest angles are opposite the middle and shortest sides, respectively. Likewise, the longest side is opposite the largest angle, the middle side is opposite the middle angle, and the shortest side is opposite the smallest angle.

EXAMPLE

List the sides of $\triangle ABC$ in order from greatest to least.

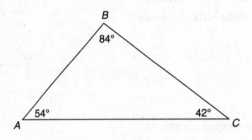

SOLUTION

The largest side is opposite the largest angle, so

$$\overline{AC} > \overline{BC} > \overline{AB}$$

Similarly, the largest angle is opposite the longest side.

EXAMPLE

List the angles in order from greatest to least.

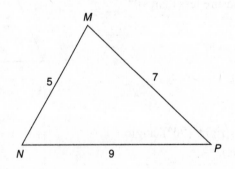

SOLUTION

$\angle M > \angle N > \angle P$

Exterior Angles

An **exterior angle** to a triangle is the angle formed by extending a side. Each exterior angle equals the sum of the other two interior angles.

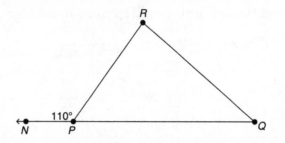

In $\triangle PRQ$, if the measure of exterior angle $\angle RPN$ is 110°, then the sum of the measures of $\angle R$ and $\angle Q$ is also 110°. You can see this also with another look at $\triangle PRQ$.

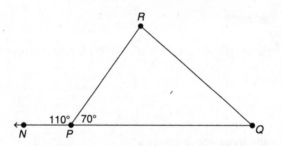

$\angle RPN$ and $\angle RPQ$ are supplementary angles. Thus, if $m\angle RPN$ is 110°, then $m\angle RPQ$ is 70° because $180 - 110 = 70$. Input the measure of $\angle RPQ$ to solve the measure of the sum of $\angle R$ and $\angle Q$.

$m\angle RPQ + m\angle R + m\angle Q = 180$

$70 + m\angle R + m\angle Q = 180$

$m\angle R + m\angle Q = 110$

Right Triangles

Right triangles are a special kind of triangle. They have one right (90°) angle. The side opposite the right angle is called the **hypotenuse**, and the other two sides are called the **legs**.

When two sides of a right triangle are known, the Pythagorean theorem can be used to calculate the measure of the third side.

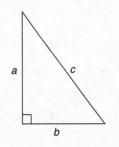

The Pythagorean Theorem

The formula for the Pythagorean theorem is $a^2 + b^2 = c^2$, where a and b are the legs and c is the hypotenuse.

EXAMPLE

Find the length of the hypotenuse in $\triangle LMN$.

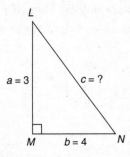

SOLUTION

Use the Pythagorean theorem, $a^2 + b^2 = c^2$, to find c.

$$3^2 + 4^2 = c^2$$
$$9 + 16 = c^2$$
$$25 = c^2$$
$$\sqrt{25} = \sqrt{c^2}$$
$$5 = c$$

EXAMPLE

In the triangle below, what is the length of $\overline{BC}$?

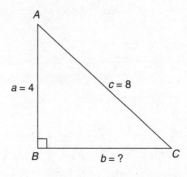

SOLUTION

Using the Pythagorean theorem we get:

$$4^2 + b^2 = 8^2$$
$$16 + b^2 = 64$$
$$b^2 = 48$$
$$b = 4\sqrt{3}$$

Pythagorean Triples

The sides 3, 4, and 5 are known as a **Pythagorean triple**. A triple exists when all the sides of the triangle are whole numbers. Below are additional triples worth knowing for the Praxis exam:

5-12-13

8-15-17

7-24-25

All multiples of triples are triples as well. If 3-4-5 is a triple, then so are 6-8-10, 9-12-15, 30-40-50, and so on.

Special Right Triangles

The Pythagorean theorem works for any right triangle problem, but there are helpful shortcuts for special right triangles. Two **special right triangles** have angles of 45°-45°-90° and 30°-60°-90°, as shown on the next page.

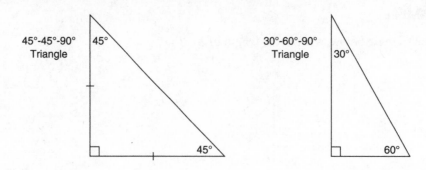

It should be no surprise that the 45°-45°-90° triangle has two equal sides because if the measures of two angles in a triangle are equal, then the sides opposite those angles also have equal measures. Using the Pythagorean theorem, the sides of a 45°-45°-90° triangle are in the ratio $x:x:x\sqrt{2}$, where the x's are the legs, and $x\sqrt{2}$ is the hypotenuse. This ratio, $1:1:\sqrt{2}$, holds for all 45°-45°-90° triangles, so if one leg is 10, the other leg is 10, and the hypotenuse is $10\sqrt{2}$.

The sides of a 30°-60°-90° triangle also have an easy-to-remember relationship. The shorter leg (the side opposite the 30° angle) is exactly half the length of the hypotenuse, and the longer leg (the one opposite the 60° angle) is $\sqrt{3}$ times the shorter leg. What makes this easy to remember is that the ratio is $1:2:\sqrt{3}$. In other words, if the hypotenuse is 12, the two legs are 6 (the shorter one) and $6\sqrt{3}$ (the longer one). This ratio comes from the Pythagorean theorem, but by remembering $1:2:\sqrt{3}$, the lengths of the sides of a 30°-60°-90° triangle can be found right away.

EXAMPLE

Find the hypotenuse of $\triangle ABC$.

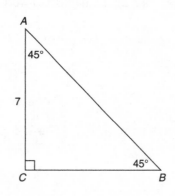

SOLUTION

Using the model for a 45°-45°-90° triangle, the other leg is 7 and the hypotenuse is $7\sqrt{2}$.

EXAMPLE

Find the hypotenuse of △*DEF*.

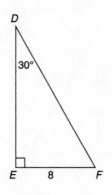

SOLUTION

Using the model for a 30°-60°-90° triangle, we find the other leg and the hypotenuse to be $8\sqrt{3}$ and 16, respectively.

Sometimes algebraic manipulation is needed to compute the length of a side.

EXAMPLE

What is the measure of $\overline{MN}$ in △*MNP*?

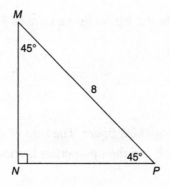

SOLUTION

The hypotenuse, $\overline{MP}$, is length 8. Set 8 equal to $x\sqrt{2}$ to solve for x, the length of $\overline{MN}$.

$$x\sqrt{2} = 8$$

$$\frac{x\sqrt{2}}{\sqrt{2}} = \frac{8}{\sqrt{2}}$$

$$x = \frac{8}{\sqrt{2}} \times \frac{\sqrt{2}}{\sqrt{2}} = \frac{8\sqrt{2}}{2} = 4\sqrt{2}$$

The length of $\overline{MN}$ (and $\overline{NP}$) is $4\sqrt{2}$.

EXAMPLE

Find the hypotenuse of $\triangle RST$.

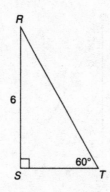

SOLUTION

The side opposite 60° is 6. In the general model, the side opposite 60° is $x\sqrt{3}$. Set 6 equal to $x\sqrt{3}$ and solve for x, the shorter leg.

$$x\sqrt{3} = 6$$

$$\frac{x\sqrt{3}}{\sqrt{3}} = \frac{6}{\sqrt{3}}$$

$$x = \frac{6}{\sqrt{3}} \times \frac{\sqrt{3}}{\sqrt{3}} = \frac{6\sqrt{3}}{3} = 2\sqrt{3}$$

The hypotenuse is double the shorter leg, so its measure is $4\sqrt{3}$.

QUADRILATERALS

A **quadrilateral** is a closed, four-sided figure. The sum of the measures of the four angles is 360°. A list of common quadrilaterals and their properties is shown below:

Trapezoid:

1. Has exactly two parallel sides.

2. The sides are not necessarily equal.

Parallelogram:

1. The opposite sides are parallel and have equal length.

2. The opposite angles are congruent and consecutive angles are supplementary.

3. The diagonals bisect each other.

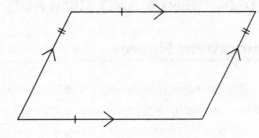

Rhombus:

1. Has all the properties of parallelograms.

2. Has four equal sides.

3. The diagonals are perpendicular.

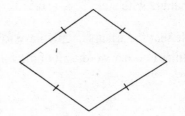

Rectangle:

1. Has all the properties of parallelograms.

2. Has four right angles.

3. The diagonals are congruent.

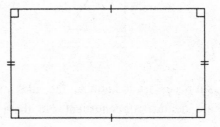

Square:

1. Has all the properties of parallelograms.

2. Has all the properties of rhombuses.

3. Has all the properties of rectangles.

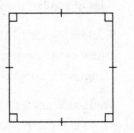

Kite:

1. The adjacent sides are congruent.

2. The diagonals are perpendicular.

CONGRUENCE AND SIMILARITY

Congruent Figures

Two objects are **congruent** if they are identical. Two triangles are congruent if they have the same side lengths. Because triangles are rigid, once the three sides are chosen, the angles are automatically determined. So once you have a triangle with sides 3, 4, and 5, you know the largest angle is 90° since this is a Pythagorean triple, and the other two angles have to match the angles in every other triangle with sides 3, 4, and 5.

Note that the triangles only have to match side for side but they don't have to be in the same orientation. In other words, all of the following triangles are congruent.

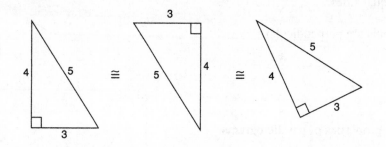

Is it necessary to know all the sides and all the angles for two triangles to be able to state that they are identical, or congruent? No, there are several ways to prove that triangles are congruent.

- Side-side-side (SSS): If three sides of a triangle are congruent to three corresponding sides of another triangle, the triangles are congruent.

- Side-angle-side (SAS): If two sides and the included angle of one triangle are congruent to two corresponding sides and the included angle of another triangle, the two triangles are congruent.

- Angle-side-angle (ASA): If two angles and the included side of a triangle are congruent to two corresponding angles and the included side of another triangle, the two triangles are congruent.

- Angle-angle-side (AAS): If two angles and the side opposite one of the angles of a triangle are congruent to two corresponding angles and the side opposite one of the angles of another triangle, the two triangles are congruent.

- Hypotenuse-leg (HL): If the hypotenuse and leg of a right triangle are congruent to the hypotenuse and corresponding leg of another right triangle, the two triangles are congruent.

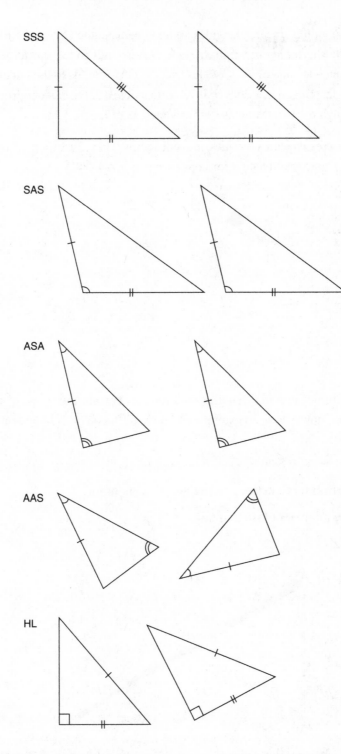

When two triangles are proven to be congruent, we get the following theorem to prove parts of congruent triangles are congruent.

**If two triangles are congruent, then corresponding parts
of the triangles are congruent (abbreviated CPCTC).**

The word "corresponding" means the sides and angles have the same relationship in each triangle. For example, the shorter leg in a right triangle corresponds to the shorter leg in a congruent right triangle. Or the unequal side of an isosceles triangle corresponds to the unequal side in a congruent isosceles triangle. (But an isosceles triangle with sides 3, 3, 5 is *not* congruent with one with sides 5, 5, 8, even though the two triangles each have a side of length 5.)

$\triangle ABC$ and $\triangle DEF$ are congruent by side-side-side (SSS). Therefore, their corresponding angles $\angle A \cong \angle D$ by CPCTC. Note that the sign for congruence is $A \cong D$.

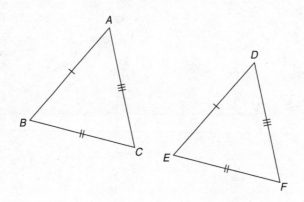

A detailed discussion of proving triangles congruent is beyond the scope of the Praxis exam. The proof shown below, however, is an example of a typical Praxis proof question.

EXAMPLE

What is the reason for Statement #4 in the following proof?

Given: E is the midpoint of $\overline{AB}$ and $\overline{CD}$.

Prove: $\angle D \cong \angle C$

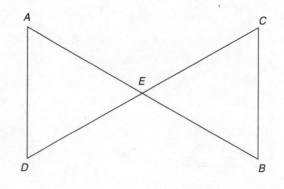

Statement	Reason
1. E is the midpoint of $\overline{AB}$ and $\overline{CD}$	1. Given
2. $\overline{AE} \cong \overline{BE}$ and $\overline{CE} \cong \overline{DE}$	2. Definition of midpoint
3. $\angle DEA \cong \angle CEB$	3. Vertical angles are congruent
4. $\triangle AED \cong \triangle BEC$	4. ?
5. $\angle D \cong \angle C$	5. CPCTC (corresponding parts of congruent triangles are congruent)

The reason for statement #4 is:

(A) SSS

(B) SAS

(C) AAS

(D) HL

SOLUTION

The answer is (B) SAS because the proof shows the congruence of two sides (in statement #2) and the included angles (in statement #3). Note that the actual lengths and angle measurements aren't even mentioned. Only the relationships are needed to prove two figures are congruent.

But what if the three angles in one triangle match the three angles in another triangle? Are these two triangles congruent? They would have the same shape, but it is possible for two triangles to have the same shape but not the same side lengths. Think of Pythagorean triples and their multiples, such as two triangles with sides 3-4-5 and 6-8-10.

Similar Figures

Consider three equiangular triangles. Each would have angles of 60°-60°-60° (because they are all equal and must add up to 180°), but one could have sides of length 4, another could have sides of length 2, and the third could have sides of length 5.

Figures with exactly the same shape, meaning matching angles, one-for-one, are called **similar**. Consider the three figures below. They certainly aren't congruent, but they are similar. In fact, two polygons are always similar if their corresponding angles match; we don't even have to know their side lengths to say they are similar.

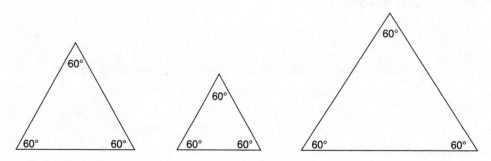

Similar geometric figures have the same shape but can have different sizes. For figures to be similar, their corresponding angles must have equal measures and their corresponding sides must be proportional. Triangles *ABC* and *DEF* are similar because their corresponding angles are equal and their corresponding sides are proportional.

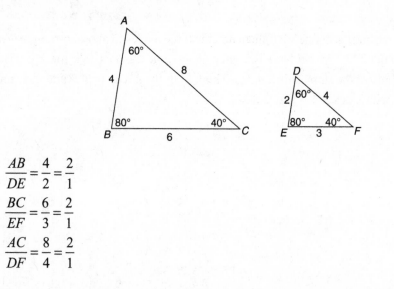

$$\frac{AB}{DE} = \frac{4}{2} = \frac{2}{1}$$

$$\frac{BC}{EF} = \frac{6}{3} = \frac{2}{1}$$

$$\frac{AC}{DF} = \frac{8}{4} = \frac{2}{1}$$

The symbol "~" means "is similar to." In the triangles above, $\triangle ABC \sim \triangle DEF$.

EXAMPLE

$\triangle CDE \sim \triangle FGH$. If $CD = 12$, $CE = 8$, and $FG = 5$, what is the measure of FH?

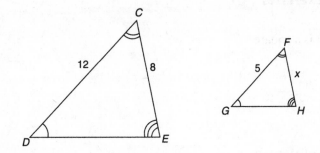

SOLUTION

Use the fact that similar triangles have sides that are proportional to solve for x.
Use the proportion

$$\frac{\text{side}1_{\text{larger}}}{\text{side}1_{\text{smaller}}} = \frac{\text{side}2_{\text{larger}}}{\text{side}2_{\text{smaller}}}$$

$$\frac{12}{5} = \frac{8}{x}$$

$$12x = 40$$

$$x = 3\frac{1}{3}$$

It is much more difficult to prove polygons with more than three sides similar, and certainly that proof is beyond the scope of the Praxis exam with one exception:

All regular polygons of *n* sides are similar to all other regular polygons of *n* sides.

All of the angles in a regular polygon are equal; therefore, the lengths of the sides will be proportional to every other regular polygon with the same number of sides (or angles). This means:

All equilateral or equiangular triangles are similar to each other.

All squares are similar to each other.

All regular pentagons are similar to each other.

And so on.

Practice Exercises

1. A parallelogram is a square

   (A) always

   (B) sometimes

   (C) never

2. A square is a parallelogram

   (A) always

   (B) sometimes

   (C) never

3. One diagonal of a rectangle measures 144 inches and the other has a measure of $7x + 18$. What is the measure of x?

   (A) 16

   (B) 17

   (C) 18

   (D) 360

Solutions

1. **(B)**

   If a parallelogram has four congruent sides and four right angles, then that parallelogram is a square.

2. **(A)**

   A square possesses all of the properties of a parallelogram.

3. **(C)**

   The diagonals of a rectangle have the same measure. Set $7x + 18$ equal to 144 and solve for x.

   $$7x + 18 = 144$$

   $$7x = 126$$

   $$x = 18$$

PERIMETER AND AREA OF POLYGONS

The **perimeter** is the distance around a closed figure.

Use your knowledge of triples to quickly solve the triangle below without resorting to the Pythagorean theorem.

EXAMPLE

Find the perimeter of $\triangle BCD$.

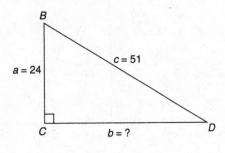

SOLUTION

Perimeter is the distance around a figure. Note that $8 \times 3 = 24$ and $17 \times 3 = 51$, so the missing side is 45 ($3 \times 15 = 45$). We have used a multiple of the 8-15-17 triple to find the missing side.

Add the three sides to find the perimeter. $24 + 45 + 51 = 120$ feet.

Not all questions using the Pythagorean theorem use whole numbers.

EXAMPLE

The perimeter of a parallelogram is 84 feet. If one of the widths measures 12 feet, what are the measures of the remaining three sides?

SOLUTION

The opposite sides of a parallelogram have equal measures. Since one of the widths is 12 feet, so is the other. Subtract the sum of the two widths, 24, from the perimeter, 84, to find the sum of the two lengths.

$$84 - 24 = 60$$

Divide 60 by 2 to find the measure of a length.

$$60 \div 2 = 30$$

The measures of the three remaining sides are 12, 30, and 30.

EXAMPLE

The diagonals of a rhombus measure 18 and 24 inches. What is the perimeter of the rhombus?

SOLUTION

The diagonals of a rhombus are perpendicular and bisect each other.

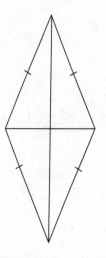

Use the Pythagorean theorem to find the length of one of the sides of the rhombus.

$$9^2 + 12^2 = c^2$$

$$225 = c^2$$

$$15 = c$$

The four sides of a rhombus are congruent; multiply 15×4 to find the perimeter.

$$4 \times 15 = 60$$

The **area** is the region contained within a plane figure. In our daily lives, we encounter terms such as square feet, square yards, etc. These square units are measures of area. If the unit of measure is not provided, then areas are listed as square units. Measures of area can be shown as "square feet," "feet²," or (abbreviated) "ft²," for example.

The Praxis exam provides no formulas for finding the area of a figure on the test. Here are some important ones to remember:

Triangle: $\frac{1}{2}$ base × height ($A = \frac{1}{2}bh$)

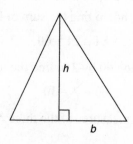

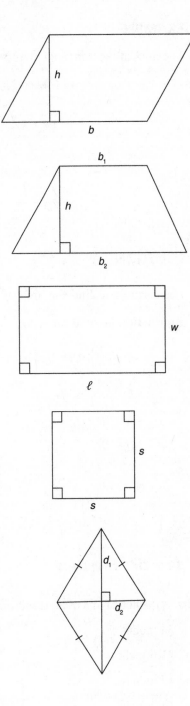

Parallelogram: base × height ($A = bh$)

Trapezoid: $A = \dfrac{1}{2}h(b_1 + b_2)$, where h is the distance between bases b_1 and b_2.

Rectangle: length × width ($A = lw$)

Square: side × side ($A = s^2$)

Rhombus: $\dfrac{1}{2}$ × diagonal #1 × diagonal #2

$\left(A = \dfrac{1}{2}d_1d_2 \right)$

EXAMPLE

The area of the trapezoid pictured below is 66 in². What is the length of b_1?

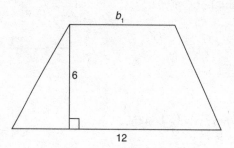

SOLUTION

The formula to find the area of a trapezoid is $A = \frac{1}{2}h(b_1 + b_2)$. Input the known information to solve for b_1.

$$66 = \left(\frac{1}{2}\right)(6)(b_1 + 12)$$

$$66 = 3(b_1 + 12)$$

$$66 = 3b_1 + 36$$

$$30 = 3b_1$$

$$10 = b_1$$

Practice Exercises

1. What is the height of a triangle with an area equal to 108.8 in² and a base that equals 12.8 inches?

    (A) 34 inches

    (B) 21.6 inches

    (C) 17 inches

    (D) 14.4 inches

2. A rectangle has a diagonal that is 5 inches long and a height of 1.4 inches. What is the perimeter of the rectangle?

    (A) 4.8 inches

    (B) 6.72 inches

    (C) 12.4 inches

    (D) 25 inches

3. Rectangle *ABCD* ~ rectangle *EFGH*. What is the ratio of the area of *ABCD* to the area of *EFGH*?

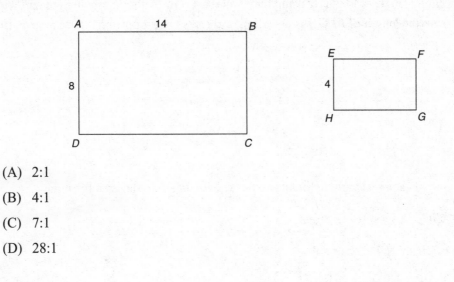

(A) 2:1

(B) 4:1

(C) 7:1

(D) 28:1

Solutions

1. **(C)**

Use the formula $A = \frac{1}{2}bh$, the formula for the area of a triangle, and input the known data.

$$108.8 = \frac{1}{2}(12.8)h$$

$$108.8 = 6.4h$$

$$h = 17 \text{ inches}$$

2. **(C)**

The diagonal of a rectangle creates two right triangles. Use the Pythagorean theorem to calculate the base of the rectangle.

$$a^2 + b^2 = c^2$$

$$1.4^2 + b^2 = 5^2$$

$$1.96 + b^2 = 25$$

$$b^2 = 23.04$$

$$b = 4.8 \text{ inches}$$

The perimeter of a rectangle is found by using the formula $P = 2l + 2w$

$$P = (2)(4.8) + (2)(1.4) = 12.4 \text{ inches}$$

3. **(B)**

The area of a rectangle is found by using the formula $A = lw$. Although the length and width of $ABCD$ are known, the length of $EFGH$ is not. Similar figures are proportional. Use a proportion to find EF.

$$\frac{14}{x} = \frac{8}{4}$$

$$56 = 8x$$

$$7 = x$$

Find the area of each rectangle by inputting the known data into the area formula.

Area $ABCD$: $14 \times 8 = 112$ units²

Area $EFGH$: $7 \times 4 = 28$ units²

Find the ratio of the areas:

$$\frac{112}{28} = \frac{4}{1}$$

A quicker way to answer this question is to square the ratio of the corresponding sides.

$$\frac{AD}{EH} = \frac{8}{4} = \frac{2}{1}$$

$$\left(\frac{2}{1}\right)^2 = \frac{4}{1}$$

CIRCLES

A **circle** is the set of points equidistant from a given point. A circle measures 360°.

Following are some parts of a circle. A **diameter** goes from one side of a circle to the other and passes through the center, so it is twice as large as a radius. A **tangent** touches the circle at just one point and is perpendicular to the radius to the tangent point.

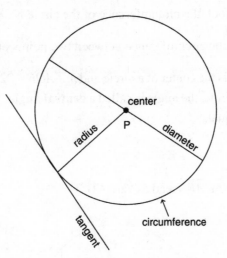

Circumference of a Circle and an Arc

The perimeter of a circle is called the **circumference**. The formulas for the circumference are:

$$C = 2\pi r$$

$$C = \pi D$$

In the circumference formulas, r is the radius and D is the diameter. The formulas are equivalent because two radii are equal to one diameter. The symbol π (pronounced "pie") is approximately equal to 3.14 or $\frac{22}{7}$.

EXAMPLE

A circle has a radius that measures 6 feet. To the nearest foot, what is its circumference?

SOLUTION

The problem provides the radius (6 feet), so use the formula $C = 2\pi r$. Some questions will permit you to leave π in your answer. However, when a question asks for a measure to the nearest unit, use $\pi = 3.14$ or $\frac{22}{7}$.

$$C = 2\pi r$$

$$= 2\pi(6)$$

$$= 12(3.14)$$

$$= 37.68 \text{ feet}$$

Rounded to the nearest foot, the circumference of the circle is 38 feet.

An **arc** is the portion of the circumference between two points on a circle.

In the diagram below, O is the center of a circle and $m\angle AOB = 72°$. When the vertex of an angle is located in the center of a circle, the angle is called a **central angle**. The measure of a central angle and its intercepted arc are equal.

EXAMPLE

What is the measure of $\overset{\frown}{AB}$ (read as "arc AB")?

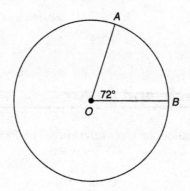

SOLUTION

A central angle equals its intercepted arc, so $m\overset{\frown}{AB}$ is also 72°.

Finding the length of an arc relates to the ratio of the central angle to 360°, the number of degrees in a circle. Find the length of an arc by using the formula for arc length, $\dfrac{m}{360}(2\pi r)$, where m represents the measure of a central angle.

EXAMPLE

In the circle with center P (represented by "$\odot P$"), find the length of $\overset{\frown}{AB}$ (express your answer in terms of π).

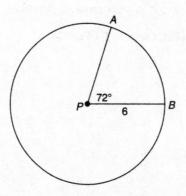

SOLUTION

Use the arc length formula, $\dfrac{m}{360}(2\pi r)$ to find the length of $\overset{\frown}{AB}$.

$$\frac{72}{360}(2 \times \pi \times 6) = 2.4\pi$$

The length of $\overset{\frown}{AB}$ equals 2.4π.

Practice Exercises

1. What is the circumference of a circle with a radius equal to 9.4? (Round your answer to the nearest tenth.)

    (A) 46.2

    (B) 59.0

    (C) 62.1

    (D) 73.3

2. A circle with a central angle measuring 72° intercepts an arc with length $(23n + 3)°$. What is the value of n?

    (A) 2

    (B) 3

    (C) 4

    (D) 5

3. A circle has a circumference that measures 256π. What is the measure of a central angle that intercepts an arc that measures 32π?

    (A) 30°

    (B) 45°

    (C) 60°

    (D) 90°

Solutions

1. **(B)**

   The formula for the circumference of a circle is $C = 2\pi r$. Input 9.4 for r and 3.14 for π.

   $$C = (2)(3.14)(9.4) = 59.032$$

   59.032 rounded to the nearest tenth is 59.0.

2. **(B)**

   A central angle and its intercepted arc have the same degree measure. Set $23n + 3$ equal to 72 to find the value of n.

   $$23n + 3 = 72$$

   $$23n = 69$$

   $$n = 3$$

3. **(B)**

   Use the arc length formula, $\frac{m}{360}(2\pi r)$, to find the measure of m, the central angle. To find m, use the circumference formula, $C = 256\pi = 2\pi r$ and substituting it into the arc length formula.

   $$256\pi = 2\pi r$$

   $$32\pi = \frac{m}{360°}(256\pi)$$

   $$\frac{32\pi}{256\pi} = \frac{m}{360°}$$

   $$\frac{1}{8} = \frac{m}{360°}$$

   $$8m = 360°$$

   $$m = 45°$$

Area of a Circle and a Sector

The formula for the **area of a circle** is

$A = \pi r^2$, where r is the radius of the circle.

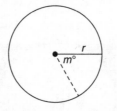

A **sector** of a circle is the area bounded by two radii and the arc between them, like a slice of pie.

The area of a sector of a circle is computed by multiplying the fraction of the circle represented by the sector $\left(\dfrac{\text{measure of central angle}}{360} \right)$ by the area of the circle $A = \pi r^2$:

$$\text{Area of a sector} = \left(\frac{\text{measure of central angle}}{360} \right)(\pi r^2) = \frac{m}{360}(\pi r^2)$$

EXAMPLE

Find the area of a circle with a diameter that measures 28.6 meters.

SOLUTION

The area of a circle is found by using the formula $A = \pi r^2$. The question provides the diameter, so divide 28.6 by 2 to find the radius.

$28.6 \div 2 = 14.3$

$A = \pi(14.3)^2 = 204.49\pi$ (approximately 642.1 square meters)

Practice Exercises

1. A circle is inscribed in square *ABCD*. If the perimeter of the square is 64 ft, what is the area of the shaded portion?

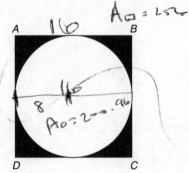

(A) 256 ft²

(B) 200.96 ft²

(C) 110.08 ft²

(D) 55.04 ft²

2. $\overline{OA}$ measures 4 meters and $\overline{OB}$ measures 8 meters. What is the area of the shaded ring?

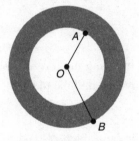

(A) 64π m²

(B) 48π m²

(C) 32π m²

(D) 16π m²

3.   The area of the shaded portion of $\odot P$ is 18π. What is the circumference of $\odot P$?

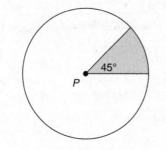

(A) 144π

(B) 84π

(C) 24π

(D) 12π

Solutions

1.   **(D)**

Find the area of the circle and subtract it from the area of the square. The area of the square is found by using the formula $A = s^2$, where s is the side length of the square. Find the length of a side by dividing the perimeter by 4.

$64 \div 4 = 16$

$A = s^2$

$A = 16^2 = 256$

The area of a circle is found by using the formula $A = \pi r^2$. Note that the side of the square is equal to the circle's diameter. The radius can be found by dividing one side of the square by 2 to get $r = 8$.

$A = \pi(8)^2 = 64\pi = 200.96$

Subtract the area of the circle from the area of the square.

$256 - 200.96 = 55.04$ ft²

2. **(B)**

To find the area of the ring, subtract the area of the smaller circle with radius $\overline{OA}$ from the area of the larger circle with radius $\overline{OB}$. Use the formula $A = \pi r^2$ to find the area of each circle.

Larger circle: A = $\pi(8)^2$ = 64π

Smaller circle: A = $\pi(4)^2$ = 16π

$64\pi - 16\pi = 48\pi$ m^2

3. **(C)**

The formula for a sector of a circle is $A = \pi r^2 \left(\dfrac{m}{360} \right)$ where r is the radius and m is the measure of the central angle.

$$18\pi = \pi r^2 \left(\frac{45}{360} \right)$$

$$18 = \frac{r^2}{8}$$

$$144 = r^2$$

$$12 = r$$

The formula for the circumference of a circle is $C = 2\pi r$. Thus, the circumference of the circle is $2(12)\pi = 24\pi$.

THREE-DIMENSIONAL FIGURES

Three-dimensional figures, also called **solids**, have length, width, and height. A sphere is also a solid figure with surface points equidistant from the center. Two important measurements for solids are surface area and volume.

Surface Area

Surface area (SA) is the region that spans the outside of a solid object. Similar to the area of plane figures, surface area is measured in square units. Basically, the surface area can be thought of as the wrapping paper on a solid (with no overlapping).

The Praxis exam will not have any sophisticated surface area questions. However, no formulas are provided on the exam so the most useful ones are included here.

A **rectangular solid** (also called a **right prism**) is a rectangle with height, like a shoe box. The surface area is the sum of the areas of the two base rectangles ($2B$) plus the area of the four sides (ph), where p is the perimeter of the base and h is the height.

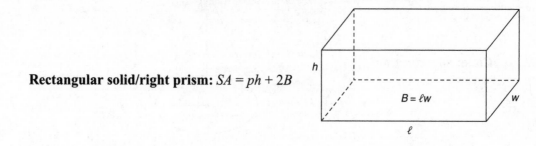

Rectangular solid/right prism: $SA = ph + 2B$

A **cube** is actually a rectangular solid with $l = w = h$. There are six squares in a cube, each with area e^2, where e represents the length of an edge. So the surface area is $SA = 6e^2$.

A **cylinder** is shaped like a can. Its surface area is calculated similarly to the rectangular solid, but the bases are now two circles with area $2\pi r^2$, and the area of the side has a perimeter that is the circumference of the circle, so the area of the side (think of the label on a can) is $2\pi rh$.

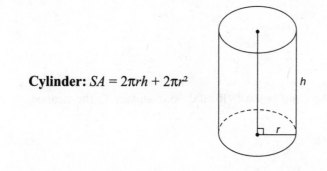

Cylinder: $SA = 2\pi rh + 2\pi r^2$

The next two solids have a point rather than a second identical base.

A **regular pyramid** has a base of area $B = lw$. The sides are all triangles, and the height from the edge of the base to the point is s, which stands for slant height. The base of each triangle is a side of the base of the pyramid. So the area of all the triangles equals $\frac{1}{2}ps$, where p is the perimeter of the base.

Pyramid: $SA = \frac{1}{2}ps + B$

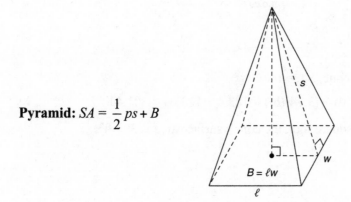

A **cone** looks like an ice cream cone. The base is a circle with area πr^2, and the slanted side that wraps around has an area of πrs, where s is the slant height from the edge of the base to the point.

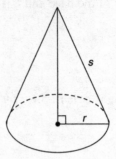

Cone: $SA = \pi rs + \pi r^2$

Finally, a **sphere** is a ball, with r being the only dimension.

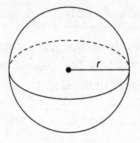

Sphere: $SA = 4\pi r^2$

EXAMPLE

What is the surface area of the cone below? (Round your answer to the nearest square foot.)

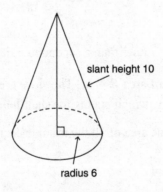

slant height 10

radius 6

SOLUTION

Use the formula for the cone, $SA = \pi rs + \pi r^2$.

$$SA = (3.14)(6)(10) + (3.14)(6^2) = 188.4 + 113.04 = 301.44$$

Rounded to the nearest square foot, the cone's surface area is 301 ft².

EXAMPLE

The rectangular solid pictured below has a surface area measuring 268 square inches. The length and width of the base are 11 and 6 inches, respectively. What is the height of the rectangular solid?

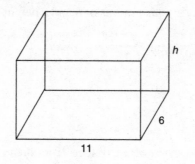

SOLUTION

Use the formula $SA = ph + 2B$ to calculate the height. The perimeter of the base, p, is found by adding its sides:

$$6 + 6 + 11 + 11 = 34$$

The base is a rectangle, so its area, B, is found by using the formula $A = lw$.

$$B = 6 \times 11 = 66 \text{ square inches.}$$

Input the measures of p and B to calculate the height.

$$268 = 34h + 2(66)$$

$$268 = 34h + 132$$

$$136 = 34h$$

$$4 = h$$

EXAMPLE

A sphere has a surface area of 288π cm². What is the measure of its radius?

SOLUTION

Use the formula $SA = 4\pi r^2$ to calculate the measure of the radius.

$$288\pi = 4\pi r^2$$

$$\frac{288\pi}{4\pi} = \frac{4\pi r^2}{4\pi}$$

$$72 = r^2$$

$$\sqrt{72} = \sqrt{r^2}$$

$$6\sqrt{2} = r$$

The radius measures $6\sqrt{2}$ cm (approximately 8.5 cm).

Practice Exercises

1. Find the surface area of a cone with a radius of 8 and a height of 15. (Leave π in your answer.)

    (A) 200π

    (B) 150π

    (C) 100π

    (D) 50π

2. A container of salt is in the shape of a cylinder. If its diameter is 6 inches and its height is 10 inches, find its surface area after the top has been removed. Use $\pi = 3.14$ and round your answer to the nearest tenth.

    (A) 602.9 inches²

    (B) 489.8 inches²

    (C) 244.9 inches²

    (D) 216.7 inches²

Solutions

1. **(A)**

    Use the formula $A = \pi rs + \pi r^2$ to find the surface area of the cone. Although the radius and height are known, the slant height, s, is not.

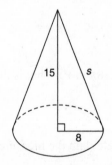

    Use the Pythagorean theorem to find the slant height.

    $8^2 + 15^2 = s^2$

    $64 + 225 = s^2$

    $289 = s^2$

    $17 = s$

You may remember this is a Pythagorean triple, 8-15-17.

$$SA = \pi(8)(17) + \pi(8)^2 = 200\pi$$

2. **(D)**

The formula to find the surface area of a cylinder is $SA = 2\pi rh + 2\pi r^2$ with r representing the radius of the cylinder and h representing its height. Since the top, which is one of the circles, is removed, the formula becomes $SA = 2\pi rh + \pi r^2$. Input the known values for radius and height. Remember to divide the diameter, 6, by 2 to find the radius.

$$SA = 2(3.14)(3)(10) + (3.14)(3)^2 = 216.7 \text{ inches}^2$$

VOLUME

Volume is the measure of the region within a solid object. Volume is measured in cubic units such as cubic inches, cubic meters, etc. Cubic units are labeled as follows:

cubic feet   or   feet³   or   ft³

Although the volume questions on the Praxis exam will not be too complicated, there are no volume formulas provided on the test. It is worth familiarizing yourself with the formulas below. Essentially, for solids with identical bases, the volume is base area × height. For the following volume formulas, as for the surface area formulas,

B = base area r = radius h = height $\pi = 3.14$

Rectangular solid (also known as a rectangular prism): $V = Bh$

Cylinder: $V = \pi r^2 h$

For solids that have a base and a point (pyramid and cone), the formula is $\frac{1}{3}$ times the formula for the corresponding solid with two bases (rectangular prism and cylinder, respectively).

Pyramid: $V = \frac{1}{3}Bh$

Cone: $V = \frac{1}{3}\pi r^2 h$

Even for a sphere, the $\frac{1}{3}$ comes into play, as the volume is $\frac{1}{3}$ the formula for the surface area ($4\pi r^2$) times the radius r.

Sphere: $V = \frac{4}{3}\pi r^3$

Cube: Since a cube is a rectangular prism with all sides (edges) equal to e, $V = e^3$.

EXAMPLE

What is the volume of the cone shown below? (Leave π in your answer.)

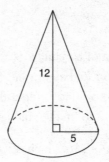

12

5

SOLUTION

Use the formula $V = \dfrac{1}{3}\pi r^2 h$ to calculate the volume.

$$V = \frac{1}{3}\pi(5^2)(12)$$

$$V = \frac{1}{3}(\pi)(300)$$

$$V = 100\pi \text{ units}^3$$

EXAMPLE

A square pyramid has a volume of $391.08\overline{3}$ in³. If the height of the pyramid is 13 inches, what is the perimeter of the base?

SOLUTION

Use the formula $V = \dfrac{1}{3}Bh$ and input the known data.

$$391.08\overline{3} = \frac{1}{3}(B)(13)$$

$$391.08\overline{3} = \frac{13}{3}B$$

$$\frac{3}{13}(391.08\overline{3}) = \left(\frac{13}{3}\right)(B)\left(\frac{3}{13}\right)$$

$$90.25 = B$$

The base area, B, is the area of a square, $A = s^2$. Find the square root of 90.25 to find the length of one side, s.

$$\sqrt{90.25} = 9.5$$

One side of the square base is 9.5. Multiply 9.5 by 4 to find the perimeter.

$$9.5 \times 4 = 38$$

The perimeter of the base of the pyramid is 38 inches.

EXAMPLE

The volume of a sphere is 288π feet³. What is the surface area of the sphere? (Leave π in your answer.)

SOLUTION

The volume of a sphere is found by using the formula $V = \frac{4}{3}\pi r^3$. Use the formula to calculate the radius, then input that value into the formula for the surface area of a sphere, $SA = 4\pi r^2$.

$$288\pi = \frac{4}{3}\pi r^3$$

$$\left(\frac{3}{4\pi}\right)(288\pi) = \frac{4}{3}\pi r^3\left(\frac{3}{4\pi}\right)$$

$$216 = r^3$$

$$\sqrt[3]{216} = \sqrt[3]{r^3}$$

$$6 = r$$

$$SA = 4\pi r^2$$

$$SA = 4\pi(6^2) = 144\pi$$

EXAMPLE

The radii of two spheres are 2 and 5. What is the ratio of the larger volume to the smaller volume?

SOLUTION

Since all spheres are similar, find the volume of each to find the ratio.

$$V = \frac{4}{3}\pi r^3$$

Smaller sphere: $V = \frac{4}{3}\pi(2)^3 = \frac{32}{3}\pi$

Larger sphere: $V = \frac{4}{3}\pi(5)^3 = \frac{500}{3}\pi$

Find the ratio of their volumes:

$$\frac{\frac{500}{3}\pi}{\frac{32\pi}{3}} = \frac{500\pi}{3} \times \frac{3}{32\pi} = \frac{500}{32} = \frac{125}{8}$$

A quicker way to answer this question is to cube the ratios of the radii.

$$\left(\frac{5}{2}\right)^3 = \frac{125}{8}$$

Practice Exercises

1. What is the surface area of a cube with a volume that equals 216 mm³?

    (A) 6 mm²

    (B) 36 mm²

    (C) 216 mm²

    (D) 432 mm²

2. A rectangular solid has a volume of 720 cubic inches. If the rectangular base has a length of 8 inches and a width of 6 inches, what is the height of the solid?

    (A) 15

    (B) 20

    (C) 36

    (D) 72

3. An aquarium in the shape of a rectangular solid is 6 feet long, 2 feet wide, and 4 feet high. Water is poured into the aquarium and rises to a height of 1.5 feet. The water is poured into another aquarium that is 5 feet long, 3 feet wide, and 4 feet high. What will be the height of the water in the second aquarium?

    (A) 1 foot

    (B) 1.2 feet

    (C) 1.8 feet

    (D) 2.1 feet

4. How many times greater is the volume of a sphere with a radius of 8 units compared to a sphere with a radius of 3 units?

    (A) $\dfrac{9}{512}$

    (B) $\dfrac{27}{64}$

    (C) $\dfrac{216}{169}$

    (D) $\dfrac{512}{27}$

5. The two trapezoids below are similar. What is the height of the smaller trapezoid?

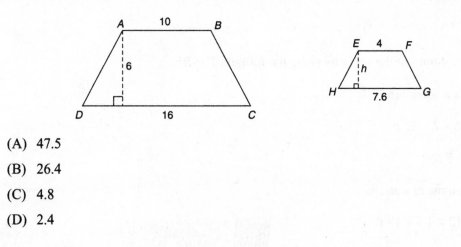

    (A) 47.5

    (B) 26.4

    (C) 4.8

    (D) 2.4

Solutions

1. **(C)**

    Use the formula $V = e^3$, where e is the measure of an edge. Once the edge's value is known, put it in the formula $SA = 6e^2$.

    $$216 = e^3$$
    $$\sqrt[3]{216} = \sqrt[3]{e^3}$$
    $$6 = e$$
    $$SA = 6e^2$$
    $$SA = 216 \text{ mm}^2$$

    Note that the numerical value of the volume and surface area of a cube are *not* always the same. For a cube with edges of 4 units, the volume is $(4)^3 = 64$ cubic units, but the surface area is $6(4^2) = 96$ square units.

2. **(A)**

The volume of a rectangular solid is found by using the formula $V = Bh$. Find B by finding the area of the rectangular solid.

$A = lw$

$A = 6 \times 8 = 48$ in²

Input 48 for B in the volume formula.

$V = Bh$

$720 = 48h$

15 inches $= h$

3. **(B)**

Find the volumes of the water by using the formula $V = Bh$.

For the first aquarium,

$B = 6 \times 2 = 12$ ft²

$h = 1.5$ feet

So the volume of water is

$V = 12 \times 1.5 = 18$ ft³

The same 18 ft³ of water is poured into the new aquarium, whose base is $5 \times 3 = 15$ ft².

$V = Bh$

$18 = (5 \times 3)h$

$18 = 15h$

$h = 1.2$ feet

4. **(D)**

Compute each volume and compare the measures. Use the formula $V = \frac{4}{3}\pi r^3$.

8 unit radius: $\frac{4}{3}\pi(8)^3 = \frac{2048}{3}\pi$

3 unit radius: $\frac{4}{3}\pi(3)^3 = \frac{108}{3}\pi$

$$\frac{\dfrac{2048}{3}\pi}{\dfrac{108}{3}} = \frac{2048}{3} \times \frac{3}{108} = \frac{2048}{108} = \frac{512}{27}$$

Since spheres are similar, an easier way to do this problem is to cube the ratio of the radii:

$$\left(\frac{8}{3}\right)^3 = \frac{512}{27}$$

5. **(D)**

Similar figures have parts that are proportional. Use the proportion $\dfrac{AB}{EF} = \dfrac{h_{ABCD}}{h_{EFGH}}$.

$$\frac{10}{4} = \frac{6}{h}$$

$$10h = 24$$

$$h = 2.4$$

Note that you don't even need the lengths of the other two sides, 19 and 7.6, but if you use them, the answer is still the same.

TRANSFORMATIONS, NETS, AND CONSTRUCTIONS

Transformations

Transformations map figures into new figures. The new figure is called the **image** and the original figure is called the **pre-image**. One of the following three types of transformations is likely to be on the Praxis exam.

Reflection: A transformation that uses a line like a mirror to map (reflect) an image.

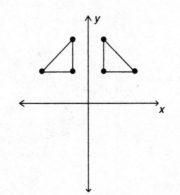

Rotation: A transformation that turns (rotates) a figure about a fixed point. Rotations can be clockwise or counterclockwise.

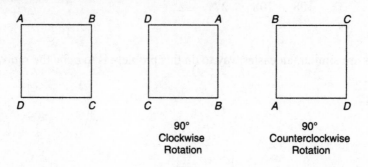

90°
Clockwise
Rotation

90°
Counterclockwise
Rotation

Translation: A transformation that changes the location of (translates) an image, but not its size or orientation.

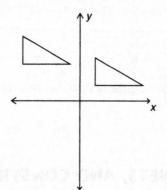

A translation in a coordinate plane can be described by the following coordinate notation:

$$(x, y) \rightarrow (x + a, y + b)$$

EXAMPLE

If $\triangle ABC$ is translated to $\triangle A'B'C'$ by using the formula $(x, y) \rightarrow (x + 2, y - 4)$, what are the coordinates of $\triangle A'B'C'$?

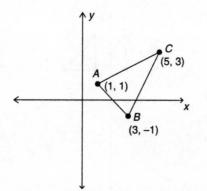

SOLUTION

Add 2 to each x-coordinate and subtract 4 from each y-coordinate to get the new image, $A'B'C'$.

$$A\,(1, 1) \rightarrow A'\,(3, -3)$$
$$B\,(3, -1) \rightarrow B'\,(5, -5)$$
$$C\,(5, 3) \rightarrow C'\,(7, -1)$$

The pre-image $\triangle ABC$ and the image $\triangle A'B'C'$ are shown below.

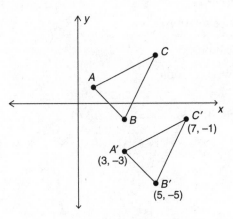

Practice Exercises

1. What type of reflection maps $\triangle ABC \rightarrow \triangle A'B'C'$?

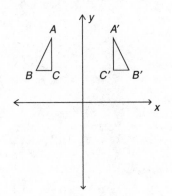

(A) Reflection across the y-axis

(B) Reflection across the x-axis

(C) Reflection across the origin

(D) Reflection across $y = x$

2. What rotation maps square $ABCD$ onto square $A'B'C'D'$?

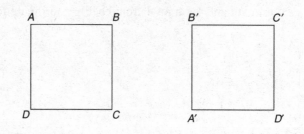

(A) 90° clockwise rotation

(B) 90° counterclockwise rotation

(C) 180° clockwise rotation

(D) 180° counterclockwise rotation

3. What translation maps $\overline{AB}$ to $\overline{A'B'}$?

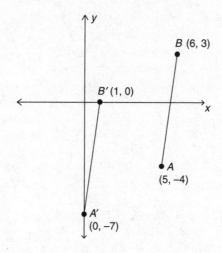

(A) $(x, y) \rightarrow (x + 5, y + 3)$

(B) $(x, y) \rightarrow (x + 5, y - 3)$

(C) $(x, y) \rightarrow (x - 5, y - 3)$

(D) $(x, y) \rightarrow (x - 5, y + 3)$

Solutions

1. **(A)**

Imagine flipping $\triangle ABC$ side-over-side across the y-axis. The new image will be $\triangle A'B'C'$.

2. **(B)**

$A'B'C'D'$ is a quarter turn (90°) in the counterclockwise direction.

3.   **(C)**

One set of coordinates is sufficient to deduce the rule for this translation.

Point A has coordinates $(5, -4)$ and A' has coordinates $(0, -7)$. Thus, the x-value goes from 5 to 0, or $0 - 5 = -5$ units and the y-value goes from -4 to -7, or $-7 - (-4) = -3$ units.

x is shifted 5 units to the left and y is shifted 3 units down.

$$(x, y) \rightarrow (x - 5, y - 3)$$

If we used B and B' as the points, the answer would be the same.

Nets

A **net** deconstructs a geometric solid into two-dimensional plane figures. The cube below is shown along with its net.

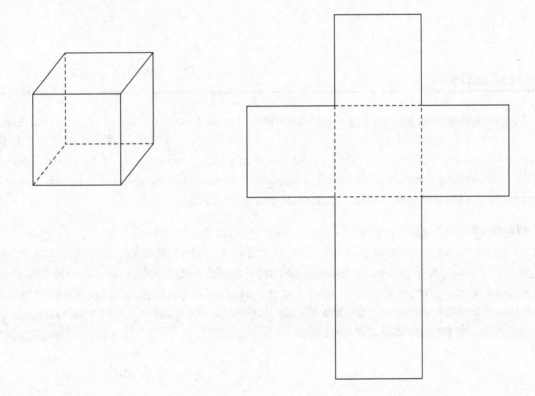

The Praxis exam will probably feature at least one problem about turning a common solid into its net.

EXAMPLE

Draw the net of a pyramid with a square base.

SOLUTION

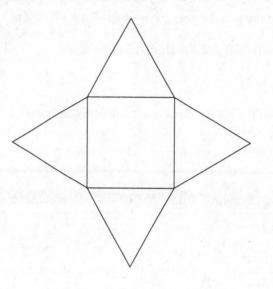

Constructions

Constructions involve drawing shapes accurately. For many constructions, all that is needed is a compass and a straightedge. A compass draws circles or arcs. Constructions use the fact that all points on a circle are the same distance from the center, which is the location of the compass point. So the opening of a compass can be used to measure distance. The straightedge is used to connect two points in a straight line. A ruler can be used as a straightedge.

Duplicating a Line Segment: To draw a line segment that is the same length as a given line segment (*AB*) using just a compass and a straightedge (not a ruler), pick a point (*C*) away from the original line segment to be one endpoint of the duplicate line segment. To measure the length of the original line, put the point of the compass at one endpoint (*A*) and open the compass so that the pencil is at the other endpoint (*B*). Then put the point of the compass at point *C* and draw an arc. All the points on the arc will be the same distance from *C* as the length of the original line segment.

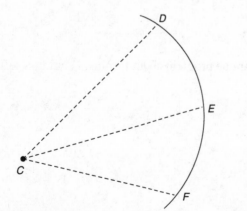

Duplicating an Angle: This construction uses the idea that a compass can measure distance. To construct an angle equal to a given angle, put the point of the compass at the vertex of the original angle (B) and draw an arc that intersects both sides of the angle at D and E. Pick a point to be the vertex of the new angle (G), and draw a line GH to be one side of the new angle. Put the point of the compass at G and draw an arc with the compass open the same size as for the original angle. Now use the compass to duplicate the size (opening) of the original angle ($\angle ABC$). Put the compass point at the intersection of one of the sides of the original angle (D) and open the compass so the pencil is at the other intersection (E). Then, keeping the compass open the same amount, put the point of the compass at the intersection (J) of the drawn line and the arc, and draw a new arc (arc JK). The point of intersection of the arcs (K) will be a point on the other side of the new angle. Using a straightedge, draw a line from this point (K) to the vertex (G) to get a duplicate ($\angle FGH$) of the original angle.

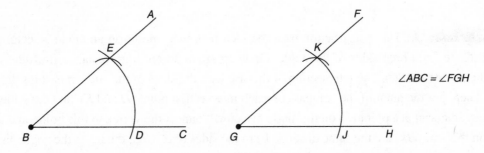

$\angle ABC = \angle FGH$

Segment Bisector: This is a point that divides a segment into two equal parts. Use a compass to find a line that goes through the center of a line segment. Draw an arc at a distance (more than halfway) from one of the endpoints (A) of the segment, and then draw an arc from the other endpoint (B) at the same distance (with the compass open the same amount). The two points where these arcs cross (C and D) are thus at equal distances from the endpoints. Connect those points (line CD). The point (E) where that line touches the line segment is the bisector of the segment. Also, line CD is perpendicular to AB.

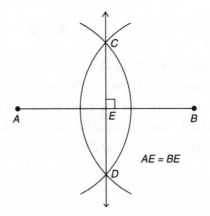

$AE = BE$

Line Perpendicular to a Given Line from a Given Point: Put the point of the compass on the given point (H) and draw an arc that intersects the line (FG) at two points (J and K). Then use these two points (rather than the endpoints of a line segment) and do the same construction as for a segment bisector (remember to open the compass the same amount). The resulting line will be perpendicular to the given line ($LM \perp FG$).

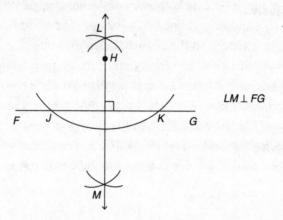

$LM \perp FG$

Angle Bisector: This construction uses the idea that every point on an angle bisector is the same distance from both sides of the angle. Draw an arc at an arbitrary distance from the vertex (B) of the angle ($\angle ABC$). The intersection of this arc with the sides of the angle measures the same length. Then, put the point of the compass on each intersection point (D and E), and draw identical arcs. They intersect at a point (F) on the angle bisector. Connect the vertex to this point, and all the points on this line (BF) are the same distance from the sides of $\angle ABC$; thus, it is the angle bisector.

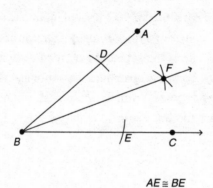

$AE \cong BE$

Line Parallel to a Given Line: Use the fact that if two parallel lines are intersected by a transversal, the corresponding angles are equal. Draw an arbitrary line (AB) and a point (C) outside of it through which the parallel will be drawn. Now draw any line (CD) that intersects the original line at a point (E). This transversal (CD) forms an angle ($\angle BED$), and now just use the same construction as for duplicating an angle. The side of this angle (CF) will be parallel to the given line (AB).

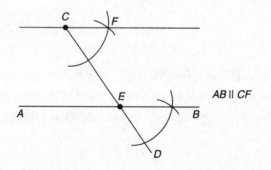

$AB \parallel CF$

Practice Exercises

1. For what construction is the figure below the final step?

    (A) Bisecting an angle

    (B) Duplicating an angle

    (C) Rotating an angle

    (D) Measuring an angle

2. In constructions, a compass is used for which of the following?

    (A) Drawing a straight line

    (B) Only drawing circles

    (C) Duplicating distances

    (D) Duplicating only angles

Solutions

1. **(A)**

    The final figure shows an angle that is divided into two halves, or bisected.

2. **(C)**

    The distance between the point of the compass and the pencil is actually the radius of a circle, and all radii on a circle are equal, so the compass can be used for duplicating distances.

UNITS OF MEASURE

Questions on the Praxis exam require an understanding of U.S. (sometimes called standard, or English) and metric units of measure. You should be proficient in converting units within each system. However, you are not required to convert units of measure between the two systems.

The U.S. System

Below is a list of common U.S. measurements that are used in Praxis questions.

Length

> 1 foot = 12 inches
>
> 3 feet = 1 yard
>
> 36 inches = 1 yard

Liquid Measure

> 1 cup = 8 ounces (oz)
>
> 1 pint = 2 cups = 16 oz
>
> 1 quart = 32 oz
>
> 1 gallon = 4 quarts

Time

> 60 seconds = 1 minute
>
> 60 minutes = 1 hour
>
> 24 hours = 1 day
>
> 7 days = 1 week
>
> 52 weeks = 1 year
>
> 12 months = 1 year
>
> 10 years = 1 decade
>
> 100 years = 1 century
>
> 1000 years = 1 millennium

Weight

> 1 pound (lb) = 16 ounces (oz)
>
> 1 ton = 2,000 lb

Two rules are used to convert from one unit to another:

1. When converting from larger units to smaller units, multiply by the conversion factor.

2. When converting from smaller units to larger units, divide by the conversion factor.

The conversion factor is how many smaller units there are in one larger unit.

EXAMPLE

Convert 8 pounds into ounces.

SOLUTION

Since pounds are larger than ounces, multiply 8 by 16, the number of ounces in 1 pound.

$$8 \times 16 = 128$$

8 pounds is equivalent to 128 ounces.

Sometimes more than one conversion is needed.

EXAMPLE

Convert 7.5 tons into ounces.

SOLUTION

Although a direct conversion from tons to ounces is not usually known, it can be derived. Multiply the number of ounces in 1 pound, 16, by the number of pounds in 1 ton, 2,000.

$$16 \times 2,000 = 32,000$$

Now multiply 7.5 by 32,000 to find the number of ounces in 7.5 tons.

$$7.5 \times 32,000 = 240,000$$

There are 240,000 ounces in 7.5 tons.

EXAMPLE

Convert 1,080 inches into yards.

SOLUTION

Inches are smaller than yards, so divide 1080 by 36, the number of inches in 1 yard.

$$1,080 \div 36 = 30$$

1,080 inches is equal to 30 yards.

EXAMPLE

Convert 5,184 minutes into days.

SOLUTION

Although we do not have a direct conversion from minutes to days, we can derive it.

1 day = 24 hours

1 hour = 60 minutes

Multiply 24 by 60 to find the number of minutes in 1 day.

$$24 \times 60 = 1,440$$

Finally, divide 5,184 by 1,440 to find the number of days that are equal to 5,184 minutes.

$$5,184 \div 1,440 = 3.6$$

Thus, 5,184 minutes is equal to 3.6 days.

The Metric System

There are three standard units of measure in the metric system.

Gram: a unit of weight (about the weight of a U.S. dime)

Liter: a liquid measure (a little more than a quart)

Meter: a measure of distance (a little more than a yard).

The metric system is based on powers of 10. The following prefixes are used with metric measure:

milli-: $\dfrac{1}{1,000}$ of a standard unit

centi-: $\dfrac{1}{100}$ of a standard unit

deci-: $\frac{1}{10}$ of a standard unit

deka-: 10 times a standard unit

hecto-: 100 times a standard unit

kilo-: 1,000 times a standard unit

The prefixes, used with the standard metric units, yield, for example:

a kilogram is 1,000 grams

a milliliter is $\frac{1}{1000}$ of a liter

a centimeter is $\frac{1}{100}$ of a meter

The two rules for U.S. unit conversion apply also to metric conversion, but since the conversion factors are based on 10, metric calculations are easier.

1. When converting from larger units to smaller units, multiply by the conversion factor.

2. When converting from smaller units to larger units, divide by the conversion factor.

EXAMPLE

Convert 7.7 kilometers into meters.

SOLUTION

Kilometers are larger than meters, so multiply 7.7 by 1,000, the number of meters in a kilometer.

$$7.7 \times 1,000 = 7,700$$

There are 7,700 meters in 7.7 kilometers.

Sometimes more than one conversion is needed.

EXAMPLE

Convert 511.2 hectograms into centigrams.

SOLUTION

Hectograms are larger than centigrams, so use multiplication. Although a direct conversion from hectograms to centigrams is not shown, it can be derived. There are 100 centigrams in every gram and 100 grams make a hectogram. Multiply 100 by 100 by 511.2 to find the number of centigrams that are equal to 511.2 hectograms.

$$100 \times 100 \times 511.2 = 5{,}112{,}000$$

There are 5,112,000 (5.112×10^6 in scientific notation) centigrams in 511.2 hectograms.

EXAMPLE

Convert 471 liters into kiloliters.

SOLUTION

Liters are smaller than kiloliters, so use division. Divide 471 by 1000, the number of liters in a kiloliter. This can be accomplished easily by moving the decimal point three units to the left.

$$471 \div 1{,}000 = 0.471$$

EXAMPLE

Convert 97.2 decimeters into dekameters.

SOLUTION

Decimeters are smaller than dekameters, so use division. Although a direct conversion from decimeters to dekameters is not shown, it can be derived. There are 10 decimeters in a meter and 10 meters make a dekameter, so multiply 10 by 10 to find the number of decimeters in a dekameter:

$$10 \times 10 = 100.$$

Next, divide 97.2 by 100 to find how many dekameters 97.2 decimeters is.

$97.2 \div 100 = 0.972$ (9.72×10^{-1}) dekameters, which is equal to 97.2 decimeters.

Practice Exercises

1. 17 pints is equal to how many gallons?

    (A) 6.625

    (B) 4.375

    (C) 2.125

    (D) 1.875

2.   9.71 grams equals how many milligrams?

    (A) 9,710

    (B) 971

    (C) 97.1

    (D) 0.971

3.   A vendor of copper cable charges $0.15 per inch or $1.55 per foot. What is the savings on an order of 7 yards of cable if it is purchased on a per-foot basis rather than a per-inch basis?

    (A) $5.25

    (B) $4.65

    (C) $1.40

    (D) $0.15

Solutions

1.   **(C)**

2 pints = 1 quart and 4 quarts = 1 gallon. Thus, there are $2 \times 4 = 8$ pints in a gallon. Divide 17 by 8 to find how many gallons are equivalent to 17 pints.

$$17 \div 8 = 2.125$$

2.   **(A)**

1,000 milligrams = 1 gram. When converting from larger units to smaller units, grams to milligrams, multiply by the conversion factor.

$$9.71 \times 1,000 = 9,710$$

3.   **(A)**

Find the number of feet and inches in 7 yards.

    1 yard = 36 inches

    7 yards = 252 inches

    1 yard = 3 feet

    7 yards = 21 feet

Find the cost of 252 inches at $0.15 per inch:

    $(252)(\$0.15) = \$37.80$

Find the cost of 21 feet at $1.55 per foot:

$(21)(\$1.55) = \$32.55$

So the savings is

$\$37.80 - \$32.55 = \$5.25$

Probability, Statistics, and Discrete Mathematics

In this chapter we will review the following topics:

- Interpreting data displays

- The counting principle

- Probability

- Measures of central tendency

- Discrete mathematics

INTERPRETING DATA DISPLAYS

Many questions on the Praxis exam will be answered by referring to various data displays. Data may be displayed in the form of tables, bar graphs, pie charts, and line graphs, among other forms. It is important to know how to interpret these displays.

Tables

Tables are a convenient way to present data clearly. Often the data are presented in two columns, with the item being measured in one column and the number (or percentage) of data points for that item in the other column. For example, if students are asked how many pets they have, the responses might be:

Student	Number of Pets
Amy	1
Beth	3
Chloe	0
Darryl	3
Emily	5
Francesco	1
Gina	0
Hillary	2
Ingrid	2
Jason	0
Kara	2
Luis	0
Mike	1
Noah	0
Olivia	2

To show data on how many pets students have, it would be more useful to present a table such as the following.

Number of Pets	How Many Students
0	5
1	3
2	4
3	2
4	0
5	1
More than 5	0

The following facts (among others) can easily be seen in such a table, but not so easily seen from the original data presentation.

1. Most students have 2 or fewer pets.

2. One-third of the students have no pets.

3. No one has more than 5 pets.

A similar table could be set up with percentages of the class. Using the same data, it would look like:

Number of Pets	Percentage of Students
0	33.3
1	20.0
2	26.7
3	13.3
4	0
5	6.7
More than 5	0

Note that when using percentages, the total should equal 100%. Sometimes, because the numbers are rounded, the total may be a little more or a little less than 100%.

Tables can also present a range of values for the item being measured. For example, it would be unwieldy for a table to have too many lines. An example would be presenting the weights of football players in the NFL, which actually range from 160 to 360 pounds. To present such data in a table, rather than listing each weight individually, it is best to use a range of weights, such as 160–179, 180–199, 200–219, etc., which would make the table only 10 lines long.

The tables discussed above are for **quantitative** data, or data having to do with quantities as the items being measured. Tables for **categorical** data, or data having to do with categories as the items being measured, are informational but lack the ability for some statistical analyses, such as finding the "average" political party in the following table.

Political Party (2012 election)	Number of Registered Members (× 100,000)
Constitution Party	3.7
Democratic Party	431.0
Green Party	2.5
Independent	240.0
Libertarian Party	2.8
Republican Party	307.0
Other	0.7

Two features in this table should be noted.

1.   The list of political parties is alphabetical, but could have been presented from the highest to lowest number of registered members, which might have been more useful.

2. The "($\times$ 100,000)" designation for the right-hand column means that each of the data points should be multiplied by 100,000. This makes the table more readable than listing the large number of digits of the actual data points. A designation like this is often used for thousands, in which case it appears as "$\times$ 1,000," "(thousands)," or simply "000."

Bar Graphs and Histograms

Bar graphs and **histograms** convey information by using rectangular bars. Bar graphs are used for categorical data, whereas histograms show quantitative data.

Bar Graphs

EXAMPLE

The bar graph below shows the number of metal cans collected for recycling by a local elementary school.

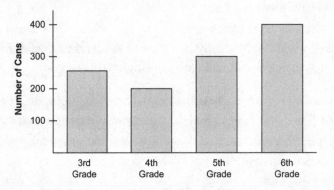

The sixth and fourth grades together collected how many more cans than did the fifth and third grades together?

SOLUTION

Find the sum of the sixth and fourth grade collections and subtract the sum of the fifth and third grade collections.

Sixth and fourth grades: $400 + 200 = 600$

Fifth and third grades: $300 + 250 = 550$

$600 - 550 = 50$

The sixth and fourth grades collected 50 more cans than did the fifth and third grades.

Double bar graphs show the same type of data for two groups on the same graph, usually for different years, genders, etc. These graphs use two colors to differentiate the groups. The typical double bar graph below shows average annual savings in thousands of dollars for a sample population. From the graph, we can read not only total savings, but also how much of each total was for male savers and how much was for female savers.

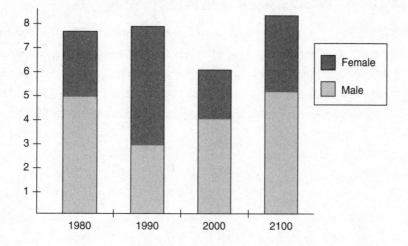

Histograms

Histograms are used to display how numerical data are distributed. The histogram for the prior example of the number of pets each of the 15 children have is the following.

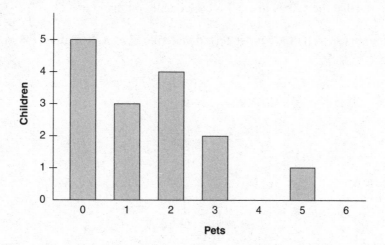

The histogram gives a better visual for the distribution of the number of pets than the individual data points do, and even better than the table does. The following observations from the table can more easily be seen in the histogram.

1.   Most students have 2 or fewer pets.

2.   One-third of the students have no pets.

3.   No one had more than 5 pets.

Stem-and-Leaf Plots

As we have seen above, quantitative data can be presented as a table or as a histogram. A third choice is as a stem-and-leaf plot. Histograms and stem-and-leaf plots are better visual representations of data than a table. The advantage of a stem-and-leaf plot is that the original data points aren't lost, as they are in a histogram when data are grouped into intervals.

A stem-and-leaf plot is just another way to visually present data. The plot is presented in two columns. Usually, the "stem," which appears in the left column, contains the data values except for the last digit (units), in order; the "leaves," in the right column, show all of the unit values for their corresponding stems. The stem-and-leaf plot for data points {12, 20, 33, 43, 37, 14, 38, 46, 38, 17}, representing the annual number of snowy days in the winter in Massachusetts for ten years is shown below.

Stem	Leaf
1	2 4 7
2	0
3	3 7 8 8
4	3 6

Although this plot doesn't look so impressive (because it involves only 10 values), we can still see that there are more values in the 30s in this data set because each data point is represented. In addition, we can see that the values in the 30s are actually on the high side.

Turn this stem-and-leaf plot a quarter turn counterclockwise. It mimics the histogram for the same data.

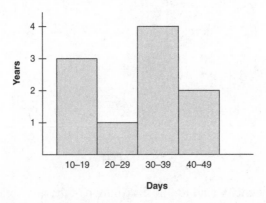

Note that the horizontal leaves in the stem-and-leaf plot correspond to the vertical bars in the histogram. But the histogram simply shows that the frequency for the 30s is twice as high as for the 10s, 20s, and 40s. We can't tell that the data for the 30s are mostly on the "high" side, since the individual values are not shown. That information is presented on the stem-and-leaf plot, though.

The differences among the three presentations for quantitative data—frequency tables, histograms, and stem-and-leaf plots—are shown clearly in the following example.

EXAMPLE

The following 20 test scores were recorded for a math test:

99, 89, 99, 88, 97, 79, 78, 85, 99, 100, 77, 84, 75, 88, 85, 69, 83, 78, 75, 87

Show these data in a table, histogram, and stem-and-leaf plot, grouping them into intervals of 10.

SOLUTION

The frequency distribution table that groups the values into intervals of ten (61–69, 70–79, 80–89, etc.) is the following:

Test Score	Number of Students
60–69	1
70–79	6
80–89	8
90–99	4
100	1

The histogram for the same data is the following:

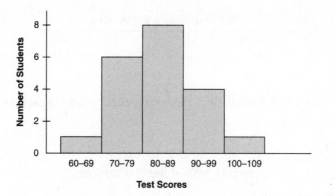

And the stem-and-leaf plot for the same data is the following:

Stem	Leaf
6	9
7	5 5 7 8 8 9
8	3 4 5 5 7 8 8 9
9	7 9 9 9
10	0

The stem-and-leaf plot shows that the scores, for the most part, were on the high side of each interval, whereas the table and histogram do not convey that information clearly. This is because the stem-and-leaf plots show the original data points.

Pie Charts

The **pie chart** gets its name because it displays data as "wedges" in a circular "pie." Pie charts are also called circle graphs. A pie chart is useful because it visually portrays data in a simple, eye-appealing fashion. Pie charts are used for categorical data.

The pie chart below shows the percentages of the 800 high school students who attend each grade. The wedges represent percentages of the total. If presented as the actual percentages, they must total 100%, or the entire circle.

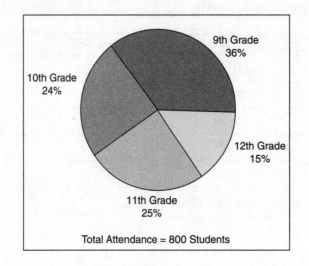

Total Attendance = 800 Students

EXAMPLE

How many more ninth graders than eleventh graders attend the school?

SOLUTION

The ninth grade class represents 36% of the 800 students.

$$(0.36)(800) = 288$$

The eleventh grade class represents 25% of the 800 students.

$$(0.25)(800) = 200$$

$$288 - 200 = 88$$

There are 88 more ninth graders attending the school than eleventh graders.

The pie chart for the same data could also be presented as actual counts, as shown below.

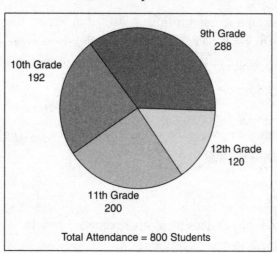

The pie looks the same, but the numbers are different. It is important to determine whether actual counts or percentages are being presented in a pie chart. If counts, the total must be the total count (here, 800 students).

Line Graphs

Line graphs plot one variable against another. They are similar to linear equations graphed in the coordinate plane. The slope of the line graph gives information about the data, such as rate of change or percentage gain or loss between data points. For example, a positive slope indicates an increase and a negative slope indicates a decrease.

Line graphs can simply connect data points, and information can be read from the graph. Often, the line graphs are plotted with time as the *x*-axis.

EXAMPLE

The weekly downloads of a YouTube video over a six-week period are shown below.

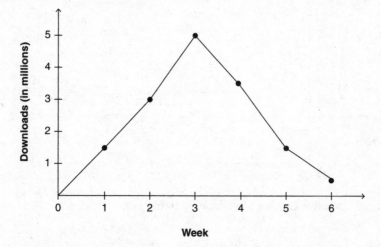

What was the number of downloads during the fifth week?

SOLUTION

The x-axis in the graph represents time measured in weeks, and the y-axis represents the number of downloads measured in millions. At week 5, the volume is midway between 1 and 2 million. Thus, the number of downloads during week 5 was 1.5 million.

We can also estimate values between the actual data points by **interpolation**, or reading a value on the graph between the given points.

EXAMPLE

Using the graph on the previous page, approximately how long did it take for the number of downloads to reach 2 million?

SOLUTION

The answer is about 1.5 weeks, which is where the graph crosses the 2 million download mark. In fact, if we continue the 2 million mark, we can see that the downloads cross the 2 million mark again (after reaching the peak in week 3) about 5.75 weeks after it started on YouTube.

If a graph isn't changing direction, it is possible to estimate a future value by extending the graph beyond what is plotted. This is called **extrapolation**, and usually is used when the graph shows a clear trend in the data.

Line graphs may be used to convey information of more than one function simultaneously.

A company that started operations in 2009 plotted its annual costs and revenues (income) through 2013.

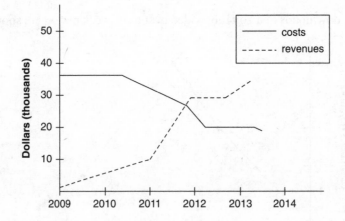

We can read several features of the data from this graph:

1. In 2009, the difference between costs and revenues was the greatest (about $36,000).

2. The lines intersect when revenues and costs are equal, known as the break-even point in a business. The break-even point for this company occurred in 2012.

3. Extrapolating the data to 2014, revenues should increase and costs should decrease.

    If there are many data points, connecting each point won't give a clear picture of the trend of the data. If the data points are correlated in some way, a **line of best fit** shows an overall trend in the data. In such cases, **scatter plots** are useful, and one line of best fit through the data points gives the needed information. This line doesn't go through each of the points, but it shows the trend of the data. Therefore, the information from the line of best fit is important, even though determining how to find the line of best fit is beyond the scope of the Praxis exam. Sometimes, however, the data points don't seem to show a trend at all. The three scatter plots below show (a) high correlation with a line of best fit, (b) moderate correlation with a line of best fit, and (c) no correlation.

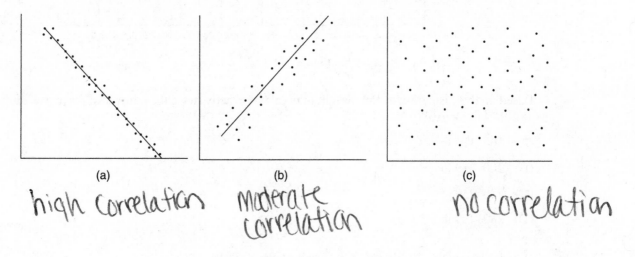

(a)   (b)   (c)

high correlation   moderate correlation   no correlation

Practice Exercises

Questions 1 and 2 refer to the graph below, which shows a hypothetical (but realistic) distribution for the weights of a group of NFL football players. Note that weights are rounded to the nearest pound. The horizontal axis shows intervals of data, whereas the vertical axis shows the number of data points in each interval.

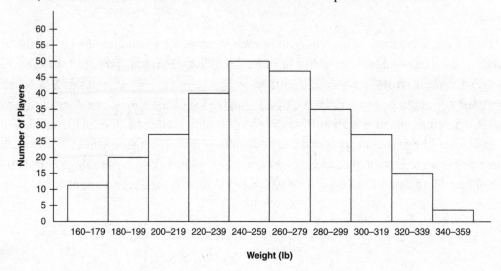

1. Based on this histogram, which weight interval has exactly twice the number of players as the 180–199 lb interval?

    (A) 160–179 lb

    (B) 200–219 lb

    (C) 220–239 lb

    (D) 280–299 lb

2. Which two weight intervals have the same number of players?

    (A) 180–199 and 320–339

    (B) 200–219 and 300–319

    (C) 220–239 and 280–299

    (D) 240–259 and 260–279

3. Which of the following pie charts represents responses to the question "What is your favorite pie?" for the same data as the bar graph shown below?

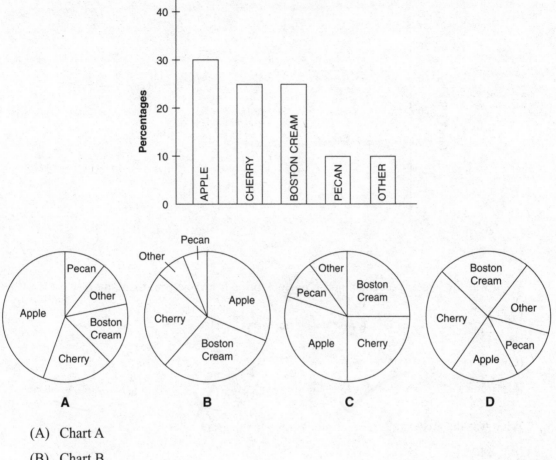

(A) Chart A

(B) Chart B

(C) Chart C

(D) Chart D

CHAPTER 6

Questions 4 and 5 refer to the graph below.

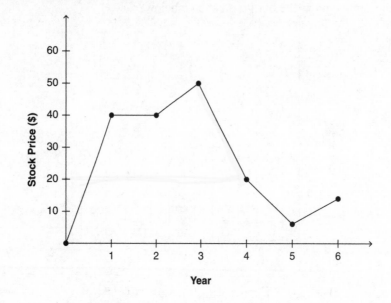

4. What was the largest percentage drop in stock price from one year to another?

    (A) 15%

    (B) 25%

    (C) 50%

    (D) 75%

    Year 3–4 $\dfrac{30,000}{50,000} = 60\%$

    Year 4–5 $\dfrac{15,000}{20,000} = 75\%$

5. What was the greatest decrease in stock price in the graph?

    (A) $40

    (B) $30

    (C) $25

    (D) $10

Solutions

1. **(C)**

    The 180–199 lb interval has 20 players, so the answer would be the interval with 40 players, which is the 220–239 lb interval.

2. **(B)**

    The intervals for 200–219 and 300–319 each have 27 players.

3. **(C)**

Based on the data, the pie chart should show two equal sectors (Cherry and Boston Cream, 25% each) that take up half the circle. That eliminates choices (A) and (B). In addition, the sectors for Pecan and Other should be equal and total less than the sector for Apple. That eliminates choice D.

4. **(D)**

The greatest percentage drop is 75%. Drops are seen only in the intervals from years 3 to 4 and years 4 to 5. Although the values dropped more from year 3 to year 4 ($30,000 drop) than from year 4 to year 5 ($15,000), the percentage drop, calculated as

$$\text{Percentage change } (n) = \frac{\text{change}}{\text{original}},$$

is $\frac{30,000}{50,000} = 60\%$ for years 3 to 4, and $\frac{15,000}{20,000} = 75\%$ for years 4 to 5.

5. **(B)**

In year 3, the stock price was $50. In year 4, the stock price decreased to $20.

$$\$50 - \$20 = \$30$$

THE COUNTING PRINCIPLE

The **counting principle** says that if one activity can be done in a ways and another can be done in b ways, both can be done in $a \times b$ ways. This is true for any number of activities, so for four activities, a, b, c, and d, all four can be done in $a \times b \times c \times d$ ways.

EXAMPLE

If a pre-school lunch menu offers 2 different types of sandwiches, 3 different side orders, and 2 different drinks, how many different combinations of sandwich, side order, and drink are available?

SOLUTION

To calculate the number of combinations of lunch options, multiply all the possibilities.

$$2 \quad \times \quad 3 \quad \times \quad 2 \quad = 12$$

$$\text{sandwiches} \times \text{side orders} \times \text{drinks} = \text{combinations of lunches}$$

Another way to find the answer is by using a **tree diagram**.

S = Sandwich
SO = Side Order
D = Drinks

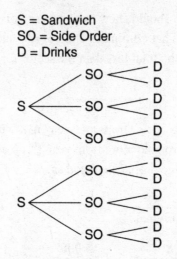

The tree diagram is a useful visual aid to demonstrate that there are a total of 12 different combinations of sandwich, side order, and drink.

Practice Exercises

1. A vegan restaurant offers 5 salads, each with a choice of 3 different types of lettuce and 4 different salad toppings. How many different kinds of salads are available at the restaurant?

    (A) 12

    (B) 24

    (C) 32

    (D) 60

2. Carla packed 4 skirts, 3 blouses, and 2 pairs of shoes for her weekend trip. How many combinations of skirts, blouses, and shoes are available for her trip?

    (A) 9

    (B) 18

    (C) 21

    (D) 24

Solutions

1. **(D)**

    Use the counting principle to find the number of salads:

    (5 salads) × (3 types of lettuce) × (4 salad toppings) = 60 salads

2. **(D)**

    Multiply the number of skirts by the number of blouses by the number of pairs of shoes to find the number of outfit combinations.

    $4 \times 3 \times 2 = 24$ outfits

PROBABILITY

A raffle for a prize is an example of probability. How many tickets did you buy? How many were sold? These questions affect the probability of your winning the raffle. Probability can be expressed by using the formula:

$$\text{Probability} = \frac{\text{favored outcomes}}{\text{all outcomes}}$$

Probability can be expressed as a fraction, a decimal, or a percentage. For example, for the toss of a coin, the probability that it will land heads up is $Pr = \frac{1}{2}$, 0.5, or 50%. When people say there is a 50:50 chance, they are expressing a win:lose ratio, not a probability.

Probabilities range from 0 to 1. A probability of 1 means the favored outcome will always happen (such as the probability of picking a red marble from a jar that contains only red marbles). A probability of 0 means no favored outcomes will happen (such as picking a red marble from a jar that contains only blue marbles). All the probabilities in between are expressed as fractions, decimals, or percentages (0% to 100%).

EXAMPLE

Larry purchased a package of baseball trading cards. He knows among the ten cards in the package, there is one Dustin Pedroia card. What is the probability he will select the Dustin Pedroia card on the first draw?

SOLUTION

$$Pr = \frac{\text{favored outcomes}}{\text{all outcomes}} = \frac{1}{10}$$

The answer, $\frac{1}{10}$, may also be expressed in decimal form, 0.1, or as a percentage, 10%.

We can use our knowledge of probability to calculate the probability of independent and dependent events occurring.

Independent Events

Independent events are two events that occur with one outcome not affected by the other. The following example demonstrates the probability of independent events. As we saw with the counting principle, the probability of more than one independent event occurring is the product of each of their probabilities.

EXAMPLE

Alice flips a coin and then rolls a die (singular of dice). What is the probability that the coin will land on heads and the die will land on an odd number?

SOLUTION

Since these are independent events, calculate the probabilities of each event occurring and multiply those probabilities.

Probability of a coin landing on heads: $\frac{1}{2}$

Probability of a die landing on an odd number: $\frac{3}{6} = \frac{1}{2}$

Multiply the probabilities: $\frac{1}{2} \times \frac{1}{2} = \frac{1}{4}$

There is a $\frac{1}{4}$ probability (0.25) that the coin lands on heads and the die lands on an odd number.

When calculating probabilities, be careful of what is meant by "all outcomes." All outcomes do not necessarily mean the whole population, only the population from which the selection is made.

EXAMPLES

The chart below shows the enrollment at a small middle school.

Grade	Boys	Girls
7th grade	27	28
8th grade	34	31
Total	61	59

Use the formula Probability = $\dfrac{\text{favored outcomes}}{\text{all outcomes}}$ to answer all of the questions.

1.   What is the probability of a randomly selected student being a 7th-grade boy?

   SOLUTION

   Here, "all outcomes" is the total of 120 students in the school (61 + 59 = 120). There are 27 7th-grade boys.

   $$Pr = \frac{27}{120} = 0.225 = 22.5\%$$

2.   What is the probability of a randomly selected girl being an 8th grader?

   SOLUTION

   Here, "all outcomes" is the girls only. There are 59 girls in the school and 31 are in the 8th grade.

   $$Pr = \frac{31}{59} \approx 0.525 \approx 52.5\%$$

3.   What is the probability of a randomly selected 8th grader being a girl?

   SOLUTION

   Here, "all outcomes" is all 8th graders. There are 65 8th graders (34 + 31), of which 31 are girls.

   $$Pr = \frac{31}{65} \approx 0.477 \approx 47.7\%$$

Notice the difference between questions 2 and 3 above. The "all outcomes" is different for each. This points out the importance of reading probability questions carefully to determine what "all outcomes" means for that particular problem.

Dependent Events

With **dependent events**, the outcome of one event affects the outcome of the next event. This happens, for example, when selecting two marbles from a jar containing 5 blue, 4 yellow, and 11 red marbles. We already know that the probability of picking a blue marble is $\frac{5}{20} = \frac{1}{4}$; the probability of picking a yellow marble is $\frac{4}{20} = \frac{1}{5}$; and the probability of picking a red marble is $\frac{11}{20}$. For a second pick from the jar, if the marbles from the first pick are replaced, these probabilities remain the same. These are independent events.

However, if we do not replace the first marble, the probabilities change. The probabilities for the second pick are dependent on the first pick. The events are dependent. If the first marble picked is red, and it is not replaced, the jar now contains 19 marbles, 5 blue, 4 yellow, and 10 red. The probabilities for each color, respectively, have changed to $\frac{5}{19}$, $\frac{4}{19}$, and $\frac{10}{19}$. It is important to pay attention to whether or not there is replacement in any problem of this type on the Praxis test.

Practice Exercises

1. Chad has 4 pairs of black socks, 3 pairs of white socks, and 3 pairs of brown socks in a drawer. If he reaches into the drawer to pick a pair of socks (without looking), what is the probability that it is a pair of black socks?

    (A) $\frac{10}{10}$

    (B) $\frac{2}{5}$

    (C) $\frac{3}{10}$

    (D) $\frac{7}{10}$

2. Based on the information in question 1, what is the probability that Chad will pick a pair of black socks and then a pair of white socks the next morning? (Assume no replacement.)

    (A) $\frac{2}{5}$

    (B) $\frac{1}{3}$

(C) $\dfrac{2}{15}$

(D) $\dfrac{11}{15}$

3. What is the probability that a coin flipped three times will land on heads all three times?

(A) $\dfrac{1}{8}$

(B) $\dfrac{1}{2}$

(C) $\dfrac{3}{4}$

(D) $\dfrac{4}{4}$

Solutions

1. **(B)**

To find the probability of selecting a pair of black socks, use the formula:

$$\frac{\text{favored outcomes}}{\text{all outcomes}}$$

$$\frac{4}{10} = \frac{2}{5}$$

2. **(C)**

These are dependent events because there is no replacement. The probability of picking a pair of black socks on day 1 is $\dfrac{2}{5}$, as we saw in Exercise 1 above. However, now there are 3 pairs of each color and only 9 pairs left for day 2. Therefore, the probability of both events is found by multiplying the individual probabilities, or $\dfrac{2}{5} \times \dfrac{3}{9}$, which reduces to $\dfrac{2}{15}$. Answer choice (D) is wrong because it is the sum, not the product, of the two probabilities.

3. **(A)**

Each flip of the coin is an independent event because landing on heads on one flip has no effect on future flips. The probability of a coin landing on heads is $\frac{1}{2}$. Multiply each probability by the others to find the probability of all three flips landing on heads.

$$\frac{1}{2} \times \frac{1}{2} \times \frac{1}{2} = \frac{1}{8}$$

Geometric Probability

When geometric measures, such as length and area, are involved in a probability question, the question is asking about **geometric probability**. Hitting a bull's-eye on a dartboard is a form of geometric probability, such as the likelihood of hitting the center versus other locations on the board. When answering a question involving geometric probability, use the formula

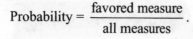

$$\text{Probability} = \frac{\text{favored measure}}{\text{all measures}}.$$

EXAMPLE

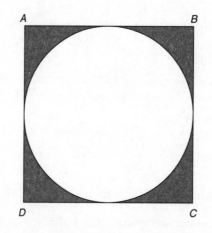

If the perimeter of square *ABCD* is 64 inches, what is the probability of not hitting the inscribed circle on a coin toss (use π = 3.14)?

SOLUTION

Use $Pr = \dfrac{\text{favored measure}}{\text{all measures}}$ to answer the question. Find the area of the square and subtract the area of the circle to find the shaded area.

A square has a perimeter of $4s$ and an area of s^2, where s is the measure of one side. Find the measure of a side by substituting 64 into the perimeter formula:

$$P = 4s$$

$$64 = 4s$$

$$16 = s$$

Next, substitute 16 for s in the area formula.

$$A = s^2$$

$$A = 16^2$$

$$A = 256$$

To find the measure of the shaded area, subtract the area of the circle from 256, the area of the square. The formula for the area of a circle is $A = \pi r^2$, where r is the radius of the circle. Notice that the width of the square is the diameter of the circle. Thus, the circle's diameter is 16 and its radius is 8.

$$A = \pi r^2$$

$$A = (3.14)(8)^2 = 200.96$$

Thus, the area of the shaded area is:

$$256 - 200.96 = 55.04$$

Finally, to find the probability of a coin landing on the shaded area, use the formula

$$Pr = \frac{\text{favored measure}}{\text{all measures}}$$

$$\frac{55.04}{256} = 0.215 = 21.5\%$$

MEASURES OF CENTRAL TENDENCY

Any group of data, such as monthly checking account balances or Major League Baseball batting averages, can be collected and analyzed. Each data set can be used to calculate the following statistics: mean, median, mode, and range. Taken together, the first three of these statistics are called **measures of central tendency**. In addition, the range tells about the spread of the data. These measures are useful for drawing conclusions quickly about sets of data.

The Mean

The **mean**, also known as the average, indicates what a typical data value is for a specific set of data. It is the sum of a group of numbers divided by the quantity of numbers. For example, if an archer had scores of 213, 186, and 234, her mean score would be calculated as:

$$\frac{213+186+234}{3} = \frac{633}{3} = 211$$

The mean score of the archer's three scores is 211.

When the mean of a series of numbers is known, specific data points can be calculated.

EXAMPLE

Vince needs an average of 80% on his three exams to earn a B in math. On his first two exams, he received grades of 65% and 75%. What score must he receive to get an 80% average for the three exams?

SOLUTION

Let x = the score needed on the third test to raise his average to 80%.

$$\frac{65+75+x}{3} = 80$$

$$\frac{140+x}{3} = 80$$

$$(3)\left(\frac{140+x}{3}\right) = (80)(3)$$

$$140+x = 240$$

$$x = 100$$

Vince needs to score 100% on his third test to average 80% for the three exams.

When certain values are repeated in a data set, it is often useful to calculate a **weighted mean**, which takes into account repetitions when calculating the mean of a set of data.

EXAMPLE

The girls on a swimming team, to the closest year, were the following ages:

Age	# of girls
12	4
11	3
10	7
9	6

What is the mean age of the girls?

SOLUTION

It would be incorrect to simply find the average of the ages [(12 + 11 + 10 + 9) ÷ 4 = 10.5]. Since there are more girls of one age than others, it is necessary to find a weighted average.

$$\frac{(12 \times 4) + (11 \times 3) + (10 \times 7) + (9 \times 6)}{20} =$$

$$\frac{205}{20} = 10.25$$

The weighted average is lower than the mean of the ages because there were more girls in lower age brackets than in the higher age brackets.

If data are **skewed**, meaning at least one value is very different from the rest of the values, the mean may not represent a typical value.

Consider the incomes of four families (incomes in thousands of dollars).

47.6   71.3   62.4   611.2

The average income of the four families is calculated as

$$\frac{47.6 + 71.3 + 62.4 + 611.2}{4} = 198.1, \text{ or } \$198,100$$

An income of $198,100 per year is much greater than three of the four families. The family with an annual income of $611,200 skewed the data set to a greater average income. This large value, called an **outlier**, is the reason we cannot rely solely on the mean as a representative statistic of a data set. Often, other measures of central tendency, such as the median, are needed to accurately represent a data group.

The Median

The **median** is the middle value in a data set that is arranged in order. In the set of numbers {2, 4, 6, 8, 10}, 6 is the median because it is the value in the middle. In the data set {4, 11, 7, 6, 9}, the median is not immediately apparent because the numbers are not in order. When arranged in ascending order, {4, 6, 7, 9, 11}, it is clear that 7 is the median.

Data sets with an even number of values have two numbers in the middle. For example, in the data set {4, 9, 11, 17, 20, 26}, 11 and 17 are the middle values. In this case, find the average of the two numbers to get the median:

$$\frac{11+17}{2} = \frac{28}{2} = 14$$

The median of the data set {4, 9, 11, 17, 20, 26} is 14. The median of a data set is not necessarily a member of the group.

Sometimes, the median is better than the mean to represent a data set. Let's look again at the example of four families with incomes of $47,600, $62,400, $71,300, and $611,200. When we determine the median value, we get the average of the two middle values, or ($62,400 + $71,300) ÷ 2 = $66,850. This figure is a better representative of the data than the $198,000 mean.

EXAMPLE

The following are the lengths (in inches) of fish caught off of a pier during a one-hour period.

6, 8, 10, 11, 12, 40

Find the median and the mean of the lengths of the fish.

SOLUTION

Find the median by arranging the lengths in ascending order:

6   8   10   11   12   40

There are two measures in the middle, 10 and 11, so find their mean.

$$\frac{10+11}{2} = \frac{21}{2} = 10.5$$

Now find the mean.

$$\frac{6+8+10+11+12+40}{6} = \frac{87}{6} \approx 14.5$$

The median, 10.5, is a useful statistic to represent this particular data set. Three of the fish measure below 10.5 inches and three measure above, whereas the mean, 14.5, is greater than five of the six values in the data set. The greatest length of any of the fish, 40 inches, is an outlier, and it skews the mean toward higher values. In this situation, the median is a better representative of the data set than is the mean.

The Mode

The mode is the value that occurs most frequently in a data set. In the group of numbers {7, 8, 8, 11, 15}, 8 is the mode because it appears twice whereas the rest of the numbers appear only once.

Some data sets have no mode. In the set {22, 33, 44, 55}, no number appears more frequently than the rest. Thus, this data set has no mode.

Some data sets have more than one mode. In the group {1, 7.4, 7.4, 9.2, 11.6, 11.6, 13}, 7.4 and 11.6 appear twice and all of the other numbers show up only once. Thus, 7.4 and 11.6 are modes of this group. This group is thus called "bimodal" ("bi" means 2).

The Range

In a group of numbers, the difference between the least and greatest values is called the **range**. In the data set {15.2, 17.4, 22.4, 46.2}, the range is 31 because $46.2 - 15.2 = 31$.

EXAMPLE

The data set {17.6, 19.1, 56.3, x} is arranged in ascending order. If the range is 74.9, what is the value of x?

SOLUTION

The range is found by calculating the difference between the least and greatest values. Use the fact that x must be the greatest value of the set since the numbers are arranged in ascending order.

$$x - 17.6 = 74.9$$

$$x = 92.5$$

Using the Best Measures of Central Tendency

On the Praxis exam, you may be required to determine the best measure(s) of central tendency to assess a particular situation.

In particular, keep in mind that the median is a better measure than the mean for skewed data. For nonskewed data, the mean and median are usually close in value. The mode is more of a descriptive value.

EXAMPLE

The engineering department of a small corporation has only six employees—a supervisor who makes $216,000 per year, and five engineers with salaries of $65,000, $65,000, $72,000, $73,000, and $79,000.

The mean of the salaries is

$$\frac{65,000 + 65,000 + 72,000 + 73,000 + 79,000 + 216,000}{6} = \$95,000$$

and the median is $72,500.

The engineers want a raise, but the company management cites an average salary of $95,000 in the department, and says no raise is warranted. The engineers cite a median salary of $72,500. Who is correct?

SOLUTION

Actually, each is using a true statistic and promoting the one that helps their case. The engineers should insist on knowing the range of salaries, which in this case is $216,000 – $65,000 = $151,000, twice the median, making the mean salary meaningless.

EXAMPLE

A set of data is given as follows:

$$\{0, 1, 2, 2, 2, 12, 15, 18, 20\}$$

Should the mean or median be used as a measure of central tendency?

SOLUTION

The median is 2. The mean is $\frac{0 + 1 + 2 + 2 + 2 + 12 + 15 + 18 + 20}{9} = 6$. While neither statistic is truly representative of the data, the mean is the more accurate measure.

These examples point out the fact that if the mean and median differ greatly, further information is needed to determine the best measure of central tendency.

Boxplots

Boxplots provide visual data on the median value of a set of data as well as its variation. A typical boxplot of nonskewed data has the following appearance:

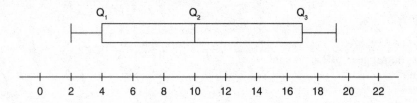

The features of a boxplot are Q_2 (quartile 2), which is the median; Q_1 and Q_3, which are the first and third quartiles, respectively; and the highest and lowest data points. The first quartile is actually the median value for the data below the median; likewise, the third quartile is the median value of the data above the median. This boxplot is for a data set with a low value of 2, a high value of 19.5, and a median of 10. Because Q_2 appears to be close to the middle of the box that has a low (Q_1) value of 4 and high (Q_3) value of 17, and there are no outliers in the data (which would be indicated by an asterisk), this data set is not skewed.

For the example above with a data set of {0, 1, 2, 2, 2, 12, 15, 18, 20}, the boxplot is shown below.

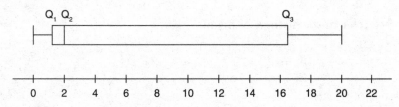

This boxplot shows a clear left skew to the data, meaning many low data points, which pulls the median to the left.

Practice Exercises

Questions 1–4 refer to the data set below.

{11.43, 19.76, 14.41, 3.86, 7.86, 17.68}

1. What is the mean of the data set?

    (A) 12.5

    (B) 12.92

    (C) 15.9

    (D) 19.76

2. What is the median of the data set?

    (A) 12.5

    (B) 12.92

    (C) 15.9

    (D) 19.76

3. What is the range of the data set?

    (A) 12.5

    (B) 12.92

    (C) 15.9

    (D) 19.76

4. What is the mode of the data set?

    (A) 12.5

    (B) 12.92

    (C) Each number is a mode.

    (D) There is no mode.

Questions 5–6 refer to the histogram below.

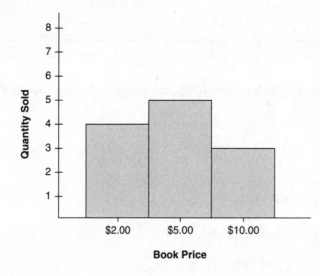

5. What is the median cost of the books sold?

    (A) $2.00

    (B) $5.00

    (C) $7.50

    (D) $10.00

6.   What is the mean cost of the books sold?

   (A) $9.95

   (B) $7.35

   (C) $6.45

   (D) $5.25

7.   After a chapter test, the following scores were entered for the class:

60%	70%	80%	90%	100%
X	X	X	X	X
X		X	X	

   What score must a ninth student earn for the median and mode to be the same?

   (A) 70

   (B) 80

   (C) 90

   (D) 100

Solutions

1.   **(A)**

   The mean is the average of the numbers. Find the sum of the numbers and divide by 6.

   $(11.43 + 19.76 + 14.41 + 3.86 + 7.86 + 17.68) \div 6 = 12.5$

2.   **(B)**

   The median is the number in the middle. Arrange the numbers in ascending order to identify the median.

   $\{3.86, 7.86, 11.43, 14.41, 17.68, 19.76\}$

   Both 11.43 and 14.41 are middle values. In this case, the median is the average of the middle numbers.

   $(11.43 + 14.41) \div 2 = 12.92$

3.   **(C)**

   The range of a group of numbers is the difference between the greatest and least values.

   $19.76 - 3.86 = 15.9$

4.   **(D)**

The mode is the value that occurs most frequently. Each number in the group appears the same number of times, once, so there is no mode.

5.   **(B)**

Array the number of books sold; there are four $2 books, five $5 books, and three $10 books.

   2   2   2   2   5   5   5   5   5   10   10   10

The middle numbers are both 5s, so their mean average is 5.

   $(5 + 5) \div 2 = 5$, or $5.00

6.   **(D)**

Add the costs of the books and divide the sum by 12, using weighted means to simplify the calculation

$$\frac{(4(2) + 5(5) + 3(10))}{12} = 5.25, \text{ or } \$5.25$$

7.   **(B)**

Array the scores from least to greatest.

   60   60   70   80   80   90   90   100

The median score is 80 and the modes are 60, 80, and 90. When another student scores an 80% on the test, the scores are:

   60   60   70   80   80   80   90   90   100

The median remains 80, but the third score of 80 makes 80 the sole mode of the group.

DISCRETE MATHEMATICS

Solutions to problems, especially those with **discrete** (as opposed to continuous) data points, can be simplified with visual aids, including Venn diagrams, algorithms, and flow charts.

Venn Diagrams

A **Venn diagram** is a diagram that shows all possible relations among a finite collection of data points.

Consider all the whole number factors of 24 and 15.

24: 1, 2, 3, 4, 6, 8, 12, 24

15: 1, 3, 5, 15

If you were asked to find the common whole number factors of both 24 and 15, you could express the information by using a Venn diagram. A Venn diagram helps us picture relationships. In the diagram below:

A shows the whole number factors of 24

B shows the whole number factors of 15.

W represents the group of all whole numbers.

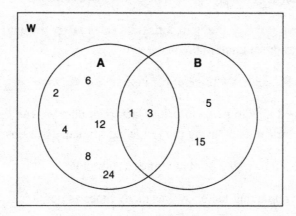

The Venn diagram helps us to see that the common factors of 15 and 24 are 1 and 3.

EXAMPLE

The Venn diagram below represents 132 students in a high school who study French or Spanish or both.

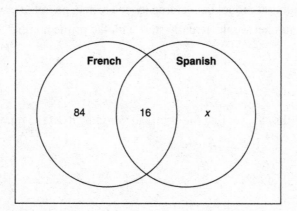

How many students study only Spanish?

SOLUTION

From the diagram, 84 students study only French, 16 students study both languages, and x students study only Spanish. The total represented in the diagram is 132, so

$$84 + 16 + x = 132$$

$$100 + x = 132$$

$$x = 32 \text{ students study only Spanish.}$$

Algorithms

An **algorithm** is a set of rules or steps that always leads to the correct solution.

The algorithm for calculating the total cost of an item at a store is:

1. Multiply the price of the item times the sales tax percentage expressed in decimal form to find the amount of the tax.

2. Add the sales tax to the price of the item to find the total cost.

Previously, we learned how to perform prime factorizations. We can use an algorithm to correctly create a prime factorization by using the following sequence of steps:

1. Divide the number by 2 as many times as possible.

2. Divide the remaining factor by 3 as many times as possible.

3. Divide the remaining factor by 5 as many times as possible.

4. Divide the remaining factor by 7 as many times as possible.

5. Continue factoring using prime numbers (for example, 11, 13, 17, 19, …) until the number is expressed in terms of all its prime factors.

Note that once the number cannot be factored by one prime, go to the next prime. Therefore, the factorization of an odd number would actually start with the prime number 3, since an odd number is not factorable by 2.

EXAMPLE

Using the algorithm above, find the prime factored form of the number 2,520.

SOLUTION

$$2,520 \div 2 = 1,260$$

$$1,260 \div 2 = 630$$

$$630 \div 2 = 315$$

$$315 \div 3 = 105$$

$$105 \div 3 = 35$$

$$35 \div 5 = 7$$

The prime factored form of 2,520 is thus $2 \times 2 \times 2 \times 3 \times 3 \times 5 \times 7$. The prime factorization of 2,520 is $2^3 \times 3^2 \times 5 \times 7$.

Flow Charts

A **flow chart** is a graphical representation of the successive steps in solving a problem. A flow chart uses symbols connected by lines.

EXAMPLE

This flow chart shows the percentage of income tax to be paid, depending upon a person's income. Find the percentage of income tax for someone whose income is $40,000.

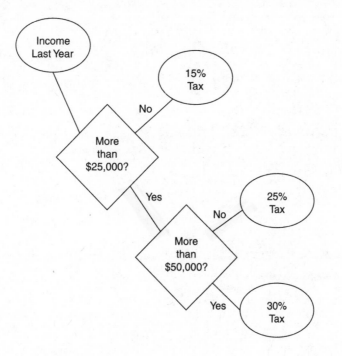

SOLUTION

Consulting the flow chart, we see that a person with an income of $40,000 would have to pay 25% in income tax.

Posttest

Now that you have reviewed all the topics for the Praxis Middle School Mathematics (5169) exam, go to the online REA Study Center to take the posttest. Your score report will automatically identify topics in need of further study.

(www.rea.com/studycenter)

Practice Tests 1 and 2

Available at the online REA Study Center (www.rea.com/studycenter)

The Praxis Middle School Mathematics (5169) exam is computer-based, so we strongly recommend that you take our online practice exams to simulate test-day conditions and to receive these added benefits:

- **Timed testing conditions**—helps you gauge how much time you can spend on each question

- **Automatic scoring**—find out how you did on the test, instantly

- **On-screen detailed explanations of answers**—give you the correct answer and explain why the other answer choices are wrong

- **Diagnostic score reports**—pinpoint where you're strongest and where you need to focus your study

If your study time allows, you can continue preparing for your exam by taking additional Practice Tests 3 and 4 in this book.

PRACTICE TEST 3

Praxis II
Middle School Mathematics

Praxis II Middle School Mathematics Practice Test 3

TIME: 2 hours

QUESTIONS: 55 selected-response and numeric-entry questions

> **Directions:** Each of the following questions or statements below is followed by four suggested answers or completions. Select the one that is best in each case.

(Answer Sheets appear in the back of the book.)

1. $-\sqrt{361}$ is an example of which of the following categories?

   (A) Integers

   (B) Irrational numbers

   (C) Whole numbers

   (D) Natural numbers

2. What is the area in square inches of a triangle with one leg measuring 9 inches and hypotenuse measuring 41 inches? Enter your answer in the spaces below. (Round to the nearest tenth.)

   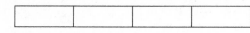

3. What is the domain of the following relation?

   $$(6, 2)\ (5, 3)\ (7, 5)\ (3, 1)$$

   (A) $\{5, -2, 4\}$

   (B) $\{6, 5, 7, 3\}$

   (C) $\{5\}$

   (D) $\{1, 2, 3, 5\}$

4. The probability of rain for the next three days is given in the table.

Day	Sun.	Mon.	Tue.
Probability of rain	45%	80%	30%

Based on the data in the table, what is the probability that it will rain on Sunday and Monday but not Tuesday? Place your answer as a percentage in the boxes below.

5. In the graph of the equation $6x + 4y = 12$, what is the x-intercept?

   (A) $(0, 2)$

   (B) $(0, 3)$

   (C) $(2, 0)$

   (D) $(3, 0)$

6. The net shown below can be constructed to form a:

   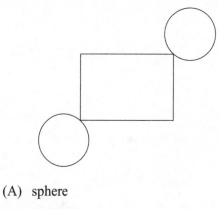

   (A) sphere

   (B) pyramid

   (C) cylinder

   (D) cone

7. One square face of a cube has an area measuring 49 cm². What is the volume of the cube in cm³? Fill in the spaces below.

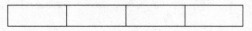

8. What is the y-intercept of a line perpendicular to $y = -\frac{2}{3}x + 5$ that passes through $(-6, -6)$?

(A) $(3, 0)$

(B) $(0, 3)$

(C) $(-6, 4)$

(D) $(0, 2)$

9. Arrange the following values from least to greatest:

$$\frac{2}{7}, \frac{6}{25}, 0.26, 23.9\%$$

(A) $0.26, \frac{6}{25}, 23.9\%, \frac{2}{7}$

(B) $\frac{6}{25}, 0.26, \frac{2}{7}, 23.9\%$

(C) $23.9\%, \frac{6}{25}, 0.26, \frac{2}{7}$

(D) $23.9\%, \frac{6}{25}, \frac{2}{7}, 0.26$

10. What type of construction is shown below?

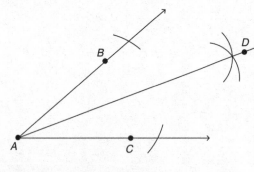

(A) Line segment bisector

(B) Perpendicular bisector of a line

(C) Angle bisector

(D) Ray bisector

11. How many yards are there in 7 miles? Express your answer in scientific notation.

(A) 1.76×10^3

(B) 17.6×10^2

(C) 12.32×10^3

(D) 1.232×10^4

12. What is the value of the following expression?

$$-2(2 - 7)^3 - (1.5)(4)^4$$

Place your answer in the boxes below.

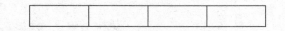

13. What are the domain and range of $f(x) = -(x + 2)^2 - 3$?

(A) Domain: all real numbers; Range: $y \geq -3$

(B) Domain: $x \geq -3$; Range: $y \geq -2$

(C) Domain: all real numbers; Range: $y \leq -3$

(D) Domain: $x \geq -2$; Range: all real numbers

14. A coin is flipped four times. What is the probability that the coin will land on tails three consecutive times and tails on the final flip?

(A) $\frac{1}{2}$

(B) $\frac{1}{8}$

(C) $\frac{1}{16}$

(D) 1

15. What is the area of a square that has a side length of $x + 3$ units? (Answers are in square units.)

(A) $x^2 + 9$

(B) $x^2 + 6x + 9$

(C) 9

(D) $9x^2$

16. What is the area in square units of the triangle shown below?

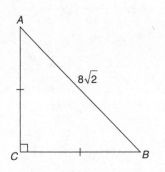

Enter your answer in the boxes below.

17. If $f(x) = 2x^2 - 20$ and $g(x) = 4x + 3$, what is the value of $g(f(8))$?

Fill in your answer in the boxes below.

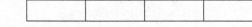

18. What is the slope, m, and the y-intercept, b, of the equation $4x - 3y = 7$?

(A) $m = -\dfrac{7}{3}, b = \dfrac{4}{3}$

(B) $m = 4, b = 7$

(C) $m = \dfrac{4}{3}, b = -\dfrac{7}{3}$

(D) $m = \dfrac{2}{3}, b = \dfrac{5}{3}$

19. The area of the shaded section of $\odot P$ (below) is 54π, and $m\angle APB = 135°$. What is the circumference of $\odot P$?

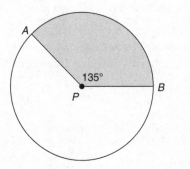

(A) 12

(B) 12π

(C) 24π

(D) 144π

20. What is two-thirds of one-sixth of one thousand eighty? Place your answer in the boxes below.

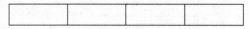

21. The following chart shows the daily temperatures of a local beach and the attendance each day (in thousands).

Temperature	Attendance
74	17
78	19
78	18
80	19
81	21

This chart is:

(A) not a function because the input 78 has two outputs, 18 and 19.

(B) not a function because two outputs are the same.

(C) a function because there are repeated inputs.

(D) a function because there are repeated outputs.

22. A restaurant's lunch special offers three different sandwiches, three different side orders, and five different beverages. How many different lunch combinations are available to the diners?

(A) 11

(B) 12

(C) 45

(D) 54

23. In the following two-column proof, what is the missing statement?

Given: $7x = 98$

Prove: $x = 14$

Statement	Reason
1. $7x = 98$	1. Given
2. ?	2. Division Property

(A) $x = 12$

(B) $x = 13$

(C) $x = 14$

(D) $x = 2$

24. What inequality describes the graph below?

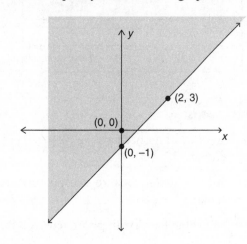

(A) $y > 2x - 1$

(B) $y < 2x - 1$

(C) $y \geq 2x - 1$

(D) $y \leq 2x - 1$

25. What geometric solid is represented by the net below?

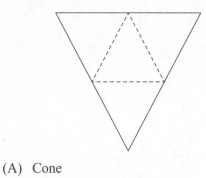

(A) Cone

(B) Rectangular prism

(C) Cylinder with a triangle base

(D) Pyramid with a triangle base

26. $-9, -4, 1, 6, 11 \ldots$

Find the 17th term in the series above by using the formula $c_n = c_1 + (n - 1)(r)$ where:

n = place in the series

c_1 = the first term in the series

r = difference among succeeding values in the series

Place your answer in the boxes below.

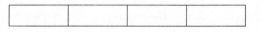

27. What is the slope and y-intercept in the equation $y = -4x + 3$?

(A) Slope is 1, y-intercept is 1.

(B) Slope is 3, y-intercept is -4.

(C) Slope is -4, y-intercept is 3.

(D) Slope is -3, no y-intercept.

28. Find the surface area of a cone with a radius of 8 and a height of 15. (Leave π in your answer.)

(A) 200π

(B) 320π

(C) 136π

(D) 64π

Questions 29–31 refer to the data set below.

17.25 6.73 8.29 15.17 10.26 11.30

29. What is the mean of the data set?

(A) 11.5

(B) 10.78

(C) 6.25

(D) 18.5

30. What is the median of the data set?

(A) 11.5

(B) 10.78

(C) 10.00

(D) 12.15

31. What is the range of the data set?

(A) 11.5

(B) 10.78

(C) 10.52

(D) 8.37

32. Simplify the quantity below and express your answer in scientific notation.

$$\frac{(81.9 \times 10^9)(3.69 \times 10^{-4})}{(27.3 \times 10^3)}$$

(A) 11.07×10^2

(B) 1.107×10^3

(C) 1.107×10^2

(D) 0.1107×10^4

33. $\overline{RS}$ has its endpoints at $R(-4, -4)$ and $S(12, 8)$. What is the length of $\overline{RS}$?

(A) 200

(B) $4\sqrt{10}$

(C) 20

(D) $20\sqrt{20}$

34. Find the value of x in the following equation. Place your answer in the boxes below.

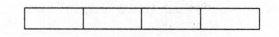

$$8^{2x} = 16^{2x-2}$$

35. What is the length of $\overarc{AB}$ in $\odot M$?

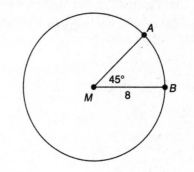

(A) 64π

(B) 16π

(C) 2π

(D) π

36. Simplify the expression:

$$\sqrt{3}(\sqrt{6} - 3\sqrt{2})$$

(A) $3 - 3\sqrt{6}$

(B) $3 + 3\sqrt{6}$

(C) $3\sqrt{2} - 3\sqrt{6}$

(D) $9 - 3\sqrt{6}$

37. Kathy has 30 pounds of candy to distribute on Halloween. If she groups the candy into $\frac{3}{10}$-pound servings, how many servings will she have?

(A) 9

(B) 30

(C) $30\frac{3}{10}$

(D) 100

38. Find the value of x. Write your answer in the boxes below.

$$\sqrt{10x+1} - 2 = 17$$

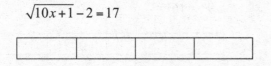

39. Two 6-sided dice are thrown. What is the probability that the first die will land on a prime number and the second will land on a number greater than 4?

(A) $\dfrac{5}{6}$

(B) $\dfrac{1}{2}$

(C) $\dfrac{1}{3}$

(D) $\dfrac{1}{6}$

Questions 40 and 41 refer to the information below.

A business measures its profit by using the following profit function:

$$P(x) = 11,000x - 6750,$$

where x is the number of units the company sells in a three-month period.

40. If the company sold 1,740 units in a three-month period, what were its profits?

(A) $19,140,000

(B) $19,133,250

(C) $18,242,360

(D) $1,913,325

41. If the company's profit over a three-month period was $9,321,250, how many units did it sell?

(A) 848

(B) 849

(C) 851

(D) 904

42. To change the equation $\dfrac{2}{3}x + 4y = \dfrac{1}{6}$ to standard form, one must

(A) multiply the equation by 3.

(B) multiply the equation by 6.

(C) divide the equation by 3.

(D) divide the equation by 6.

43. A great circle of a sphere lies on its surface and contains its center. What is the circumference of a great circle of a sphere that has a surface area that measures 1,256 cm² ($\pi = 3.14$)?

(A) 31.4

(B) 62.8

(C) 314.0

(D) 408.6

44. Solve the system of equations using the substitution method.

$$2x + 4y = 10$$
$$y = 2x - 5$$

(A) $x = 1, y = 3$

(B) $x = 2, y = 2$

(C) $x = 3, y = 1$

(D) $x = 0, y = 2.5$

45. A manufacturer of duct tape compiles data regarding the strength of its tape. The company manufactures tape with different widths: 1 inch, 2 inches, 2.5 inches, and 4 inches.

An experiment was designed to see how much pressure each of the different tapes could withstand before breaking. The pressure was measured in pounds per square inch (psi).

Input Tape Width	Output Pressure (psi)
1	2.5
2	5
2.5	6.25
4	10

The company is interested in manufacturing a tape that is 5 inches wide. How much pressure in pounds per square inch (psi) could it withstand?

(A) 8 psi

(B) 10 psi

(C) 11.5 psi

(D) 12.5 psi

46. The supplement of an angle is four times the measure of its complement. What is the measure of the angle? Place your answer in degrees in the boxes below.

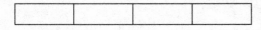

47. If $i = \sqrt{-1}$, what is the value of $(7 - 2i)^2$?

(A) $45 - 28i$

(B) $28 - 45i$

(C) 45

(D) $28i - 14$

48. Factor completely:

$x^4 - 81$

(A) $(x^2 + 9)(x^2 - 9)$

(B) $(x + 3)(x + 3)(x + 3)(x - 3)$

(C) $(x + 3)(x - 3)(x^2 + 9)$

(D) $(x^2 + 3)(x^2 - 27)$

49. The height of an object that is thrown is given by the equation $z = -16t^2 + 144t$, where z is the distance in feet and t is the time in seconds. After how many seconds will this object reach its maximum height?

(A) 3

(B) 4.5

(C) 7.5

(D) 9

50. Simplify the following expression:

$-2xy^2 - 3x^2y + 5xy - (-12xy^2)$

(A) $12x^5y^6$

(B) $10xy^2 - 3x^2y$

(C) $10xy^2 - 3x^2y + 5xy$

(D) $7x^4y^2 + 6xy$

51. A drawer contains 2 pairs of white socks, 5 pairs of blue socks, and 3 pairs of brown socks. If the socks are not replaced when drawn, what is the probability of selecting a white pair followed by a blue pair?

(A) $\dfrac{34}{45}$

(B) $\dfrac{16}{45}$

(C) $\dfrac{1}{9}$

(D) $\dfrac{1}{10}$

52. Which number below is irrational?

(A) $17.6363\ldots$

(B) $\sqrt{196}$

(C) $\sqrt{96}$

(D) $\dfrac{313}{17}$

53. Which of the following can be represented by a graph that has the same vertex as the graph of $f(x) = x^2 + 14x + 51$?

(A) $f(x) = 3(x + 7)^2 + 2$

(B) $f(x) = 4(x - 7)^2 + 51$

(C) $f(x) = 7(x - 14)^2 + 2$

(D) $f(x) = 6(x + 14)^2 + 51$

54. A trapezoid has an area that measures 288 in². The height of the figure is 18 inches and the lower base measures 28 inches. What is the measure of the upper base in inches?

    (A) 4

    (B) 8

    (C) 16

    (D) 28

55. A truck in a movie measures 16 feet across a screen that is 36 feet long. What is the measure of the same truck, in inches, on a television screen that is 2 feet wide?

    (A) $\frac{8}{9}$

    (B) $\frac{9}{8}$

    (C) $10\frac{2}{3}$

    (D) $11\frac{5}{6}$

ANSWER KEY—PRACTICE TEST 3

Question	Answer	Content Category
1.	(A)	Arithmetic and Algebra
2.	180	Geometry and Data
3.	(B)	Arithmetic and Algebra
4.	25.2	Geometry and Data
5.	(C)	Arithmetic and Algebra
6.	(C)	Geometry and Data
7.	343	Geometry and Data
8.	(B)	Arithmetic and Algebra
9.	(C)	Arithmetic and Algebra
10.	(C)	Geometry and Data
11.	(D)	Arithmetic and Algebra
12.	−134	Arithmetic and Algebra
13.	(C)	Arithmetic and Algebra
14.	(C)	Geometry and Data
15.	(B)	Geometry and Data
16.	32	Geometry and Data
17.	435	Arithmetic and Algebra
18.	(C)	Arithmetic and Algebra
19.	(C)	Geometry and Data
20.	120	Arithmetic and Algebra
21.	(A)	Arithmetic and Algebra
22.	(C)	Geometry and Data
23.	(C)	Arithmetic and Algebra
24.	(C)	Arithmetic and Algebra
25.	(D)	Geometry and Data
26.	71	Arithmetic and Algebra
27.	(C)	Arithmetic and Algebra
28.	(A)	Geometry and Data
29.	(A)	Geometry and Data
30.	(B)	Geometry and Data
31.	(C)	Geometry and Data
32.	(B)	Arithmetic and Algebra
33.	(C)	Arithmetic and Algebra
34.	4	Arithmetic and Algebra
35.	(C)	Geometry and Data
36.	(C)	Arithmetic and Algebra
37.	(D)	Arithmetic and Algebra
38.	36	Arithmetic and Algebra
39.	(D)	Geometry and Data
40.	(B)	Arithmetic and Algebra
41.	(A)	Arithmetic and Algebra
42.	(B)	Arithmetic and Algebra
43.	(B)	Geometry and Data
44.	(C)	Arithmetic and Algebra
45.	(D)	Arithmetic and Algebra
46.	60	Geometry and Data
47.	(A)	Arithmetic and Algebra
48.	(C)	Arithmetic and Algebra
49.	(B)	Arithmetic and Algebra
50.	(C)	Arithmetic and Algebra
51.	(C)	Geometry and Data
52.	(C)	Arithmetic and Algebra
53.	(A)	Arithmetic and Algebra
54.	(A)	Geometry and Data
55.	(C)	Arithmetic and Algebra

1. (A)

This question requires the test-taker to categorize all real numbers according to their sub-classifications. The correct answer is (A), integers.

$$-\sqrt{361} = -\sqrt{19}$$

Integers: $\{\ldots -2, -1, 0, 1, 2, \ldots\}$

Choice (B) is incorrect because irrational numbers cannot be expressed as $\frac{a}{b}$ where a and b are integers. Numbers under a radical sign that are not squares, such as $\sqrt{17}$, are irrational numbers. Choice (C) is incorrect because the set of whole numbers is $\{0, 1, 2, 3, \ldots\}$. Choice (D) is incorrect because the set of natural numbers is $\{1, 2, 3, 4, \ldots\}$.

2. 180

This question tests the examinee's knowledge of the Pythagorean theorem and the process for finding the area of a triangle. The correct answer is 180.

The triangle is a right triangle since it has a hypotenuse. Given that two sides are known, use the Pythagorean theorem, $a^2 + b^2 = c^2$, to calculate the missing leg.

$$9^2 + b^2 = 41^2$$

$$81 + b^2 = 1681$$

$$b^2 = 1600$$

$$b = 40$$

The formula for the area of a triangle is Area = $\frac{1}{2}$(base)(height) or $A = \frac{1}{2}bh$. Input the known values for the base and height to find the area of the triangle:

$$\text{Area} = \frac{1}{2}(9)(40) = 180 \text{ square inches}$$

3. (B)

This question tests the examinee's ability to discern the domain of a relation. The correct answer is (B), $\{6, 5, 7, 3\}$.

The domain of a set of values consists of the input values of the relation. Here, the inputs are the x values of each coordinate pair.

Choice (A) is incorrect because it contains elements that are not part of the relation. Choice (C) is incorrect because it contains solely one element of the domain. Choice (D) is incorrect because it is the range of the relation.

4. 25.2

Solving this problem requires knowledge of compound probability. The correct answer is 25.2.

Begin by converting each percentage into a decimal.

$$45\% = 0.45$$

$$80\% = 0.80$$

$$30\% = 0.30$$

To find the probability of no rain on Tuesday, subtract .30 from 1.00.

$$100\% - 30\% = 70\%$$

To find the probability of rain on Sunday and Monday but not Tuesday, multiply the three probabilities together.

$$(0.45)(0.80)(0.70) = 0.252$$

Finally, convert the decimal into a percentage.

$$0.252 = 25.2\%$$

5. (C)

This question tests the student's knowledge of intercepts in linear equations. The correct answer is (C), (2, 0).

To find the x-intercept, let $y = 0$.

$$6x + 4(0) = 12$$

$$6x = 12$$

$$\frac{6x}{6} = \frac{12}{6}$$

$$x = 2$$

The x-intercept is (2, 0).

Choice (A) is incorrect because it juxtaposes the coordinates of the x-intercept. Choice (B) is incorrect because it is the y-, rather than the x-intercept. Choice (D) is incorrect because it is the result of improper calculation.

6. (C)

This question tests the examinee's knowledge of nets. The correct answer is (C), cylinder.

A net is a geometric solid that has been deconstructed into plane figures. A cylinder would have two circular bases and a rectangle that, when curved, creates the lateral area.

Choice (A) is incorrect because a sphere would not contain a rectangle when deconstructed. Choice (B) is incorrect because a pyramid would show at least three triangular faces. Choice (D) is incorrect because a cone contains only a single circular base.

7. 343 cm³

This question tests the examinee's knowledge of volume. The correct answer is 343 cm³.

The volume of a cube is found by using the formula $V = e^3$, where e is the length of an edge. Since one of the square faces has an area that measures 49 cm², find the length of a side by using the formula $A = s^2$, where s is the length of a side.

$$49 = s^2$$

$$7 = s$$

The length of one of the square's sides is also the length of an edge of the cube. Input 7 for e in the volume formula.

$$V = 7^3$$

$$V = 343 \text{ cm}^3$$

8. (B)

This question tests the examinee's knowledge of perpendicular lines. The correct answer is (B), (0, 3).

Perpendicular lines have slopes that are the opposite reciprocals of one another. In the equation $y = -\frac{2}{3}x + 5$, the slope is $-\frac{2}{3}$. Therefore, the slope of a line perpendicular to $y = -\frac{2}{3}x + 5$ is $\frac{3}{2}$.

Input $\frac{3}{2}$ for the slope in the equation $y = mx + b$:

$$y = \frac{3}{2}x + b$$

Substitute (–6, –6) for x and y, respectively, to find the value of b, the y-intercept.

$$-6 = \frac{3}{2}(-6) + b$$

$$-6 = -9 + b$$

$$3 = b$$

The y-intercept, b, has coordinates (0, 3).

Choice (A) is incorrect because it juxtaposes the actual x- and y-coordinates. Choice (C) is incorrect because any y-intercept will have 0 as the x-coordinate. Choice (D) is incorrect because it calculates the y-intercept erroneously.

9. **(C)**

This question tests the examinee's ability to compare fractions, decimals, and percentages.

The correct answer is (C), 23.9%, $\frac{6}{25}$, 0.26, $\frac{2}{7}$.

The quickest way to solve this problem is to convert each value into a decimal.

$$\frac{2}{7} = 0.286$$
$$\frac{6}{25} = 0.24$$
$$0.26 = 0.26$$
$$23.9\% = 0.239$$

$$0.239 < 0.24 < 0.26 < 0.286$$

$$23.9\% < \frac{6}{25} < 0.26 < \frac{2}{7}$$

Choices (A), (B), and (D) all fail to arrange the values in ascending order.

10. **(C)**

This question tests the examinee's ability to recognize specific geometric constructions. The correct answer is (C), angle bisector.

Place the point of the compass at point A and create equally placed arcs on $\overrightarrow{AB}$ and $\overrightarrow{AC}$. Keeping the compass angle, place the point of the compass where the arcs cross $\overrightarrow{AB}$ and $\overrightarrow{AC}$ and make intersecting arcs in the interior of $\angle BAC$. Draw $\overrightarrow{AD}$ from the vertex of

$\angle BAC$ through the intersecting arcs. $\overrightarrow{AD}$ is the angle bisector of $\angle BAC$.

Choice (A) is incorrect because $\angle BAC$ is not a line segment. Choice (B) is incorrect because a line, which extends infinitely in opposite directions, cannot be bisected. Choice (D) is incorrect because a ray, which extends infinitely in one direction, cannot be bisected.

11. **(D)**

This question tests the examinee's knowledge of measurement conversion and scientific notation. The correct answer is (D), 1.232×10^4.

Use the fact that 1 mile = 5,280 feet and 1 yard = 3 feet to calculate the number of yards in one mile:

$$5,280 \div 3 = 1,760 \text{ yards.}$$

There are 1,760 yards in one mile. Multiply 1,760 by 7 to find the number of yards in 7 miles.

$$1,760 \times 7 = 12,320 \text{ yards}$$

Convert 12,320 yards into scientific notation,

$$12,320 = 1.232 \times 10^4.$$

Choice (A) is incorrect because it provides solely the number of yards in one mile in scientific notation. Choice (B) is incorrect because it also provides the number of yards in one mile but not in scientific notation. Choice (C) is incorrect because it is not in scientific notation, although the figure is the number of yards in 7 miles.

12. **−134**

This question tests the examinee's ability to simplify expressions using the order of operations. The correct answer is −134.

Use PEMDAS to simplify the expression.

Parentheses: $-2(2-7)^3 - (1.5)(4)^4 =$
$$-2(-5)^3 - (1.5)(4)^4$$

Exponents: $-2(-5)^3 - (1.5)(4)^4 =$
$$-2(-125) - (1.5)(256)$$

Multiplication/Division: $-2(-125) - (1.5)(256) =$
$$250 - 384$$

Addition/Subtraction: $250 - 384 = -134$

13. (C)

This question tests the examinee's ability to determine the domain and range of a quadratic function. The correct answer is (C), Domain: all real numbers; Range: $y \leq -3$.

The function $f(x) = -(x+2)^2 - 3$ is a parabola that opens down and has a vertex $(-2, -3)$.

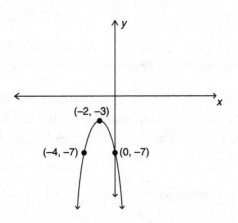

The domain and range represent the sets of x and y values, respectively. By inspection, we see that all x values are possible, so the domain is all real numbers. The y values are all of the values that are less than or equal to -3.

Choices (A), (B), and (D) are all incorrect because they include points that don't satisfy the function. For example, they all include $(0, 0)$, but $0 \neq -4 - 3$.

14. (C)

This question tests the examinee's knowledge of the probability of independent events. The correct answer is (C), $\frac{1}{16}$.

The result of a coin landing on heads or tails is $\frac{1}{2}$. No successive result of a coin flip depends on previous flips; the results are independent. To find the probability of four flips landing a certain way, multiply all of the probabilities.

$$\frac{1}{2} \times \frac{1}{2} \times \frac{1}{2} \times \frac{1}{2} = \frac{1}{16}$$

Choice (A) is incorrect because it is the probability of only a single coin flip landing on heads or tails. Choice (B) is incorrect because it is the result of three, not four, successive flips landing a certain way. Choice (D) is incorrect because it is the result of a coin flip landing on heads and tails simultaneously, which is impossible.

15. (B)

This question tests the examinee's ability to use algebra to find the area of a square. The correct answer is (B), $x^2 + 6x + 9$.

The area of a square is found by using the formula $A = s^2$, where s is the length of one side.

$$A = s^2$$

$$A = (x+3)^2 = (x+3)(x+3) = x^2 + 6x + 9$$

Choice (A) is incorrect because it erroneously multiplies $(x+3)^2$. Choice (C) is incorrect because it assumes that $s = 3$. Choice (D) is incorrect because it assumes that $s = 3x$.

16. 32

This question tests the examinee's knowledge of 45-45-90 triangles and the area formula of a triangle. The correct answer is 32.

A 45-45-90 triangle has legs of equal measure and hypotenuse $\sqrt{2}$ times the length of one of the sides. Since the hypotenuse is $8\sqrt{2}$, the legs each measure 8.

Input the base and height into the area formula.

$$A = \frac{1}{2}bh$$

$$A = \frac{1}{2}(8)(8)$$

$$A = 32$$

17. 435

This question tests the examinee's knowledge of composite functions. The correct answer is 435.

Find $f(8)$ by substituting 8 for x in $f(x)$:

$$f(x) = 2x^2 - 20$$

$$f(8) = 2(8)^2 - 20$$

$$f(8) = 108$$

Next, replace x with 108 in $g(x)$.

$$g(x) = 4x + 3$$

$$g(108) = 4(108) + 3$$

$$g(108) = 435$$

18. (C)

This question tests the examinee's knowledge of the slope-intercept form of a line. The correct answer is (C), $m = \frac{4}{3}$, $b = -\frac{7}{3}$.

The equation $4x - 3y = 7$ is a line in standard form. Change it to slope-intercept form, $y = mx + b$, by isolating y.

$$4x - 3y = 7$$

$$-3y = -4x + 7$$

$$y = \frac{4}{3}x - \frac{7}{3}$$

The slope of the line is $\frac{4}{3}$ and the y-intercept is $-\frac{7}{3}$.

Choice (A) is incorrect because it juxtaposes the value of the slope with the value of the y-intercept. Choice (B) is incorrect because it fails in the last step to divide the equation by –3. Choice (D) is incorrect because it is the result of improper calculation.

19. (C)

This question tests the examinee's knowledge of the sector of a circle. The correct answer is (C), 24π.

The formula for the circumference of a circle is $C = 2\pi r$, where r is a radius of the circle. Calculate the measure of the radius, r, by using the formula for the area of a sector, $S = \left(\frac{m}{360}\right)(\pi r^2)$, where m is the measure of the central angle.

$$54\pi = \left(\frac{135}{360}\right)\pi r^2$$

$$54 = \frac{3}{8}r^2$$

$$144 = r^2$$

$$12 = r$$

Then use the formula for the circumference of the circle, $C = 2\pi r$, replacing r with 12.

$$C = 2(\pi)(12) = 24\pi$$

Choice (A) is incorrect because it is the radius of ⊙*P*, not the circumference. Choice (B) is incorrect because it is the length of a semi-circle of ⊙*P*. Choice (D) is incorrect because it is the area of ⊙*P*.

20. 120

This question tests the examinee's ability to translate English phrases into mathematical expressions. The correct answer is 120.

The phrase "two-thirds of one-sixth of one thousand eighty" translates to the following mathematical expression:

$$\left(\frac{2}{3}\right)\left(\frac{1}{6}\right)(1080) = 120$$

21. (A)

This question tests the examinee's ability to discern a function from an input-output table. The correct answer is (A), not a function because the input 78 has two outputs, 18 and 19.

A function can have only one output for each input. The input 78 has two outputs, 19 and 18.

Choice (B) is incorrect because the outputs of a function can repeat. For example, the set of ordered pairs (6, 9), (7, 9), (8, 9) is a function because each input has only one output (9 in each case). Choices (C) and (D) are incorrect because the table does not represent a function.

22. (C)

This question tests the examinee's knowledge of the counting principle. The correct answer is (C), 45.

Multiply all of the different options.

(3 sandwiches) × (3 side orders) × (5 beverages) = 45 combinations

Choice (A) is incorrect because it adds rather than multiplies the lunch options. Choices (B) and (D) are incorrect because they each are the result of inaccurate calculation.

23. (C)

This question tests the examinee's knowledge of algebraic proofs. The correct answer is (C), *x* = 14.

The reason in step 2 suggests we had completed a step in division. Therefore, the step must have indicated the quotients of $\frac{7x}{7} = \frac{98}{7}$. Simplifying, we arrive at *x* = 14.

Choices (A), (B), and (D) are incorrect because they do not accurately divide 98 by 7.

24. (C)

This question tests the examinee's ability to discern the graph of an algebraic inequality. The correct answer is (C), *y* ≥ 2*x* – 1. The line in the graph is solid to show that *y* = 2*x* – 1 is part of the inequality.

Test the point (0, 0) to verify that the shading for *y* ≥ 2*x* – 1 is correct.

$$0 \geq 2(0) - 1$$

$$0 \geq -1$$

Choice (A) is incorrect because it implies that the line *y* = 2*x* – 1 is not a part of the inequality, but it *is* a part because the line is solid. Choice (B) is incorrect because it erroneously implies the line is not part of the graph and it would shade below the line. Choice (D) is incorrect because it correctly indicates that the line is part of the graph, but it shades the area below the line rather than above it.

25. (D)

This question tests the examinee's knowledge of the nets of geometric figures. The correct answer is (D), pyramid with a triangle base. Imagine the central triangle as the base of a pyramid. Next, visualize the adjacent triangles as the lateral sides of the pyramid. Bring the three adjacent triangles up into the third dimension, meeting at a central vertex. The figure will be a pyramid with a triangle base.

Choice (A) is incorrect because a cone's net will have a circle as a component. Choice (B) is incorrect because the net of a rectangular prism is composed solely of rectangles. Choice (C) is incorrect because a cylinder with a triangular base cannot exist; a cylinder has two circular bases.

26. 71

This question tests the examinee's ability to understand arithmetic and geometric patterns. The correct answer is 71.

Place the known values in the formula to calculate the 17th term.

$$c_{17} = -9 + (17 - 1)(5)$$

$$c_{17} = 71$$

27. (C)

This question tests the examinee's knowledge of the slope and y-intercept of a linear equation. The correct answer is (C), slope is -4, y-intercept is 3.

The slope-intercept form of a linear equation is $y = mx + b$, where m = slope and b = y-intercept.

For $y = -4x + 3$, the slope, m, is -4 and the y-intercept, b, is 3.

Choice (A) is incorrect because if m and b are 1, the equation would be $y = x + 1$. Choice (B) is incor-

rect because it juxtaposes the values of the slope and the y-intercept. Choice (D) is incorrect because all non-vertical linear equations have a y-intercept.

28. (A)

This question tests the examinee's ability to calculate the surface area of a cone. The correct answer is (A), 200π.

Use the formula $A = \pi rs + \pi r^2$, where r is the radius and s is the slant height, to find the surface area of the cone. Although the radius and height are known, the slant height, s, is not.

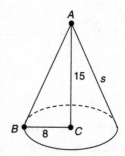

Use the Pythagorean theorem to find the slant height.

$$8^2 + 15^2 = c^2$$

$$64 + 225 = c^2$$

$$289 = c^2$$

$$17 = c$$

You may remember this is a Pythagorean triple, $8 - 15 - 17$.

$$SA = \pi(8)(17) + \pi(8)^2 = 200\pi$$

Choice (B) is incorrect because it is the volume of the cone. Choice (C) is incorrect because it is the cone's lateral area but doesn't include the base area. Choice (D) is incorrect because it is the area of the cone's circular base but doesn't include the lateral area.

29. (A)

This question tests the examinee's knowledge of the mean of a data set. The correct answer is (A), 11.5. The mean is the average of the numbers. Find the sum of the numbers and divide by 6.

$$(17.25 + 6.73 + 8.29 + 15.17 + 10.26 + 11.30) \div 6 = 11.5$$

Choice (B) is incorrect because it is the median of the data set. Choice (C) is incorrect because the mean cannot be less than the lowest data point. Choice (D) is incorrect because the mean cannot be more than the highest data point.

30. (B)

This question tests the examinee's ability to identify the median of a data set. The correct answer is (B), 10.78.

The median is the number in the middle of a data set when arranged in order. Arrange the numbers in ascending order to identify the median.

6.73   8.29   10.26   11.30   15.17   17.25

Both 10.26 and 11.30 are the middle values. In this case, the median is the mean of the middle numbers.

$$(10.26 + 11.30) \div 2 = 10.78$$

Choice (A) is incorrect because it is the mean of the data set. Choices (C) and (D) are incorrect because the median has to be between the two middle numbers, 10.26 + 11.30.

31. (C)

This question tests the examinee's ability to calculate the range of a data set. The correct answer is (C), 10.52.

The range of a group of numbers is the difference between the greatest and least values.

$$17.25 - 6.73 = 10.52$$

Choice (A) is incorrect because it is the mean of the data set. Choice (B) is incorrect because it is the median of the data set. Choice (D) is incorrect because it mistakenly uses 15.17 as the largest member of the data set.

32. (B)

This question tests the examinee's skill in using exponents to fashion answers in scientific notation. The correct answer is (B), 1.107×10^3.

Multiply and divide the first numbers in each parenthesis.

$$(81.9 \times 3.69) \div 27.3 = 11.07$$

Multiply and divide the 10's:

$$(10^9 \times 10^{-4}) \div 10^3 = 10^{9+(-4)-3} = 10^2$$

$$\frac{(81.9 \times 10^9)(3.69 \times 10^{-4})}{(27.3 \times 10^3)} = 11.07 \times 10^2$$

Convert the number to scientific notation by moving the decimal point one place to the left and adding 1 to the power of 10.

$$11.07 \times 10^2 = 1.107 \times 10^3$$

Choice (A) is incorrect because it fails to place the correct answer in scientific notation. Choice (C) is incorrect because it fails to add the additional power of 10 in the final step. Choice (D) is incorrect because it is not in scientific notation.

33. (C)

This question tests the examinee's ability to use the distance formula. The correct answer is (C), 20.

Use the distance formula to calculate the length of $\overline{RS}$.

$$\text{Distance} = \sqrt{(x_1 - x_2)^2 + (y_1 - y_2)^2}$$

$$\text{Distance} = \sqrt{(12 - (-4))^2 + (8 - (-4))^2}$$
$$= \sqrt{16^2 + 12^2}$$
$$= \sqrt{400} = 20$$

Choice (A) is incorrect because it fails to find the square root of 400. Choices (B) and (D) are incorrect because they are the results of improperly simplifying the radical.

34. 4

This question tests the examinee's ability to work with exponents. The correct answer is 4.

Convert each base number to a power of 2 and multiply the exponents.

$$8^{2x} = 16^{2x-2}$$

$$(2^3)^{2x} = (2^4)^{2x-2}$$

$$2^{6x} = 2^{8x-8}$$

Since the bases are the same, the exponents must be equal.

$$6x = 8x - 8$$

$$-2x = -8$$

$$x = 4$$

35. (C)

This question tests the examinee's ability to calculate arc length. The correct answer is (C), 2π.

Use the formula arc length $= \left(\dfrac{m}{360}\right)(2\pi r)$, where m is the measure of the arc's central angle and r is the length of a radius.

$$\text{arc length} = \left(\frac{45}{360}\right)(2 \times \pi \times 8)$$

$$= \left(\frac{1}{8}\right)(16\pi) = 2\pi$$

Choice (A) is incorrect because it is the area of $\odot M$. Choice (B) is incorrect because it is the circumference of $\odot M$. Choice (D) is incorrect because it is the result of improper calculation.

36. (C)

This question tests the examinee's ability to multiply and simplify radicals. The correct answer is (C), $3\sqrt{2} - 3\sqrt{6}$.

Multiply each term in the parentheses by $\sqrt{3}$.

$$\sqrt{3}(\sqrt{6} - 3\sqrt{2}) = \sqrt{18} - 3\sqrt{6}$$
$$= \sqrt{9} \times \sqrt{2} - 3\sqrt{6}$$
$$= 3\sqrt{2} - 3\sqrt{6}$$

Choice (A) is incorrect because it assumes $\sqrt{3}\sqrt{6} = \sqrt{9} = 3$. Choice (B) is incorrect because it assumes $\sqrt{3}\sqrt{6} = \sqrt{9} = 3$, and has the wrong sign for $3\sqrt{6}$. Choice (D) is incorrect because it assumes $\sqrt{18} = 9$.

37. (D)

This question tests the examinee's ability to solve real-world problems by using arithmetic. The correct answer is (D), 100.

The word "grouped" means divide, so divide 30 by $\frac{3}{10}$.

$$30 \div \frac{3}{10} = 100$$

Choice (A) is incorrect because it multiplies rather than divides by $\frac{3}{10}$. Choice (B) is incorrect because it divides 30 by 1. Choice (C) is incorrect because it is the sum of 30 and $\frac{3}{10}$.

38. 36

This question tests the examinee's ability to solve radical equations. The correct answer is 36.

Step 1: Isolate the radical by adding 2 to both sides of the equation.

$$\sqrt{10x+1} - 2 = 17$$
$$\sqrt{10x+1} - 2 + 2 = 17 + 2$$
$$\sqrt{10x+1} = 19$$

Step 2: Begin to isolate the variable by squaring both sides of the equation.

$$(\sqrt{10x+1})^2 = 19^2$$
$$10x+1 = 361$$

Step 3: Finish solving for the variable.

$$10x+1-1 = 361-1$$
$$10x = 360$$
$$\frac{10x}{10} = \frac{360}{10}$$
$$x = 36$$

Check your solution by replacing x with 36.

$$\sqrt{10(36)+1} - 2 = 17$$
$$\sqrt{361} - 2 = 17$$
$$19 - 2 = 17$$
$$17 = 17$$

39. (D)

This question tests the examinee's ability to solve problems dealing with the probability of independent events. The correct answer is (D), $\frac{1}{6}$.

Since the two events are independent of each other, find the probability of each event and then multiply the two probabilities.

For the first die,

$$Pr = \frac{\text{prime numbers}}{\text{all numbers}} = \frac{\{2, 3, 5\}}{\{1, 2, 3, 4, 5, 6\}} = \frac{3}{6} = \frac{1}{2}$$

Remember, 1 is not a prime number.

For the second die,

$$Pr = \frac{\text{numbers} > 4}{\text{all numbers}} = \frac{\{5, 6\}}{\{1, 2, 3, 4, 5, 6\}} = \frac{2}{6} = \frac{1}{3}$$

$$\frac{1}{2} \times \frac{1}{3} = \frac{1}{6}$$

Choice (A) is incorrect because it adds, rather than multiplies, the two probabilities. Choice (B) is incorrect because it is the probability of rolling a prime number only, and does not include the probability associated with the second roll. Choice (C) is incorrect because it is the probability of rolling a number greater than 4 and does not include the probability of the first roll.

40. (B)

This question tests the examinee's ability to find results in a real-world setting by using an algebraic function. The correct answer is (B), $19,133,250.

Replace x with 1,740, the number of units sold in a three-month period.

$$P(1,740) = 11,000(1,740) - 6,750$$
$$= \$19,133,250$$

Choice (A) is incorrect because it fails to subtract 6,750, as required by the function. Choice (C) is incorrect because it is the result of erroneous calculation. Choice (D) is incorrect because it misplaces the decimal point in the final answer.

41. (A)

This question tests the examinee's ability to find results in a real-world setting using an algebraic function. The correct answer is (A), 848.

Replace $P(x)$ with $9,321,250, the company's profit.

$$9,321,250 = 11,000x - 6,750$$

$$9,328,000 = 11,000x$$

$$848 = x$$

Choice (B) is incorrect because it would produce $9,332,250 in profit. Choice (C) is incorrect because it would produce $9,354,250 in profit. Choice (D) is incorrect because it would produce $9,993,250 in profit.

42. (B)

This question tests the examinee's ability to differentiate among different forms of linear equations. The correct answer is (B), multiply the equation by 6.

A line in standard form is one in the form of $Ax + By = C$ in which A, B, and C are integers. A must be greater than or equal to 0.

$$6\left(\frac{2}{3}x + 4y = \frac{1}{6}\right)$$
$$4x + 24y = 1$$

When transformed into standard form, $\frac{2}{3}x + 4y = \frac{1}{6}$ becomes $4x + 24y = 1$.

Choice (A) is incorrect because multiplying by 3 will leave the C term as $\frac{1}{2}$. Choices (C) and (D) are incorrect because dividing the equation by an integer will leave A, B, and C as fractions.

43. (B)

This question tests the examinee's ability to integrate knowledge of circles and spheres. The correct answer is (B), 62.8.

Use the formula for the surface area of a sphere, $A = 4\pi r^2$, to find the radius.

$$4\pi r^2 = 1,256$$

$$4(3.14)r^2 = 1,256$$

$$r^2 = 100$$

$$r = 10$$

Place the value of the radius in the circumference formula.

$$C = 2\pi r$$

$$C = 2(3.14)(10) = 62.8 \text{ cm}$$

Choice (A) is incorrect because it assumes the circumference of a circle is found by using the formula $C = \pi r$. Choice (C) is incorrect because it is the area rather than the circumference of the great circle. Choice (D) is incorrect because it is the result of improper calculation.

44. (C)

This question tests the examinee's ability to solve systems of equations. The correct answer is (C), $x = 3$, $y = 1$.

$$2x + 4y = 10$$

$$y = 2x - 5$$

Substitute $2x - 5$ for y in the first equation.

$$2x + 4(2x - 5) = 10$$

$$2x + 8x - 20 = 10$$

$$10x - 20 = 10$$

$$10x - 20 + 20 = 10 + 20$$

$$10x = 30$$

$$\frac{10x}{10} = \frac{30}{10}$$

$$x = 3$$

Substitute 3 for x in either original equation.

$$2x + 4y = 10$$

$$2(3) + 4y = 10$$

$$6 + 4y = 10$$

$$6 - 6 + 4y = 10 - 6$$

$$4y = 4$$

$$\frac{4y}{4} = \frac{4}{4}$$

$$y = 1$$

Choice (A) is incorrect because it juxtaposes the actual values for x and y. Choice (B) is incorrect because it erroneously calculates the value for both x and y. Choice (D) is incorrect because it is a solution for the first equation, but not the second.

45. (D)

This question tests the examinee's ability to recognize and use a linear function to accrue results in real-world situations. The correct answer is (D), 12.5 psi.

When you multiply each input by 2.5, you get the output shown in the table. For example, $1 \times 2.5 = 2.5$, $2 \times 2.5 = 5$, $2.5 \times 2.5 = 6.25$ and $4 \times 2.5 = 10$. Therefore, a tape that is 5 inches wide should be able to withstand 12.5 psi. $5 \times 2.5 = 12.5$.

Choice (A) is incorrect because it is <10, the strength of a 4-inch tape. Choice (B) is incorrect because it is shown in the table to be the strength of a 4-inch tape. Choice (C) is incorrect because it is the strength of a tape that is 4.6 inches wide.

46. 60

This question tests the examinee's ability to use algebra to solve geometry problems. The correct answer is 60.

Let $x = $ the angle's measure

$180 - x = $ the angle's supplement

$90 - x = $ the angle's complement

$$180 - x = 4(90 - x)$$

$$180 - x = 360 - 4x$$

$$3x = 180$$

$$x = 60$$

Check your solution. If x is 60°, then the supplement is $180 - 60 = 120$ and the complement is $90 - 60 = 30$.

$$120 = 4 \times 30$$

$$120 = 120$$

47. (A)

This question tests the examinee's ability to understand an algebraic pattern. The correct answer is (A), $45 - 28i$.

Use FOIL to expand $(7 - 2i)^2$:

$$(7 - 2i)^2 = (7 - 2i)(7 - 2i)$$

$$= 49 - 14i - 14i + 4i^2$$

$$= 49 - 28i + 4i^2$$

Since $i = \sqrt{-1}$, then $i^2 = (\sqrt{-1})^2 = -1$.

Substitute -1 for i^2.

$$49 - 28i + 4(-1) = 45 - 28i$$

Choice (B) is incorrect because it juxtaposes the constant and coefficient in the correct answer. Choice (C) is incorrect because it assumes $(7 - 2i)^2 = 7^2 - (2i)^2$. Choice (D) is incorrect because it executes FOIL incorrectly.

48. (C)

This question tests the examinee's knowledge of factoring the difference of squares. The correct answer is (C), $(x + 3)(x - 3)(x^2 + 9)$.

Use the model $a^2 - b^2 = (a + b)(a - b)$ to begin factoring the expression.

$$x^4 - 81 = (x^2 + 9)(x^2 - 9)$$

The first factor, $x^2 + 9$, is prime and will not factor further. The second factor, $x^2 - 9$, is in the form of $a^2 - b^2$.

$$x^2 - 9 = (x + 3)(x - 3)$$

Putting the components together, we get:

$$x^4 - 81 = (x + 3)(x - 3)(x^2 + 9)$$

Choice (A) is incorrect because it fails to factor $x^2 - 9$. Choice (B) is incorrect because it erroneously factors $x^2 + 9$ as $(x + 3)(x + 3)$. Choice (D) is incorrect because it does not acknowledge that $x^4 - 81$ factors as $(x^2 + 9)(x^2 - 9)$.

49. (B)

This question tests the examinee's ability to calculate values using quadratic functions. The correct answer is (B), 4.5.

The maximum height of any parabola in the form $y = Ax^2 + Bx + C$, where A is negative, is given by the y value of the vertex. In this example, z replaces y, and t replaces x, so $A = -16$ and $B = 144$.

The x value of the vertex (or here, time) is given by $x = -\dfrac{b}{2a} = \dfrac{-144}{-32} = 4.5$, and this is the time of the maximum height in seconds. (The maximum height is 324 feet.)

Choice (A) is incorrect because using the given function $z = -16t^2 + 144t$, at $t = 3$, the height is only 288. Choice (C) is incorrect because at 7.5 seconds the object has an altitude of only 180 feet. Choice (D) is incorrect because at 9 seconds, $y = 0$, and the item is now on the ground.

50. (C)

This question tests the examinee's skill in simplifying algebraic expressions. The correct answer is (C), $10xy^2 - 3x^2y + 5xy$.

To add or subtract algebraic terms, the variables and the exponents in the terms must be identical, creating like terms. In the expression $-2xy^2 - 3x^2y + 5xy - (-12xy^2)$, only $-2xy^2$ and $-12xy^2$ are like terms.

$$-2xy^2 - (-12xy^2) - 3x^2y + 5xy =$$

$$10xy^2 - 3x^2y + 5xy$$

Choice (A) is incorrect because it adds all of the coefficients of terms that are not like terms. Further, it adds all of the exponents, an operation limited to multiplication. Choice (B) is incorrect because it does not acknowledge that $5xy$ will be part of the final answer. Choice (D) is incorrect because there is no x^4y^2 term in the original equation.

51. (C)

This question tests the examinee's knowledge of dependent probability. The correct answer is (C), $\frac{1}{9}$.

Find the probability of selecting a pair of white socks.

$$Pr = \frac{\text{white socks}}{\text{all socks}} = \frac{2}{2+3+5} = \frac{2}{10} = \frac{1}{5}$$

Find the probability of next selecting a pair of blue socks. Remember, there are now only 9 pair of socks because one pair was removed.

$$Pr = \frac{\text{blue socks}}{\text{all socks}} = \frac{5}{9}$$

Find the probability of selecting a white pair of socks followed by a blue pair of socks by multiplying each probability.

$$\frac{1}{5} \times \frac{5}{9} = \frac{1}{9}$$

Choice (A) is incorrect because it adds rather than multiplies the two probabilities. Choice (B) is incorrect because it subtracts rather than multiplies the two probabilities. Choice (D) is incorrect because it is the probability of the two selections with replacement, not without replacement.

52. (C)

This question tests the examinee's knowledge of the subsets of the real number system. The correct answer is (C), $\sqrt{96}$.

A rational number can be expressed in the form of $\frac{a}{b}$ (and its decimal equivalent) where a and b are integers. A decimal that neither repeats nor terminates is an irrational number. Since 96 is not a square, $\sqrt{96}$ is irrational; its value is approximately $9.797958971\ldots$.

Choice (A) is incorrect because it is a decimal that does not terminate but does repeat a pattern. Choice (B) is incorrect because $\sqrt{196} = 14$, and 14 can be expressed as $\frac{14}{1}$. Choice (D) is incorrect because 313 and 17 are integers expressed as $\frac{a}{b}$.

53. (A)

This question tests the examinee's knowledge of quadratic functions. The correct answer is (A), $f(x) = 3(x + 7)^2 + 2$.

The general form of a quadratic function in vertex form is $f(x) = a(x - h)^2 + k$, where (h, k) is the vertex. So we must rewrite the function as $f(x) = (x^2 + 14x + ?) + 51$ and find the value of ? so that $x^2 + 14x + ?$ is a perfect square. That value would be 49; of course, we must add 49 to the left side as well. Then $f(x) + 49 = (x^2 + 14x + 49) + 51$. This simplifies to $f(x) + 49 = (x + 7)^2 + 51$ and finally to $f(x) = (x + 7)^2 + 2$.

Thus, the vertex for $f(x) = (x + 7)^2 + 2$ is $(-7, 2)$. Of the answer choices, only $3(x + 7)^2 + 2$ shares the same vertex $(-7, 2)$.

Choice (B) is incorrect because its vertex is $(7, 51)$. Choice (C) is incorrect because its vertex is $(14, 2)$. Choice (D) is incorrect because its vertex is $(-14, 51)$.

54. (A)

This question tests the examinee's ability to apply algebraic techniques to measure geometric figures. The correct answer is (A), 4.

The area of a trapezoid is found by using the formula $A = \frac{1}{2}(h)(b_1 + b_2)$, where h represents the height and b_1 and b_2 represent the two bases. Let b_1 equal the unknown base and input the known value of $b_2 = 28$ into the formula.

$$288 = \left(\frac{1}{2}\right)(18)(b_1 + 28)$$

$$288 = (9)(b_1 + 28)$$

$$32 = b_1 + 28$$

$$4 = b_1$$

Choice (B) is incorrect because it omits the factor of $\frac{1}{2}$ in the area formula. Choice (C) is incorrect because it is the result of improper calculation. Choice (D) is incorrect because an upper base that measures 28 would mean the figure is a rectangle, not a trapezoid.

55. (C)

This question tests the examinee's ability to use proportions to solve problems in real-world situations. The correct answer is (C), $10\frac{2}{3}$.

Use the proportion $\dfrac{\text{truck length}_1}{\text{screen length}_1} = \dfrac{\text{truck length}_2}{\text{screen length}_2}$ to find the length of the truck on the television screen in feet.

$$\frac{16}{36} = \frac{x}{2}$$

$$36x = 32$$

$$x = \frac{8}{9}$$

The truck will measure $\frac{8}{9}$ foot on the television screen. Since the question requires the answer to be expressed in inches, convert $\frac{8}{9}$ foot to inches by multiplying by 12, the number of inches in a foot.

$$\frac{8}{9} \times 12 = 10\frac{2}{3}$$

Choice (A) is incorrect because it is the length of the truck in feet, not inches. Choices (B) and (D) are incorrect because they are the results of improper calculations.

PRACTICE TEST 4

Praxis II
Middle School Mathematics

Praxis II Middle School Mathematics
Practice Test 4

TIME: 2 hours

QUESTIONS: 55 selected-response and numeric-entry questions

> **Directions:** Each of the following questions or statements below is followed by four suggested answers or completions. Select the one that is best in each case.

(Answer Sheets appear in the back of the book.)

1. What is the y-intercept of the equation $y = x^2 + x - 110$?

   (A) $(-11, 0)$

   (B) $(10, 0)$

   (C) $(0, -110)$

   (D) $\left(-\dfrac{1}{2}, -110\dfrac{1}{4}\right)$

2. In which of the following equations is y a function of x?

   (A) $x = y^2 + 4$

   (B) $x^2 + y^2 = 7$

   (C) $y = x^2 + 3x - 7$

   (D) $y \leq x^2 + 3x - 7$

3. $\sqrt{52}$ lies between which two integers?

   (A) 7 and 8

   (B) 6 and 7

   (C) 5 and 6

   (D) 4 and 5

4. Solve the system of equations by using the linear combination method.

   $$4x + y = 7$$
   $$2x - y = 5$$

   (A) $x = 1, y = -2$

   (B) $x = -1, y = 2$

   (C) $x = 2, y = -1$

   (D) $x = 2, y = 2$

5. What are the restrictions on the variables in the expression below?

   $$\frac{7x^3y - 5yz^4}{x^2 + 6x - 27}$$

   (A) $x \neq -9, x \neq 3$

   (B) $x \neq -9$

   (C) $x \neq 3$

   (D) $x \neq 0, y \neq 0, z \neq 0$

6.

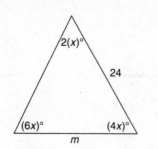

(Note: Figure not drawn to scale)

What is the value of *m*? Fill in your answer in the boxes below.

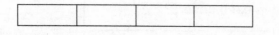

7. Which of the following figures represents a function?

(A)

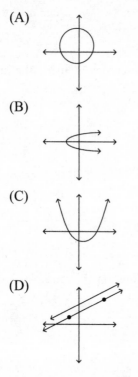

(B)

(C)

(D)

8. What value of *x* makes the mean of the data set below equal to 17.9?

$$16.8, x, 4.7, 9.6, 21.6$$

(A) 17.9

(B) 32.1

(C) 34.3

(D) 36.8

9.

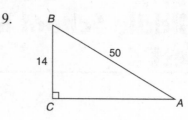

What is the length of the unknown leg?

(A) 336

(B) 112

(C) 48

(D) 36

10.

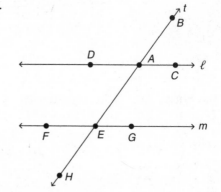

If *l* || *m*, which of the following angles are **not** congruent?

(A) $\angle HEG, \angle DAB$

(B) $\angle DAH, \angle AEG$

(C) $\angle FEA, \angle BAC$

(D) $\angle BAD, \angle AEF$

11. A carpenter is building a recreation room that will be 625 square feet in area. He must decide how to apportion each section of the room. He has decided to set aside 30% of the room for the baby grand piano and an additional 46.7 square feet for a stage. How much of the room will be set aside for the baby grand piano and stage?

(A) 76.7 square feet

(B) 234.2 square feet

(C) 390.8 square feet

(D) 578.3 square feet

12.

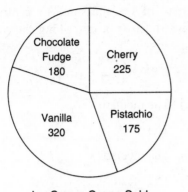

Ice Cream Cones Sold

According to the figure above, what percentage of sales was for pistachio ice cream cones?

(A) 17.5%

(B) 19.4%

(C) 20.0%

(D) 35.6%

13. Multiply the following quantities and express the product in scientific notation.

$$(41.90 \times 10^4)(6.75 \times 10^2) = ?$$

(A) 282.825×10^6

(B) 28.2825×10^7

(C) 2.82825×10^8

(D) 2.82825×10^{10}

14. The length of $\overline{AB}$ is $\sqrt{149}$. If the coordinates of A are $(6, 4)$ and the coordinates of B are $(-4, y)$, what is the value of y?

(A) 6

(B) –3

(C) 11

(D) –3, 11

15. Find the value of x.

$$9^{2x-4} = \left(\frac{1}{3}\right)^{-x+3}$$

(A) 5

(B) $\frac{5}{3}$

(C) 1

(D) $\frac{11}{5}$

16. The price of a rectangular television screen depends on the length of its diagonal. If the diagonal is 45" and the height of the screen is 27", what is the area of the screen?

(A) 486 in²

(B) 972 in²

(C) 1, 215 in²

(D) 1, 620 in²

17. A flagpole stands 18 feet high and casts an 11-foot shadow. A man standing next to the flagpole casts a shadow 3.6 feet long. How tall is the man?

(A) 5.9 feet

(B) 5.7 feet

(C) 5 feet

(D) 2.2 feet

18. Which of the following **cannot** be used to find 17.4% of 276?

(A) 0.174×276

(B) $\frac{87}{500} \times 276$

(C) $276 \div 0.174$

(D) $\frac{n}{276} = \frac{174}{1000}$

19. Which of the following equations represents the phrase: "The quantity of 7 and twice a number squared is 17."

    (A) $7(2n)^2 = 17$

    (B) $\sqrt{7+2n} = 17$

    (C) $7 + (2n)^2 = 17$

    (D) $(7 + 2n)^2 = 17$

20. What is the area of a square that has a diagonal of 28 feet? Fill in your answer in the boxes below.

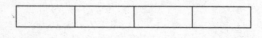

21. Solve for x:

    $$x^2 + 2x - 12 = 0$$

    (A) $-1 + \sqrt{13}$

    (B) $-1 - \sqrt{13}$

    (C) $-1 \pm \sqrt{13}$

    (D) $1 \pm \sqrt{13}$

22. What is the slope expressed in the input-output table below?

Input	Output
0	-2
3	0
6	2
9	4

    (A) $\dfrac{3}{2}$

    (B) $\dfrac{-3}{2}$

    (C) $\dfrac{2}{3}$

    (D) $\dfrac{-2}{3}$

23. Which of the measures of central tendency is **least** effective in describing the following set of numbers?

    $$12, 14, 17, 18, 976$$

    (A) The median

    (B) The mode

    (C) The inverse

    (D) The mean

24. What is the slant height of a cone with a surface area that measures 435.675 in² and a radius that measures 7.5 inches? (Use $\pi = 3.14$.) Enter your answer in the boxes below.

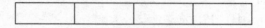

25. What is the range of the exponential function $y = 2^x$?

    (A) $y > 0$

    (B) $y \geq 0$

    (C) $x > 0$

    (D) $-\infty < y < \infty$

26. Katie can spend up to $100 on some inexpensive skirts. If each skirt cost $8, which of the following expressions reflects the conditions of Katie's purchase?

    (A) $s + 8 = 100$

    (B) $s + 8 < 100$

    (C) $8s < 100$

    (D) $8s \leq 100$

27. Solve for r:

$$-2(5-3r) = 12 - 3(5-r)$$

(A) $\dfrac{7}{3}$

(B) $\dfrac{7}{6}$

(C) 0

(D) $\dfrac{-7}{3}$

28. A jacket costing $120 is discounted 20%. After a week, the jacket is discounted another 20% and is sold. What expression below can be used to calculate the price at which the jacket was sold?

(A) $(120)(0.40)$

(B) $120 - 120(0.40)$

(C) $120 - (120)(.20) - [120 - (0.20)(120)](0.20)$

(D) $120 - (120)(0.40) - [120 - (120)(0.40)]$

29. What is the diameter of a circle that has an area equal to 484π?

(A) 88

(B) 44

(C) 33

(D) 22

30. Simplify the following expression:

$$\frac{x^3 + 6x^2 - 16x}{x^2 - 2x}$$

(A) $\dfrac{x+8}{x-2}$

(B) $\dfrac{x(x-8)}{x+2}$

(C) $x + 8$

(D) $x - 2$

31. 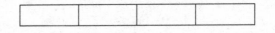 $\sqrt{2x+2} - 3 = 15$

Find the value of x and place your answer in the boxes below.

32. A cruise line ship left Port A and traveled 90 miles due west and then 400 miles due north.

At this point, the ship docked at Port B. What is the shortest distance between Port A and Port B?

(A) 41 miles

(B) 410 miles

(C) 160,000 miles

(D) 168,100 miles

33. A 1.5-gallon jug needs to be filled with water. If the jug is filled one pint at a time, how many pints are needed to fill the jug?

(A) 6

(B) 8

(C) 10

(D) 12

34. A line segment has endpoints $(-5, 1)$ and $(3, -3)$. What are the coordinates of the segment's midpoint?

(A) $(-1, -1)$

(B) $4\sqrt{5}$

(C) -0.5

(D) $(-2, -2)$

35. Simplify the following expression if $x = 0.3$, $y = 9.21$, and $z = 1.86$. Round your answer to the nearest hundredth and enter your answer in the boxes below.

$$\frac{-2x^2 y}{-3z}$$

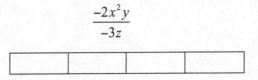

36. Which of the following graphs represents the linear equation $y = \dfrac{2}{3}x - 4$?

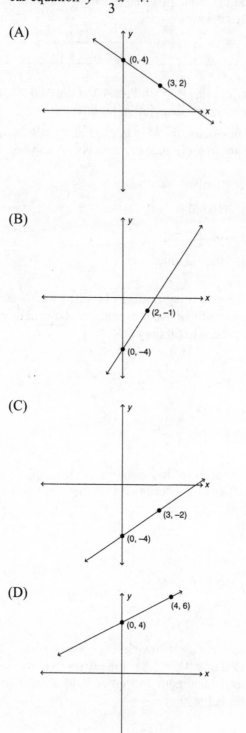

(A)

(B)

(C)

(D)

37. Any set of inputs and outputs is called a

(A) function

(B) linear function

(C) non-linear function

(D) relation

38. A line that passes through a scatterplot is called a

(A) line of best fit

(B) parallel line

(C) perpendicular line

(D) transversal

39.

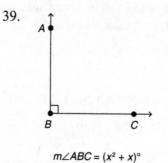

$$m\angle ABC = (x^2 + x)°$$

What is the value of x?

(A) 90

(B) 9

(C) −10

(D) 9 or −10

40. If $n > 0$ then n^2 is

(A) greater than n

(B) equal to n

(C) less than n

(D) There is not enough information to solve this problem.

41. At Joe's Hardware Store, a state tax of 5% is charged for every item. In addition, a municipal tax of 1.5% is charged for any item that exceeds $100. Steve recently purchased two items, one for $120 and the other for $90. In dollars and cents, how much tax did he pay? Fill in your answer in the boxes below.

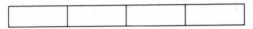

42. The graph of a function is known to contain the points (–2, 4), (5, 3), and (8, –7).

    Which of the following points **cannot** lie on this graph?

    (A) (4, –2)

    (B) (–5, –3)

    (C) (1, 4)

    (D) (8, –3)

43. Albert is a quality control manager for a department store. In a recent shipment of 900 blouses for women, 12 had defects. If he randomly selects a sample of 225 of these blouses, how many of these would be expected **not** to have any defects? Fill in your answer in the boxes below.

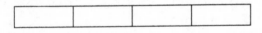

44. A local fishing pier registered the following catches (in pounds) for a six-day period:

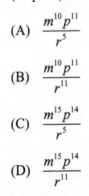

Day	Weight
1	108
2	112
3	104
4	109
5	118
6	112

    What is the difference between the median and the mean of these weights?

(A) 112

(B) 110.5

(C) 14

(D) 0

45. For which of the following intervals are *all* of its values solutions to the inequality $|3 - 4x| < 6$?

    (A) $-\frac{1}{3} < x < 3$

    (B) $-\frac{3}{4} < x < \frac{9}{4}$

    (C) $-\frac{7}{8} < x < 1$

    (D) $-\frac{9}{10} < x < \frac{5}{2}$

46. What is the simplified form of $(mp^2r^3)^3 \times (m^{-3}p^{-2}r^5)^{-4}$?

    (A) $\dfrac{m^{10}p^{11}}{r^5}$

    (B) $\dfrac{m^{10}p^{11}}{r^{11}}$

    (C) $\dfrac{m^{15}p^{14}}{r^5}$

    (D) $\dfrac{m^{15}p^{14}}{r^{11}}$

47. The dimensions of a large rectangular storage tank are as follows: 150 feet long, 100 feet wide, and 25 feet deep. A scale model of this tank has a length of 18 inches. What is the sum, in inches, of the length, width, and height of the scale model?

    Fill in your answer in the boxes below.

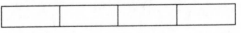

48. What is the reduced form of the fraction $\dfrac{8x^3 - 20x^2 - 48x}{8x^3 - 18x}$?

(A) $\dfrac{2x-8}{2x-3}$

(B) $\dfrac{x-8}{x-3}$

(C) $\dfrac{x-4}{2x-3}$

(D) $\dfrac{2x}{2x+3}$

49. If the average of 4, 6, 9, 1, and x is x, what is the value of x? Fill in your answer in the boxes below.

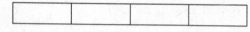

50. A gardener has 80 feet of fencing to surround a rectangular garden. If the width of the garden is w, which of the following expressions can be used to calculate the enclosed area?

(A) $80 - 2w$

(B) $80w - 2w^2$

(C) $40w - 2w^2$

(D) $40x - w^2$

51. Seven students draw numbered cards, each with a value that is a positive integer. The mean of their selections is 14. What is the largest number any student could have drawn? Place your answer in the boxes below.

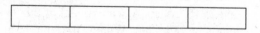

52. The coordinates of the midpoint, M, on $\overline{AB}$ is $(-7, 8)$. If the coordinates of A are $(4, -2)$, what are the coordinates of B?

(A) $(18, -18)$

(B) $(-18, 18)$

(C) $\left(-\dfrac{3}{2}, 3\right)$

(D) $\left(-\dfrac{25}{2}, 13\right)$

53. What is the sum of the first five prime numbers?

(A) 39

(B) 28

(C) 27

(D) 18

54. How many real zeroes exist for the function $f(x) = -(x-3)^2 + 2$?

(A) 3

(B) 2

(C) 1

(D) 0

55.

x	1	2	3
$g(x)$	3	5	7
x	3	4	5
$h(x)$	8	16	24

The values for $g(x)$ and $h(x)$ are listed above. What is the value for $h(g(2))$? Fill in your answer in the boxes below.

ANSWER KEY—PRACTICE TEST 4

Question	Answer	Content Category
1.	(C)	Arithmetic and Algebra
2.	(C)	Arithmetic and Algebra
3.	(A)	Arithmetic and Algebra
4.	(C)	Arithmetic and Algebra
5.	(A)	Arithmetic and Algebra
6.	12	Geometry and Data
7.	(C)	Arithmetic and Algebra
8.	(D)	Geometry and Data
9.	(C)	Geometry and Data
10.	(C)	Geometry and Data
11.	(B)	Geometry and Data
12.	(B)	Geometry and Data
13.	(C)	Arithmetic and Algebra
14.	(D)	Arithmetic and Algebra
15.	(B)	Arithmetic and Algebra
16.	(B)	Geometry and Data
17.	(A)	Arithmetic and Algebra
18.	(C)	Arithmetic and Algebra
19.	(D)	Arithmetic and Algebra
20.	392	Geometry and Data
21.	(C)	Arithmetic and Algebra
22.	(C)	Arithmetic and Algebra
23.	(D)	Geometry and Data
24.	11	Geometry and Data
25.	(A)	Arithmetic and Algebra
26.	(D)	Arithmetic and Algebra
27.	(A)	Arithmetic and Algebra
28.	(C)	Arithmetic and Algebra

Question	Answer	Content Category
29.	(B)	Geometry and Data
30.	(C)	Arithmetic and Algebra
31.	161	Arithmetic and Algebra
32.	(B)	Geometry and Data
33.	(D)	Geometry and Data
34.	(A)	Geometry and Data
35.	0.30	Arithmetic and Algebra
36.	(C)	Arithmetic and Algebra
37.	(D)	Arithmetic and Algebra
38.	(A)	Geometry and Data
39.	(D)	Geometry and Data
40.	(D)	Arithmetic and Algebra
41.	$12.30	Arithmetic and Algebra
42.	(D)	Arithmetic and Algebra
43.	222	Arithmetic and Algebra
44.	(D)	Geometry and Data
45.	(B)	Arithmetic and Algebra
46.	(D)	Arithmetic and Algebra
47.	33	Geometry and Data
48.	(A)	Arithmetic and Algebra
49.	5	Geometry and Data
50.	(D)	Geometry and Data
51.	92	Arithmetic and Algebra
52.	(B)	Arithmetic and Algebra
53.	(B)	Arithmetic and Algebra
54.	(B)	Arithmetic and Algebra
55.	24	Arithmetic and Algebra

1. (C)

This question tests the examinee's ability to find the x- and y-intercepts of an equation graphed in the coordinate plane. The correct answer is (C), $(0, -110)$.

Find the y-intercept of the equation by letting $x = 0$:

$$y = (0)^2 + (0) - 110 = -110$$

The intercept is in the coordinate plane so the coordinates are $(0, -110)$.

Choices (A) and (B) are incorrect because they are the x-intercepts of the equation. Choice (D) is incorrect because it is the vertex of the equation.

2. (C)

This question tests the examinee's ability to discern a function. The correct answer is (C), $y = x^2 + 3x - 7$.

If y is a function of x, then each x value, the domain, will have only one y value, the range. The equation $y = x^2 + 3x - 7$ is a parabola that opens up, satisfying the requirements of a function. Use the vertical line test (all vertical lines intersect the graph at only one point) to see that each x value has only one y value.

Choice (A) is incorrect because it is the equation for a parabola that opens to the right. Such a parabola would fail the vertical line test. Choice (B) is incorrect because it is a circle and would also fail the vertical line test. Choice (D) is incorrect because it is the same parabola as choice (C), but also includes those values outside of the parabola. This graph would also fail the vertical line test.

3. (A)

This question tests the examinee's ability to place a radical number on a number line. The correct answer is (A), 7 and 8.

Determine the perfect squares below and above 52, which would be 49 and 64. Then

$$\sqrt{49} < \sqrt{52} < \sqrt{64}$$
$$7 < \sqrt{52} < 8$$

Choice (B) is incorrect because $\sqrt{52}$ would have to be less than $\sqrt{49} = 7$. Choice (C) is incorrect because $\sqrt{52}$ would have to be less than $\sqrt{36} = 6$. Choice (D) is incorrect because $\sqrt{52}$ would have to be less than $\sqrt{25} = 5$.

4. (C)

This question tests the examinee's ability to solve systems of equations. The correct answer is (C), $x = 2$, $y = -1$.

Add the two equations downward to eliminate y.

$$\begin{array}{r} 4x + y = 7 \\ + 2x - y = 5 \\ \hline 6x = 12 \\ x = 2 \end{array}$$

Substitute $x = 2$ in either equation.

$$4(2) + y = 7$$
$$8 + y = 7$$
$$8 - 8 + y = 7 - 8$$
$$y = -1$$

Choice (A) is incorrect because it is the result of improper calculation. Choice (B) is incorrect because it juxtaposes the correct values for x and y. Choice (D) is incorrect because, although the y value is correct, the x value is incorrect.

5. **(A)**

This question tests the examinee's knowledge of restrictions on expressions. The correct answer is (A), $x \neq -9, x \neq 3$.

Division by 0 is not allowed, so restrict those values of x that would render the denominator equal to 0.

$$x^2 + 6x - 27 = 0$$

$$(x + 9)(x - 3) = 0$$

$$x + 9 = 0, x - 3 = 0$$

$$x \neq -9, x \neq 3$$

Choices (B) and (C) are incorrect because they cite only one of the restrictions. Choice (D) is incorrect because if x, y, and z all equal 0, the denominator does not equal 0.

6. **12**

This question tests the examinee's knowledge of special right triangles. The correct answer is 12.

Although the figure is not drawn to scale, there is enough information to discern its true shape. Since the sum of the measures of the angles in a triangle is 180°, set the sum of $6x$, $4x$, and $2x$ equal to 180.

$$6x + 4x + 2x = 180$$

$$12x = 180$$

$$x = 15$$

$$2x = 30$$

$$4x = 60$$

$$6x = 90$$

Draw the triangle to scale and compare it to the 30-60-90 model for a right triangle.

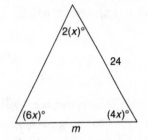

The hypotenuse is 24, and the side opposite the 30° angle is half the hypotenuse, or 12.

$$2m = 24$$

$$m = 12$$

7. **(C)**

This question tests the examinee's knowledge of the graphs of functions. The correct answer is (C).

A graph of a function passes the vertical line test. Note that (C) passes the vertical line test, whereas choices (A), (B), and (D) do not.

8. **(D)**

This question tests the examinee's ability to calculate the mean of a data set. The correct answer is (D), 36.8.

The mean of any set of numbers is found by first finding the sum of the values and then dividing by the number of values. In this case, we know the mean, but one of the values, x, is unknown.

$$\frac{16.8 + x + 4.7 + 9.6 + 21.6}{5} = 17.9$$

$$\frac{52.7 + x}{5} = 17.9$$

$$52.7 + x = 89.5$$

$$x = 36.8$$

Choice (A) is incorrect because it implies all five of the values are 17.9. Choice (B) is incorrect because it is the range of the final data set. Choice (C) is incorrect because it is the result of improper calculation.

9. (C)

This question tests the examinee's ability to use the Pythagorean theorem or to recognize a multiple of a Pythagorean triple. The correct answer is (C), 48.

Use the Pythagorean theorem, $a^2 + b^2 = c^2$, to calculate the value of b.

$$14^2 + b^2 = 50^2$$

$$196 + b^2 = 2,500$$

$$b^2 = 2,304$$

$$b = 48$$

A quicker route to calculating b would be to recognize it as a multiple of the Pythagorean triple 7-24-25.

Since $7 \times 2 = 14$ and $25 \times 2 = 50$, then the missing side is 24×2, or 48.

Choice (A) is incorrect because it is the area of the triangle. Choice (B) is incorrect because it is the perimeter of the triangle. Choice (D) incorrectly performs the Pythagorean theorem by not squaring the sides.

10. (C)

This question tests the examinee's knowledge of angle-pair measures. The correct answer is (C), $\angle FEA$, $\angle BAC$.

When two parallel lines are intersected by a transversal, several pairs of angles are congruent. These angle pairs are referred to as corresponding angles, alternate interior angles, and alternate exterior angles. $\angle FEA$ and $\angle BAC$ do not fall into any of these categories and thus are not congruent.

Choice (A) is incorrect because $\angle HEG$ and $\angle DAB$ are equal alternate exterior angles. Choice (B) is incorrect because $\angle DAH$ and $\angle AEG$ are equal alternate interior angles. Choice (D) is incorrect because $\angle BAD$ and $\angle AEF$ are equal corresponding angles.

11. (B)

This question tests the examinee's ability to apply percents to area calculations. The correct answer is (B), 234.2 square feet.

Find the area of the baby grand piano, and add that figure to the square footage set aside for the stage.

$$(625)(0.30) + 46.7 = 187.5 + 46.7 = 234.2$$

Choice (A) is incorrect because it adds the number 30, the percent allowed for the baby grand piano, to the area of the stage. Choice (C) is incorrect because it represents the area of the room that is **not** part of the stage or the baby grand piano space. Choice (D) is incorrect because it is the area of the room minus the area of the stage.

12. (B)

This question tests the examinee's ability to calculate data derived from a data display. The correct answer is (B), 19.4%.

Use the formula $\dfrac{\text{part}}{\text{whole}} = \dfrac{n}{100}$ to find the percent.

$$\frac{175}{175 + 225 + 320 + 180} = \frac{n}{100}$$

$$\frac{175}{900} = \frac{n}{100}$$

$$175 \times 100 = 900n$$

$$17,500 = 900n$$

$$19.4 = n$$

Choice (A) is incorrect because it is the result of improper calculation. Choice (C) is incorrect because it is the percentage of cones sold that were chocolate fudge. Choice (D) is incorrect because it is the percentage of cones sold that were vanilla.

13. (C)

This question tests the examinee's ability to express answers in scientific notation. The correct answer is (C), 2.82825×10^8.

First multiply 41.9 by 6.75.

$$41.9 \times 6.75 = 282.825$$

Next, when multiplying numbers with the same base, add the exponents.

$$10^4 \times 10^2 = 10^{4+2} = 10^6$$

So the product is 282.825×10^6. A number expressed in scientific notation is the product of a number greater than or equal to 1 and less than 10 ($1 \le n < 10$) and 10 to some power. Express the product in scientific notation by moving the decimal point in 282.825 two places to the left and adding 2 to the power of 10.

$$282.825 \times 10^6 = 2.82825 \times 10^8$$

Choice (A) is incorrect because the final answer is not expressed in scientific notation; the first number n must be $1 \le n < 10$. Similarly, choice (B) is incorrect because it does not express the final answer in scientific notation. Choice (D) is incorrect because it multiplied, rather than added, the exponents at the beginning of the problem.

14. (D)

This question tests the examinee's ability to calculate values using the distance formula. The correct answer is (D), (–3, 11).

Find y by using the distance formula.

$$d = \sqrt{(x_1 - x_2)^2 + (y_1 - y_2)^2}$$

Insert the known data and solve for y:

$$\sqrt{149} = \sqrt{[6 - (-4)]^2 + (4 - y_2)^2}$$

$$\left(\sqrt{149}\right)^2 = \left(\sqrt{(10)^2 + (4 - y_2)^2}\right)^2$$

$$149 = 100 + (4 - y_2)^2$$

$$49 = (4 - y_2)^2$$

$$\sqrt{49} = \sqrt{(4 - y_2)^2}$$

$$\pm 7 = 4 - y_2$$

$$y_2 = -3, y_2 = 11$$

The coordinates of B are (–4, 11) or (–4, –3). Both points are $\sqrt{149}$ (approximately 12.2) units from A.

Choice (A) is incorrect because it would mean the length of $\overline{AB}$ is $\sqrt{104} = 2\sqrt{26}$. Choices (B) and (C) are incorrect because each provides only one of the two correct answers.

15. (B)

This question tests the examinee's skills in using exponents. The correct answer is (B), $\dfrac{5}{3}$.

Convert the bases, 9 and $\dfrac{1}{3}$, into powers of 3.

$$9 = 3^2$$

$$\frac{1}{3} = 3^{-1}$$

Substitute 3^2 and 3^{-1} in the equation.

$$9^{2x-4} = \left(\frac{1}{3}\right)^{-x+3}$$

$$(3^2)^{2x-4} = (3^{-1})^{-x+3}$$

When raising one power to another, multiply the powers.

$$(3^2)^{2x-4} = (3^{-1})^{-x+3}$$

$$3^{4x-8} = 3^{x-3}$$

Since the bases are the same, set the exponents equal and solve.

$$4x - 8 = x - 3$$

$$3x = 5$$

$$x = \frac{5}{3}$$

Choice (A) is incorrect because it fails to divide by 3 in the final step of the calculation. Choice (C) is incorrect because it is the result of improper calculation. Choice (D) is incorrect because it fails to multiply $(-x + 3)$ by -1 because the 3 is in the denominator in the original equation.

16. (B)

This question tests the examinee's ability to apply the Pythagorean theorem to everyday situations. The correct answer is (B), 972 in².

The diagonal of a rectangle creates two right triangles. The diagonal of the television is the hypotenuse while the height of the screen is one of the legs. Use the Pythagorean theorem to calculate the measure of the screen's base.

$$27^2 + b^2 = 45^2$$

$$729 + b^2 = 2025$$

$$b^2 = 1,296$$

$$b = 36$$

Note that the lengths 27-36-45 are multiples of a 3-4-5 Pythagorean triple because $9 \times 3 = 27$, $9 \times 4 = 36$, and $9 \times 5 = 45$.

Find the area of the rectangular screen by using the formula for the area of a rectangle.

$$\text{Area} = \text{base} \times \text{height}$$

$$\text{Area} = 27 \times 36 = 972 \text{ in}^2$$

Choice (A) is incorrect because it erroneously uses the area formula of a triangle. Choice (C) is incorrect because it is the product of the diagonal and the height. Choice (D) is incorrect because it is the product of the diagonal and the base.

17. (A)

This question tests the examinee's ability to create and solve a proportion. The correct answer is (A), 5.9 feet.

Use the proportion $\dfrac{\text{height}_1}{\text{shadow}_1} = \dfrac{\text{height}_2}{\text{shadow}_2}$ to find the man's height.

$$\frac{18}{11} = \frac{x}{3.6}$$

Cross-multiply:

$$(18)(3.6) = 11x$$

$$64.8 = 11x$$

$$5.9 \approx x$$

Choice (B) is incorrect because it erroneously calculates the proportion. Choice (C) is incorrect because it is the quotient of the flagpole's height and the length of the man's shadow. Choice (D) is incorrect because it uses the following incorrect proportion:

$$\frac{\text{height}_1}{\text{shadow}_1} = \frac{\text{shadow}_2}{\text{height}_2}$$

18. (C)

This question tests the examinee's ability to recognize equivalent ways of finding percentages. The correct answer is (C), $276 \div 0.174$.

In order to find a percent of a number, multiply the percent, expressed as a decimal or a fraction, with that number. Choice (C) divides the number by the percent rather than multiplying it. 17.4% of 276 is 48.024, but $276 \div 17.4\%$ is 1,586.2.

Choices (A), (B), and (D) are incorrect responses because they correctly calculate 17.4% of 276.

For (A), $0.174 \times 276 = 48.024$

For (B), $\dfrac{87}{500} \times 276 = 48.024$

For (D), $\dfrac{n}{276} = \dfrac{174}{1000}$

$$1{,}000n = 48{,}024$$

$$n = 48.024$$

19. (D)

This question tests the examinee's ability to translate verbal descriptions into algebraic expressions and equations. The correct answer is (D), $(7 + 2n)^2 = 17$.

The quantity of 7 and twice a number means $(7 + 2n)$. Squaring that quantity, we get $(7 + 2n)^2$. Since $(7 + 2n)^2$ is 17, we get:

$$(7 + 2n)^2 = 17$$

Choice (A) is incorrect because the quantity of 7 and twice a number should be added, not multiplied. Choice (B) is incorrect because it finds the square root, not the square, of $(7 + 2n)$. Choice (C) is incorrect because it squares only $2n$ rather than the quantity 7 and $2n$.

20. 392

This question tests the examinee's ability to calculate area using the Pythagorean theorem. The correct answer is 392 square feet.

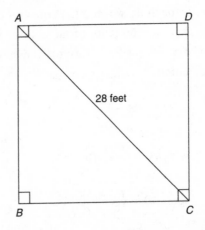

The area of a square is found by using the formula $A = s^2$, where s is the length of a side. Consider either right triangle, and use the Pythagorean theorem, $a^2 + b^2 = c^2$, to find the length of one side.

$$s^2 + s^2 = 28^2$$

$$2s^2 = 784$$

$$s^2 = 392$$

$$s = 14\sqrt{2}$$

$$A = (14\sqrt{2})^2 = 392$$

Note that we could have stopped solving the problem when we got to $s^2 = 392$.

Another way to solve the problem is to recognize that a square is a rhombus with right angles. The area of a rhombus is $\dfrac{1}{2}$(product of diagonals) and each diagonal is 28, so $A = \dfrac{1}{2}(28 \times 28) = 392$.

21. (C)

This question tests the examinee's ability to solve a quadratic equation by using the quadratic formula. The correct answer is (C), $-1 \pm \sqrt{13}$.

Upon inspection, we find the equation cannot be factored as there are no pairs of factors of –12 with a sum of 2. Using the quadratic formula is a quick way to solve the equation.

$$x = \frac{-b \pm \sqrt{b^2 - 4ac}}{2a}$$

$$a = 1, b = 2, c = -12$$

$$x = \frac{-2 \pm \sqrt{(2)^2 - 4(1)(-12)}}{2(1)}$$

$$= \frac{-2 \pm \sqrt{4 + 48}}{2}$$

$$= \frac{-2 \pm \sqrt{52}}{2}$$

$$= \frac{-2 \pm 2\sqrt{13}}{2}$$

$$= -1 \pm \sqrt{13}$$

Choices (A) and (B) are incorrect because each offers only one of the two correct solutions. Choice (D) is incorrect because it uses the quadratic formula erroneously.

22. (C)

This question tests the examinee's ability to find the slope from an input-output table. The correct answer is (C), $\frac{2}{3}$.

The slope of a linear equation can be found graphically by inspecting the rise and run of a graph. Starting from (0, –2) rise 2 and run 3 to arrive at (3, 0). Rise 2 and run 3 to arrive at (6, 2). Thus, $\frac{\text{rise}}{\text{run}} = \frac{2}{3}$.

Alternatively, recognize that the input-output table represents a linear function because the inputs have a constant difference of 3 and the corresponding outputs have a constant difference of 2. Therefore, the slope is $\frac{\text{change in output}}{\text{change in input}} = \frac{2}{3}$.

Choice (A) is incorrect because it implies slope is found by using $\frac{\text{run}}{\text{rise}}$. Choice (B) is incorrect because it is a slope perpendicular to the one expressed in the table. Choice (D) is incorrect because it erroneously calculates the rise as –2.

23. (D)

This question tests the examinee's knowledge of the measures of central tendency. The correct answer is (D), the mean.

To find the mean, add all the numbers and divide by 5.

$$\frac{12 + 14 + 17 + 18 + 976}{5} = 207.4$$

The mean is considerably larger than all the numbers, except for 976, which has skewed, or exaggerated, the result.

Choice (A) is incorrect because the median is 17, within 5 of any of the other values except for 976. Thus, it is representative of the data set. Choice (B) is incorrect because there is no mode of the data set; each value appears only once. Choice (C) is incorrect because the inverse is not a measure of central tendency.

24. 11

This question tests the examinee's ability to use geometric formulas to calculate measures of a cone. The correct answer is 11.

The surface area of a cone is found by using the formula $SA = \pi r^2 + \pi rs$, where r represents the measure of the radius and s represents the measure of the slant height. Input the known data and solve for the slant height.

$$SA = \pi r^2 + \pi rs$$

$$435.675 = (3.14)(7.5^2) + (3.14)(7.5)(s)$$

$$435.675 = 176.625 + 23.55s$$

$$259.05 = 23.55s$$

$$11 = s$$

25. (A)

This question tests the examinee's understanding of exponential functions. The correct answer is (A), $y > 0$.

An exponential function increases (or decreases) rapidly. The domain is all real numbers, but the range has an asymptote (the graph approaches this value but never reaches it). For $y = 2^x$, no matter how small x is, y is always positive.

Choice (B) is incorrect because it includes the asymptote $y = 0$. Choice (C) is incorrect because x is the domain, not the range. Choice (D) is incorrect because $y = 2^x$ is never negative and never equals 0.

26. (D)

This question tests the examinee's ability to translate a real-world situation into an algebraic inequality. The correct answer is (D), $8s \leq 100$.

The variable s represents the number of skirts Katie can purchase. Since each skirt costs \$8, $8s$ represents the cost of Katie's purchase. The phrase "up to \$100" means the cost can equal or be less than \$100. Thus, the inequality $8s \leq 100$ reflects the maximum number of skirts Katie can buy with \$100.

Choice (A) is incorrect because it implies the cost of a skirt and \$8 is equal to \$100. Choice (B) is incorrect because it implies the cost of a skirt and \$8 is less than \$100. This may be true, but it does not consider the cost of the 8 skirts. Choice (C) is incorrect because it implies the cost of the skirts cannot equal \$100; Katie can spend "up to \$100," which implies the cost may also equal \$100.

27. (A)

This question tests the examinee's ability to solve equations with variables on both sides. The correct answer is (A), $\dfrac{7}{3}$.

Use the order of operations to isolate the variable. The parentheses are in simplest form and there are no exponents, so proceed to multiplication.

$$-2(5 - 3r) = 12 - 3(5 - r)$$

$$-10 + 6r = 12 - 15 + 3r$$

Next, add the like terms.

$$-10 + 6r = 12 - 15 + 3r$$

$$-10 + 6r = -3 + 3r$$

Add 10 to both sides of the equation.

$$-10 + 6r = -3 + 3r$$

$$-10 + 6r + 10 = -3 + 3r + 10$$

$$6r = 3r + 7$$

Subtract $3r$ from both sides of the equation.

$$6r = 3r + 7$$

$$6r - 3r = 3r + 7 - 3r$$

$$3r = 7$$

Divide both sides of the equation by 3 to isolate the variable.

$$3r = 7$$

$$\frac{3r}{3} = \frac{7}{3}$$

$$r = \frac{7}{3}$$

Check your solution by replacing r with $\frac{7}{3}$ in the original equation.

$$-2\left[5 - 3\left(\frac{7}{3}\right)\right] = 12 - 3\left(5 - \frac{7}{3}\right)$$

$$-2(5 - 7) = 12 - 3\left(\frac{8}{3}\right)$$

$$-2(-2) = 12 - 8$$

$$4 = 4$$

Choice (B) is incorrect because the answer reflects the failure to subtract $3r$ from both sides of the equation. Choice (C) is incorrect because it yields a final step, $0 = 7$, which is false. Choice (D) is incorrect because it implies the last step was divided by -3 rather than 3.

28. (C)

This question tests the examinee's ability to describe mathematical processes to solve a real-world problem. The correct answer is (C), $120 - (120)(.20) - [120 - (0.20)(120)](0.20)$.

After the first 20% discount we get:

$$120 - (0.20)(120) = 96$$

After the second 20% discount, we get:

original – first discount – second discount

$$120 - (120)(.20) - [120 - (0.20)(120)](0.20)$$
$$= \$76.80$$

Choice (A) is incorrect because it would solely provide the discounted amount if the original price were discounted by 40%. Choice (B) is incorrect because it assumes successive 20% discounts are the same as a 40% discount. Choice (D) is incorrect because it assumes successive 20% discounts are the same as a 40% discount.

29. (B)

This question tests the examinee's ability to derive a diameter given a circle's area. The correct answer is (B), 44.

Find the radius of the circle by setting 484π equal to the area formula.

$$A = \pi r^2$$

$$484\pi = \pi r^2$$

$$r^2 = 484$$

$$r = 22$$

Find the diameter by multiplying the radius by 2.

$$2 \times 22 = 44$$

Choice (A) is incorrect because it is the measure of the diameter multiplied by 2. Choice (C) is incorrect because it is the result of improper calculation. Choice (D) is incorrect because it is the radius of the circle, not the diameter.

30. (C)

This question tests the examinee's ability to simplify rational expressions. The correct answer is (C), $x + 8$.

Factor the numerator and denominator completely and cancel as needed.

$$\frac{x^3 + 6x^2 - 16x}{x^2 - 2x} =$$

$$\frac{x(x^2 + 6x - 16)}{x(x - 2)} =$$

$$\frac{x(x + 8)(x - 2)}{x(x - 2)} =$$

$$\frac{\cancel{x}(x + 8)\cancel{(x - 2)}}{\cancel{x}\cancel{(x - 2)}} =$$

$$x + 8$$

Choice (A) is incorrect because it fails to cancel $x - 2$ from the denominator. Choice (B) is incorrect because there is no factor $(x + 2)$ in the denominator. Choice (D) is incorrect because it implies $x + 8$ was canceled with $x - 2$; cancellations are only allowed between identical values in the numerator and the denominator.

31. 161

This question tests the examinee's ability to solve a radical equation. The correct answer is 161.

Begin by isolating the variable.

$$\sqrt{2x + 2} - 3 = 15$$
$$\sqrt{2x + 2} = 18$$

Eliminate the radical by squaring both sides.

$$\left(\sqrt{2x + 2}\right)^2 = 18^2$$
$$2x + 2 = 324$$

Solve the equation as you normally would.

$$2x + 2 = 324$$

$$2x = 322$$

$$x = 161$$

32. (B)

This question tests the examinee's ability to use the Pythagorean theorem or recognize a Pythagorean triple. The correct answer is (B), 410 miles. The path of the ship creates the legs of a right triangle.

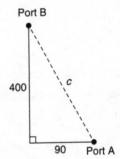

The shortest distance between Port A and Port B is the hypotenuse of the right triangle.

Use the Pythagorean theorem to calculate the distance.

$$90^2 + 400^2 = c^2$$

$$8{,}100 + 160{,}000 = c^2$$

$$168{,}100 = c^2$$

$$410 = c$$

Choice (A) is incorrect because it recognizes the 9-40-41 Pythagorean triple, but fails to realize it is a multiple, 10, of that pattern. Choice (C) is incorrect because it represents b^2 in the calculation. Choice (D) is incorrect because it represents c^2 in the calculation.

33. (D)

This question tests the examinee's ability to convert among units in the standard system of measurements. The correct answer is (D), 12.

The question is asking to find the number of pints in 1.5 gallons. Since 4 quarts equals one gallon, then 1.5 gallons equals 6 quarts because $1.5 \times 4 = 6$. Each quart equals 2 pints, so 1.5 gallons equals 12 pints.

Choice (A) is incorrect because it is the number of quarts, not pints, in the jug. Choice (B) is incorrect because 8 pints equals 1 gallon, not 1.5 gallons. Choice (C) is incorrect because 10 pints equals 1.25 gallons.

34. (A)

This question tests the examinee's ability to calculate midpoints using the midpoint formula. The correct answer is (A), $(-1, -1)$.

Use the midpoint formula to calculate the midpoint.

$$m = \left(\frac{x_1 + x_2}{2}, \frac{y_1 + y_2}{2} \right)$$

$$m = \left(\frac{-5 + 3}{2}, \frac{1 + (-3)}{2} \right)$$

$$m = \left(\frac{-2}{2}, \frac{-2}{2} \right)$$

$$m = (-1, -1)$$

Choice (B) is incorrect because it is the distance between the two points. Choice (C) is incorrect because it is the slope of the line that connects the points. Choice (D) is incorrect because it erroneously calculates the midpoint because it omits dividing each coordinate by 2.

35. 0.30

This question tests the examinee's ability to calculate values using the order of operations. The correct answer is 0.30.

Replace the values for each variable and simplify using the order of operations.

$$\frac{-2(0.3)^2(9.21)}{-3(1.86)} = \frac{-1.6578}{-5.58} = 0.297097$$

0.297097 rounded to the nearest hundredth is 0.30.

36. (C)

This question tests the examinee's ability to recognize the graphs of linear equations. The correct answer is (C).

The linear equation is in the slope-intercept form of a line. In the equation $y = \frac{2}{3}x - 4$, $\frac{2}{3}$ is the slope and -4 is the y-intercept. To graph this equation, follow these steps.

Step 1: Place a dot at -4 on the y-axis.

Step 2: The slope is also described as $\frac{\text{rise}}{\text{run}}$. From -4, rise 2 along the y-axis and "run" 3 to the right. Place another dot at that destination and connect that point, $(3, -2)$, with $(0, -4)$.

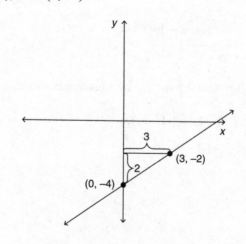

Choice (A) is incorrect because it has a negative slope and the y-intercept is $+4$. Choice (B) is incorrect because it has a slope of $\frac{3}{2}$ rather than $\frac{2}{3}$. Choice (D) is incorrect because it has a y-intercept of 4 rather than -4.

37. (D)

This question tests the examinee's skills in discerning relations and functions. The correct answer is (D), relation.

All functions are relations, but not all relations are functions. Any set of inputs and outputs is a relation.

Choices (A), (B), and (C) are incorrect because not all relations are functions.

38. (A)

This question tests the examinee's knowledge of graphical displays. The correct answer is (A), line of best fit.

When data seem to correlate in a roughly linear fashion, then a line of best fit can be drawn to create a model for the information. This model is used to make predictions about forthcoming data.

Choice (B) is incorrect because parallel lines are two or more lines that do not intersect. Choice (C) is incorrect because a perpendicular line intersects another line at right angles. Choice (D) is incorrect because a transversal intersects two or more parallel lines to create angle pairs.

39. (D)

This question tests the examinee's ability to apply algebraic techniques to geometry problems. The correct answer is (D), 9 or -10.

Rays $\overline{BA}$ and $\overline{BC}$ are perpendicular, so $m\angle ABC = 90°$. Solve for x by letting $(x^2 + x)$ equal 90.

$$x^2 + x = 90$$

$$x^2 + x - 90 = 0$$

$$(x + 10)(x - 9) = 0$$

$$x + 10 = 0 \text{ or } x - 9 = 0$$

$$x = -10 \text{ or } x = 9$$

Choice (A) is incorrect because the sum of x^2 and x is 90, not just x. Choices (B) and (C) are incorrect because each offers only one of the two correct solutions.

40. (D)

This question tests the examinee's ability to use logic to draw useful conclusions about a pattern. The correct answer is (D), there is not enough information to solve this problem.

Consider three examples that each satisfy $n > 0$:

   a. Let $n = 2$, then $n^2 = 4$

      $n^2 > n$

   b. Let $n = 1$, then $n^2 = 1$

      $n^2 = n$

   c. Let $n = \frac{1}{2}$, then $n^2 = \frac{1}{4}$

      $n^2 < n$

Without more information about n, we cannot make a conclusion about n^2.

Choices (A), (B), and (C) are incorrect because each relies solely on one condition of n. Given that n is positive, our only conclusion is that n^2 is positive.

41. $12.30

This question tests the examinee's ability to calculate percentages. The correct answer is $12.30.

For the $120 item, the tax is 5% + 1.5% = 6.5%. For the $90 item, the tax is 5%. Thus, the total tax for Steve's purchases is

$$(\$120)(0.065) + (\$90)(0.05) =$$
$$\$7.80 + \$4.50 = \$12.30$$

42. (D)

This question tests the examinee's ability to recognize the restrictions of a function. The correct answer is (D), (8, –3).

For any function, each x value may correspond to only one y value. Thus, for the graph of any function, no two points may have the same x-coordinate. Since (8, –7) is a point on the graph, this means that (8, –3) cannot be a point on the graph.

Choices (A), (B), and (C) are incorrect because each features x values distinct from those in the function. Therefore, all of the points in choices (A), (B), and (C) *can* be a part of the function that contains the points (–2, 4), (5, 3), and (8, –7).

43. 222

This question tests the examinee's ability to create and solve a proportion. The correct answer is 222.

Let x represent the expected number of defective blouses in a sample of 225. Then $\frac{12}{900} = \frac{x}{225}$. Cross-multiply to get $900x = 2,700$. Thus, $x = 3$. Therefore, the number of blouses that would not have defects would be $225 - 3 = 222$.

44. (D)

This question tests the examinee's ability to recognize different measures of central tendency. The correct answer is (D), 0.

The median of a set of numbers is the value in the middle when the numbers are arranged in order. The mean of a set of numbers is the sum of the numbers divided by the number of values.

Find the median by arranging the weights in order.

104   108   109   112   112   118

There are two numbers in the middle, 109 and 112. Find their mean to get the median.

$$(109 + 112) \div 2 = 110.5$$

Find the mean:

$$(104 + 108 + 109 + 112 + 112 + 118) \div 6 = 110.5$$

Subtract the mean from the median.

$$110.5 - 110.5 = 0$$

Choice (A) is incorrect because it is just the mode of the data set. Choice (B) is incorrect because it is the value of the mean and the median, but not their difference. Choice (C) is incorrect because it is the range of the data set.

45. (B)

This question tests the examinee's ability to solve absolute value inequalities. The correct answer is (B), $-\frac{3}{4} < x < \frac{9}{4}$.

$|3 - 4x| < 6$ is equivalent to $-6 < 3 - 4x < 6$. Then subtract 3 from each part to get $-9 < -4x < 3$. Divide each part by –4, the coefficient of x. Remember to switch the inequality signs when dividing by a negative. The inequality for x is thus $-\frac{3}{4} < x < \frac{9}{4}$. All of the members of the inequality in answer choice (B) are contained in $-\dfrac{3}{4} < x < \dfrac{9}{4}$.

Choice (A) is wrong because its upper bound of 3 exceeds $\dfrac{9}{4}$. So, for example, an x value of $\dfrac{11}{4}$ belongs to choice (A), but not to $-\dfrac{3}{4} < x < \dfrac{9}{4}$. Choices (C) and (D) are incorrect because an x value such as $-\dfrac{4}{5}$ belongs to each choice, but does not belong to $-\dfrac{3}{4} < x < \dfrac{9}{4}$.

46. (D)

This question tests the examinee's ability to accurately use the properties of exponents. The correct answer is (D), $\dfrac{m^{15}p^{14}}{r^{11}}$.

$$(mp^2r^3)^3 \times (m^{-3}p^{-2}r^5)^{-4} =$$
$$(m^3p^6r^9)(m^{12}p^8r^{-20}) =$$
$$m^{15}p^{14}r^{-11} = \dfrac{m^{15}p^{14}}{r^{11}}$$

Choices (A) and (B) are incorrect because each improperly uses the properties of exponents to calculate the exponents of m and p. Choice (C) is incorrect because it correctly calculates the exponents of m and p, but erroneously calculates the exponent of r.

47. 33

This question tests the examinee's ability to use proportions to solve scale-model problems. The correct answer is 33 inches.

Let w and d represent the width and depth, respectively, of the scale model.

Then $\dfrac{150}{100} = \dfrac{18}{w}$. Reduce $\dfrac{150}{100}$ to $\dfrac{3}{2}$, so that $\dfrac{3}{2} = \dfrac{18}{w}$. Cross-multiply to get $3w = 36$. So, $w = 12$. Similarly, $\dfrac{150}{25} = \dfrac{18}{d}$. We can reduce $\dfrac{150}{25}$ to $\dfrac{6}{1}$. Thus $\dfrac{6}{1} = \dfrac{18}{d}$, which leads to $6d = 18$. So, $d = 3$. Therefore, the sum of the length, width, and depth of the scale model is $18 + 12 + 3 = 33$ inches.

48. (A)

This question tests the examinee's ability to simplify a rational expression. The correct answer is (A), $\dfrac{2x-8}{2x-3}$.

Factor the numerator and denominator completely and cancel where possible.

$$\dfrac{8x^3 - 20x^2 - 48x}{8x^3 - 18x} = \dfrac{(4x)(2x^2 - 5x - 12)}{(2x)(4x^2 - 9)}$$
$$= \dfrac{(4x)(2x + 3)(x - 4)}{(2x)(2x + 3)(2x - 3)}$$
$$= \dfrac{(2)(x - 4)}{2x - 3}$$

which is equivalent to $\dfrac{2x-8}{2x-3}$. Note that $2x$ cannot be canceled in the final step because in each instance it is part of a binomial.

Choice (B) is incorrect because it cancels 2 from the numerator and the denominator even though each 2 is part of a binomial and cannot be canceled. Choice (C) is incorrect because it erroneously cancels 2 from the numerator. Choice (D) is incorrect because it erroneously cancels $x - 4$ from the numerator.

49. 5

This question tests the examinee's ability to use algebra to solve data questions. The correct answer is 5.

Find the mean of the 5 values by calculating their sum and dividing by 5:

$$\frac{4+6+9+1+x}{5} = x$$

$$\frac{20+x}{5} = x$$

$$(5)\left(\frac{20+x}{5}\right) = (x)(5)$$

$$20+x = 5x$$

$$20 = 4x$$

$$5 = x$$

50. (D)

This question tests the examinee's ability to apply quadratic functions to area questions. The correct answer is (D), $40w - w^2$.

The area of a rectangle is found by multiplying length by width. If both widths are subtracted from the 80 feet of fence, what remains is $80 - 2w$, which represents the two lengths of the rectangle. Divide $80 - 2w$ by 2 to get $40 - w$, a single length, then multiply that quantity by the width:

$$(40 - w)(w) = 40w - w^2$$

Choice (A) is incorrect because it is the measure of the two lengths. Choice (B) is incorrect because it multiplies the width times two lengths, not one. Choice (C) is incorrect because in finding the length, it correctly divides 80 by 2, but does not divide $2w$ by 2.

51. 92

This question tests the examinee's ability to solve for the sum before an average. The correct answer is 92.

Find the sum of the cards by multiplying the mean by the number of cards:

$$7 \times 14 = 98$$

To maximize the value of a single card, minimize the value of the other cards by assigning each a value of 1:

$$1 + 1 + 1 + 1 + 1 + 1 + 92 = 98$$

If 6 of the students drew a value of 1, then the seventh student would need to draw 92 to make the mean equal to 14.

52. (B)

This question tests the examinee's ability to calculate coordinates using the midpoint formula. The correct answer is (B), $(-18, 18)$.

The coordinates of B are found by using the midpoint formula.

$$M = \left(\frac{x_1 + x_2}{2}, \frac{y_1 + y_2}{2}\right)$$

Input the known data and solve for $B = (x, y)$.

$$(-7, 8) = \left(\frac{4+x}{2}, \frac{-2+y}{2}\right)$$

$$\frac{4+x}{2} = -7, \qquad \frac{-2+y}{2} = 8$$

$$4 + x = -14 \qquad -2 + y = 16$$

$$x = -18 \qquad y = 18$$

Choice (A) is incorrect because it juxtaposes the signs on the x and y coordinates. Choice (C) is incorrect because it is the midpoint of $\overline{AM}$. Choice (D) is incorrect because it is the midpoint of $\overline{BM}$.

53. (B)

This question tests the examinee's knowledge of prime and composite numbers. The correct answer is (B), 28.

A prime number can be divided only by one and itself. It is important to remember that 1 is not a prime number and 2 is the only even prime:

$$2 + 3 + 5 + 7 + 11 = 28$$

Choice (A) is incorrect because it omits 2 as a prime and adds 13 in its place. Choice (C) is incorrect because it adds 1 rather than 2 as the first prime, but omits 2 in the calculation. Choice (D) is incorrect because it considers 1 as the first prime, and omits 11 as the fifth prime.

54. (B)

This question tests the examinee's skill in graphing quadratic functions. The correct answer is (B), 2.

The vertex form (also known as the graphing form) of a quadratic function is $y = a(x - h)^2 + k$, where (h, k) is the vertex of a parabola. Therefore, the vertex in this equation is $(3, 2)$. Since the lead term is negative, the parabola opens down. A sketch of the graph reveals the two zeroes.

Choice (A) is incorrect because a parabola can have at most two zeroes. Choice (C) is incorrect because only one zero means the vertex is on the x-axis. Choice (D) is incorrect because the parabola wouldn't cross the x-axis.

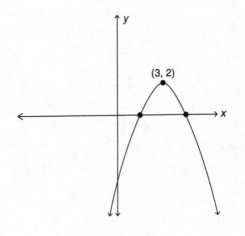

55. 24

This question tests the examinee's ability to perform composite functions. The correct answer is 24.

Using the values in the chart, note that when $x = 2$, $g(2) = 5$. Now, check the $h(x)$ value chart for $x = g(2) = 5$. We find $h(5) = 24$.

Praxis II Middle School Mathematics
Practice Test 3 Answer Sheet

1. Ⓐ Ⓑ Ⓒ Ⓓ

2. [_____]

3. Ⓐ Ⓑ Ⓒ Ⓓ

4. [_____]

5. Ⓐ Ⓑ Ⓒ Ⓓ

6. Ⓐ Ⓑ Ⓒ Ⓓ

7. [_____]

8. Ⓐ Ⓑ Ⓒ Ⓓ

9. Ⓐ Ⓑ Ⓒ Ⓓ

10. Ⓐ Ⓑ Ⓒ Ⓓ

11. Ⓐ Ⓑ Ⓒ Ⓓ

12. [_____]

13. Ⓐ Ⓑ Ⓒ Ⓓ

14. Ⓐ Ⓑ Ⓒ Ⓓ

15. Ⓐ Ⓑ Ⓒ Ⓓ

16. [_____]

17. [_____]

18. Ⓐ Ⓑ Ⓒ Ⓓ

19. Ⓐ Ⓑ Ⓒ Ⓓ

20. [_____]

21. Ⓐ Ⓑ Ⓒ Ⓓ

22. Ⓐ Ⓑ Ⓒ Ⓓ

23. Ⓐ Ⓑ Ⓒ Ⓓ

24. Ⓐ Ⓑ Ⓒ Ⓓ

25. Ⓐ Ⓑ Ⓒ Ⓓ

26. [_____]

27. Ⓐ Ⓑ Ⓒ Ⓓ

28. Ⓐ Ⓑ Ⓒ Ⓓ

29. Ⓐ Ⓑ Ⓒ Ⓓ

30. Ⓐ Ⓑ Ⓒ Ⓓ

31. Ⓐ Ⓑ Ⓒ Ⓓ

32. Ⓐ Ⓑ Ⓒ Ⓓ

33. Ⓐ Ⓑ Ⓒ Ⓓ

34. [_____]

35. Ⓐ Ⓑ Ⓒ Ⓓ

36. Ⓐ Ⓑ Ⓒ Ⓓ

37. Ⓐ Ⓑ Ⓒ Ⓓ

38. [_____]

39. Ⓐ Ⓑ Ⓒ Ⓓ

40. Ⓐ Ⓑ Ⓒ Ⓓ

41. Ⓐ Ⓑ Ⓒ Ⓓ

42. Ⓐ Ⓑ Ⓒ Ⓓ

43. Ⓐ Ⓑ Ⓒ Ⓓ

44. Ⓐ Ⓑ Ⓒ Ⓓ

45. Ⓐ Ⓑ Ⓒ Ⓓ

46. [_____]

47. Ⓐ Ⓑ Ⓒ Ⓓ

48. Ⓐ Ⓑ Ⓒ Ⓓ

49. Ⓐ Ⓑ Ⓒ Ⓓ

50. Ⓐ Ⓑ Ⓒ Ⓓ

51. Ⓐ Ⓑ Ⓒ Ⓓ

52. Ⓐ Ⓑ Ⓒ Ⓓ

53. Ⓐ Ⓑ Ⓒ Ⓓ

54. Ⓐ Ⓑ Ⓒ Ⓓ

55. Ⓐ Ⓑ Ⓒ Ⓓ

Praxis II Middle School Mathematics
Practice Test 4 Answer Sheet

1. Ⓐ Ⓑ Ⓒ Ⓓ
2. Ⓐ Ⓑ Ⓒ Ⓓ
3. Ⓐ Ⓑ Ⓒ Ⓓ
4. Ⓐ Ⓑ Ⓒ Ⓓ
5. Ⓐ Ⓑ Ⓒ Ⓓ
6. [   ]
7. Ⓐ Ⓑ Ⓒ Ⓓ
8. Ⓐ Ⓑ Ⓒ Ⓓ
9. Ⓐ Ⓑ Ⓒ Ⓓ
10. Ⓐ Ⓑ Ⓒ Ⓓ
11. Ⓐ Ⓑ Ⓒ Ⓓ
12. Ⓐ Ⓑ Ⓒ Ⓓ
13. Ⓐ Ⓑ Ⓒ Ⓓ
14. Ⓐ Ⓑ Ⓒ Ⓓ
15. Ⓐ Ⓑ Ⓒ Ⓓ
16. Ⓐ Ⓑ Ⓒ Ⓓ
17. Ⓐ Ⓑ Ⓒ Ⓓ
18. Ⓐ Ⓑ Ⓒ Ⓓ
19. Ⓐ Ⓑ Ⓒ Ⓓ

20. [   ]
21. Ⓐ Ⓑ Ⓒ Ⓓ
22. Ⓐ Ⓑ Ⓒ Ⓓ
23. Ⓐ Ⓑ Ⓒ Ⓓ
24. [   ]
25. Ⓐ Ⓑ Ⓒ Ⓓ
26. Ⓐ Ⓑ Ⓒ Ⓓ
27. Ⓐ Ⓑ Ⓒ Ⓓ
28. Ⓐ Ⓑ Ⓒ Ⓓ
29. Ⓐ Ⓑ Ⓒ Ⓓ
30. Ⓐ Ⓑ Ⓒ Ⓓ
31. [   ]
32. Ⓐ Ⓑ Ⓒ Ⓓ
33. Ⓐ Ⓑ Ⓒ Ⓓ
34. Ⓐ Ⓑ Ⓒ Ⓓ
35. [   ]
36. Ⓐ Ⓑ Ⓒ Ⓓ
37. Ⓐ Ⓑ Ⓒ Ⓓ
38. Ⓐ Ⓑ Ⓒ Ⓓ

39. Ⓐ Ⓑ Ⓒ Ⓓ
40. Ⓐ Ⓑ Ⓒ Ⓓ
41. [   ]
42. Ⓐ Ⓑ Ⓒ Ⓓ
43. Ⓐ Ⓑ Ⓒ Ⓓ
44. [   ]
45. Ⓐ Ⓑ Ⓒ Ⓓ
46. Ⓐ Ⓑ Ⓒ Ⓓ
47. [   ]
48. Ⓐ Ⓑ Ⓒ Ⓓ
49. [   ]
50. Ⓐ Ⓑ Ⓒ Ⓓ
51. [   ]
52. Ⓐ Ⓑ Ⓒ Ⓓ
53. Ⓐ Ⓑ Ⓒ Ⓓ
54. Ⓐ Ⓑ Ⓒ Ⓓ
55. [   ]

NOTES

NOTES

NOTES

NOTES

NOTES

NOTES

NOTES